IN THE
COMPANY OF EVIL
Thirty Years of California Crime
1950-1980

DEDICATION

This book is loveingly dedicated to the memory of Madison Rose, who was a constant companion during the writing of this book and many others. She was the sweetest and most loyal golden retriever a man could ever want and her calming energy and angelic presence will never be forgotten and always missed.

IN THE COMPANY OF EVIL

THIRTY YEARS OF CALIFORNIA CRIME

1950-1980

MICHAEL THOMAS BARRY

Schiffer Publishing Ltd®

1880 Lower Valley Road • Atglen, PA 19310

Printed in China

Published by Schiffer Publishing, Ltd.
4880 Lower Valley Road
Atglen, PA 19310
Phone: (610) 593-1777; Fax: (610) 593-2002
E-mail: Info@schifferbooks.com

For our complete selection of fine books on this and related
subjects, please visit our website at www.schifferbooks.
com. You may also write for a free catalog.

This book may be purchased from the publisher. Please try
your bookstore first.

We are always looking for people to write books on new
and related subjects. If you have an idea for a book, please
contact us at proposals@schifferbooks.com.

Schiffer Publishing's titles are available at special
discounts for bulk purchases for sales promotions or
premiums. Special editions, including personalized covers,
corporate imprints, and excerpts can be created in large
quantities for special needs. For more information, contact
the publisher.

CONTENTS

Introduction . . . 13

CHAPTER ONE:
The Notorious Crimes of the 1950s

CHAPTER TWO
The Sensational Crimes of the 1960s

CHAPTER THREE
The Infamous Crimes of the 1970s

"The study of crime begins with the knowledge of oneself. All that you despise, all that you loathe, all that you reject, all that you condemn and seek to convert by punishment springs from you."

—Henry Miller

American author, poet, and playwright (1891-1980), from "The Soul of Anaesthesia," *The Air-Conditioned Nightmare (1945)*

Introduction

Why is modern culture so fearful of crime but also fascinated by it? Why do the details of a gruesome murder, rape, or other heinous crimes hold our attention? For years, psychologists and criminologists have tried to answer these questions, but thus far no one has been able to come up with a solid explanation. We are both seemingly seduced and repulsed by these acts of rebellion against the morals of society. Every day we are bombarded with crime stories, whether it's in the newspapers, on television, radio, or our computers. Some of these crimes are inconspicuous and easily forgotten, while others linger forever in our collective memory because of their shock and horror.

So why write a book about notorious serial killers and evil wrongdoings? What purpose does it serve? I considered these questions while conceiving and writing this book. In the end, after hours of soul searching, the answer became clear. The retelling of these dreadful crimes does serve a purpose. It serves as a cautionary tale and helps to remind society that we need to better understand criminal behavior to help prevent and control it.

Criminologists have targeted three main theories as to why people commit violent crimes:

1. Biological
2. Socioeconomic
3. Psychological

Biological theories about the causes of crime focus on the idea that the body, through hereditary genes, evolutionary causes, brain structures, or the role of hormones, has an effect on an individual's participation in criminal behavior. Growing understanding of these theories suggests that certain genetic factors, such as neurological deficits, low serotonin activity, as well as malnourishment and environmental pollutants may all affect an individual's natural predisposition for criminal or anti-social behavior.

Socioeconomic theories of crime focus on a wide range of viewpoints but generally regard crimes as a societal phenomenon, and emphasize the cultural and group elements of criminal behavior. They also focus on the costs and benefits of criminal opportunity. Some sociological models emphasize the relationship between communal structure, such as language, ethnicity, and class, and criminal behavior. Others emphasize the effect of social conditions on an individual's tendency to become involved in crime. Theories of this type often focus on the relationship between crime and dynamics, such as social disparity, peer pressure, disorganization in the community, opportunity for success, and the role of criminal subgroups, such as gangs.

Psychological theories of crime focus on the connection between crime and individual personality, and reasoning factors. These principles focus on the individual, family, and group psychology. A key component in the development of individual characteristics, and any criminal tendencies, is the role played by parents, in terms of factors such as child-rearing practices, attachment, neglect, abuse, supervision, and the parents' own anti-social or criminal behavior.

Another aspect of the psychological theory of crime focuses on mental illness. Every day we hear about crimes that have been perpetrated by emotionally unstable people, but these sensational media reports only serve to spread misconceptions. When referring to a crime where the perpetrator had a mental illness, it is easy to define the criminal by his or her diagnosis. For example, "Paranoid Schizophrenic Murders Family of Four" is a headline that is deemed acceptable by most media outlets. However, an eye-catching caption such as this can be deceptive.

Violence is not a symptom of psychotic illnesses, such as schizophrenia. There is, however, a higher probability that someone suffering from this type of psychological disorder may become violent if they are not receiving effective treatment, have a previous history of violence, and/or misuse alcohol or drugs. Symptoms of mental health disorders, such as schizophrenia may include paranoia, as well as hallucinations and delusions. There is a chance someone who is experiencing these symptoms may become violent when they are afraid or misunderstand. However, if a person is being effectively treated for the condition and is not abusing alcohol or drugs, there is limited risk of violent behavior.

It becomes more complicated when discussing sociopaths or those afflicted with anti-social personality disorders (APD). While there are numerous ways to treat the illness, there is no known cure. One of the biggest challenges in treating sociopaths is that they don't believe they have a problem. Their outward personality is often charismatic and appealing. They often defend and rationalize their behavior and have grandiose attitudes towards themselves with a sense of superiority that makes them believe they are smarter than everyone else. They are incapable of remorse or love and are delusional, believing what they say is truth. Most people suffering from APD don't seek treatment and only reach mental health treatment under directions from the criminal justice system or pressure from family members. This sociopathic way of thinking is brilliantly illustrated by comments made by convicted murderer Charles Manson during a 1987 *Life Magazine* interview:

> I've done nothing I'm ashamed of. Nothing I couldn't face God with. I wouldn't kill a bug.

Mental health professionals are in general agreement that the most important step in preventing violence is to make sure people receive effective treatment as early as possible. It is important to understand that mental illness is not a choice. It can happen to anybody and it is equally essential to understand that violence is always unacceptable.

Beginning in the late 1950s, California became the national leader in aggressively moving mental patients from state-run facilities to private board and care homes. By the time Ronald Reagan assumed the governor's office in 1967, the state had already deinstitutionalized half of its state hospitals and released thousands of mentally disturbed patients back into the community. That same year, California passed the landmark Lanterman-Petris-Short Act, which virtually abolished involuntary hospitalizations except in extreme cases. By the early 1970s, major California cities, such as Los Angeles and San Francisco, were inundated with the mentally ill, who were wandering the streets aimlessly. They began clustering together in skid rows, which have been described as psychiatric ghettos for the emotionally disturbed.

Given the increasing number of seriously mentally ill people living in the community by the mid-1970s, it is not surprising to find that they were impacting the task of police officers. Of all the effects of deinstitutionalization's failure, the most frightening was the rise of homicides and other episodes of violence committed by mentally ill people who were not being treated properly. A few examples of this, which are discussed in detail within this book, are:

1972: Herbert Mullins, responding to auditory hallucinations, killed thirteen people over a three-month period. He had been hospitalized three times but released without further treatment.

1973: Edmund Kemper killed his mother and her friend and was charged with killing six others. Eight years earlier, he had killed his grandparents because he "tired of their company," but at the age of twenty-one had been released from a state hospital without further treatment.

1977: Edward Allaway, believing that people were trying to hurt him, killed seven coworkers at Cal State Fullerton. Five years earlier, he had been hospitalized for paranoid schizophrenia but released without further treatment.

Within the pages of this volume are listed over five dozen of the most titillating, horrifying, and ghastly crimes ever committed in the state of California. The scope of this book spans thirty-plus years, from the early 1950s into the 1980s. These accounts tell of man's inhumanity toward his fellow man and provide an inside look at infamous serial killers, assassins, sadistic rapists, bank robbers, kidnappers, Satan worshippers, and a plethora of other notorious criminals. At one point, these crimes gripped the nation, but many have faded away from our collective consciousness.

The crime stories discussed in the following pages are presented in chronological order, beginning with the date of the criminals' first documented crime, and some of these accounts overlap between decades. An example would be serial killer Mack Ray Edwards, whose reign of murder and mayhem covered three different decades beginning in the early 1950s and ending in the early 1970s. For the purpose of this book, his story is placed in the 1950s chapter. Other accounts, such as the crimes of "Score Card Killer" Randy Kraft and others overlap from the 1970s into the 1980s.

Between 1950 and 1980, California, and America as a whole, began to show dramatic social change, and this affected the way Americans learned, behaved, and thought. It was during this period that the counterculture revolution took shape, the drug culture took hold, the interstate highway system was expanded, and television became the most powerful mass medium. During this period, California took the lead in all of these categories and more.

California's golden shores have always been a magnet for outcasts, weirdos, opportunists, and criminals. Today, it is home to roughly twelve percent of the population in the United States with over thirty-eight million documented residents and millions more that are undocumented. With that comes a lot of good things but also a lot of bad. History books are filled with tales of heroics, but there is a flip side, a much more sinister and darker side to our historical past that often goes under-reported. Millions of people have come to California in search of fame and fortune, but scores have found misery and pain. Some of the following criminal accounts are more sensational than others, some more baffling, some more audacious, while others are sickening and appalling. The notorious crimes revisited in this book are all of these things and more.

It must be noted that this work is not intended to be an all-inclusive anthology but is intended to be an introductory examination of the most notorious crimes of California history between 1950 and 1980. It is a continuation of an earlier work, *Murder & Mayhem 52 Crimes that Shocked Early California, 1849-1949*. In choosing which crimes to include, an eye was kept on the well-known and obvious, as well as more obscure stories that may have been forgotten. The main intent of this book is not to glorify crime or criminals but is intended to be an unbiased description of facts and events. It is hoped that the reader will get a better understanding of the psychology and senselessness of it all.

CHAPTER ONE

The Notorious Crimes of the 1950s

"Crime is terribly revealing.
Try and vary your methods as
you will, your tastes, your
habits, your attitude of mind,
and your soul is revealed by
your actions."

—Agatha Christie
Author (1890-1976) from The ABC Murders

1950-1951

REIGN OF TERROR

Riverside and Imperial County

Billy "Cockeyed" Cook was one of the most terrifying killers of the mid-twentieth century, but today his crime spree is barely remembered. Yet, sixty plus years ago this ruthless and cold-blooded killer's name was blasted across every newspaper headline from coast to coast. He would leave a trail of death over a wide swath of the American Southwest during a brief two-week period of late December 1950 and early January 1951. The manhunt for Cook was undertaken by an army of law enforcement officers from the federal government, three states, and Mexico. This search was only rivaled by the hunt for notorious bank robber John Dillinger during the 1930s.

William Edward Cook was born on December 23, 1923, in Joplin, Missouri. His mother would die when he was 5, after which he and his siblings were placed in foster care. Cook was bullied as a child for an eye deformity, and, because of this teasing, developed an explosive temper. In his early teens, he turned to petty crime and would spend most of his high school years in and out of reformatories. After being released from the Jefferson City Penitentiary in 1950, Cook returned to Joplin for a brief period but eventually made his way to Blythe, California, where he worked in various forms of unskilled labor. To illustrate his contempt for life, he tattooed H-A-R-D-L-U-C-K across the knuckles of his left hand, and he meant it. In late December 1950, unmotivated and mad at the world, Cook headed back east. Along the way he acquired a .32-caliber handgun in Texas.

On December 30, 1950, he began his senseless crime wave by kidnapping auto-mechanic Lee Archer near Lubbock, Texas. The motorist had stopped to pick up Cook, who was hitchhiking. Armed with numerous weapons, Cook robbed Archer of $85 and forced the unfortunate mechanic into the trunk of his own car and drove to Oklahoma. Near Luther, Oklahoma, Archer was able to free himself and jumped from the moving vehicle. Not long afterward, the car developed engine trouble and had to be abandoned. By the time police discovered the vehicle, Cook had vanished.

The next day, near Tulsa, Oklahoma, Cook again posing as a hitchhiker flagged down another motorist: Carl Mosser and his wife, Thelma, and their three young children Ronald, Gary, and Pamela. The Mossers were traveling

Billy Cook with Mexican authorities after his arrest on January 15, 1951. *Courtesy of Bettmann/Corbis.*

from their home in Atwood, Illinois, to Albuquerque, New Mexico, to visit family. For the next three days, Cook forced Mosser to drive aimlessly between Oklahoma and Missouri. Then, during the early morning hours of January 2, 1951, near Joplin, Missouri, he shot and killed each member of the Mosser family (including the family dog) and dumped their bodies into an abandoned mine shaft.

Cook then fled west in his victims' car. The blood-soaked sedan was found abandoned the next day on the side of the road near Tulsa, Oklahoma. Fortunately for law enforcement, Cook had left behind incriminating evidence, such as a receipt for the gun he used to kill the Mossers. Investigators used this evidence to learn his identity and, within hours, one of the largest manhunts in United States history began.

For the next four days, Cook's whereabouts were unknown, and somehow he was able to avoid detection and reach Blythe, California. On January 6, 1951, he resumed his criminal rampage by kidnapping Riverside County Sheriff's Deputy Homer Waldrip. The deputy had gone to a local Blythe motel to look for a friend of Cook's. When Waldrip entered the room of the motel, he was immediately confronted by an armed Cook, who forced him at gunpoint to drive his own patrol car forty miles into the desert. After ordering Waldrip to pull to the side of the road, Cook forced him to lie face down in the middle of the highway. Cook then got back into the patrol car and fled the scene. He would later state that he didn't kill the deputy because of the kindness Waldrip's wife, Cecelia, had shown him during his brief employment at a local diner—a kindheartedness that he said no one else had ever given him, and he wanted to repay her generosity by letting her husband live.

After leaving Deputy Waldrip in the middle of the road, Cook then drove to Yuma, Arizona, where he abandoned the stolen patrol car. Soon after, he encountered another motorist, Robert Dewey, a traveling salesman from Seattle, who had been visiting his parents in San Diego County. Dewey was taking a side trip through the desert and Colorado River area before returning to Seattle. Unsuspecting, Dewey offered Cook a ride and soon after was abducted at gunpoint and then shot to death. Dewey's body was dumped in a ditch in Imperial County near Ogilby, California. Cook then drove in his victim's car to El Centro, where he abandoned the vehicle. He then kidnapped several hunters and forced them to drive to Santa Rosalia, Mexico, where his nine-day reign of terror would come to an end. Cook was taken into custody on January 15, 1951, by Mexican authorities without a struggle. That same day, in Joplin, Missouri, the bodies of the Mosser family were discovered in the abandoned mine shaft.

Cook was eventually extradited back to Oklahoma where he was tried under federal kidnapping statutes. Since the Lindbergh baby kidnapping case in 1932, such charges almost always meant the death penalty, and Cook told his jailers that he expected to be executed. His first trial was held in Oklahoma City before federal Judge Stephan S. Chandler. On March 21, 1951, Chandler found him to be insane but convicted him of the kidnap murder of the Mosser family. Cook was sentenced to five consecutive sixty-year prison terms and temporarily escaped the death penalty. The public was understandably outraged by the sentence and only hours after the verdict, the US Department of Justice approved plans to prosecute him in California state court for the murder of Robert Dewey.

In November 1951, an Imperial County jury took less than an hour to convict Cook of the murder of Robert Dewey and sentenced him to death. Following his trial, Cook was sent to San Quentin Prison to await his fate. In the months leading up to his execution, he became sullen and refused contact, other than simple conversation. On December 12, 1952, with all appeals exhausted, a calm and visibly bored Billy Cook was escorted to the gas chamber. He was strapped to the chair and made no final statements.

He was observed to eagerly inhale the toxic cyanide fumes. Three days later, in a macabre and ghoulish scene, his body was placed on display at a mortuary in Comanche, Oklahoma. Fifteen thousand curiosity seekers viewed his remains before outraged relatives stopped the morbid spectacle. Cook was then buried in an unmarked grave at Peace Cemetery in Joplin, Missouri. His blood-spattered rampage would later serve as inspiration and basis for Ida Lupino's 1953 cult film *The Hitch-Hiker.*

1951

THE MURDERS OF RICHARD AND DORIS COOK

Riverside County

Around 11:00 a.m. on March 26, 1951, motorists driving west on Cajalco Road in Riverside County, near March Air Force base, described seeing a tan-colored car with damage to its exterior, parked on the side of the road. With its hood up, a man, later identified as Lawrence Walker, stood beside it. The stranded driver attempted to flag down the motorist's vehicle but they did not stop. Twenty minutes later, a green Ford, belonging to Richard and Doris Cook was found several miles away by another passing motorist. The body of eighteen-year-old Richard Cook, a maintenance worker at a local aluminum factory, was found shot to death on the ground next to his vehicle, and laying on a blanket nearby was his unharmed infant son. The whereabouts of Doris Cook, also eighteen, was unknown. The Riverside County Sheriffs Department was immediately dispatched to the scene and an intensive search was begun for Mrs. Cook, who was presumed to have been

kidnapped. The Cooks had been returning to their
Maywood home after spending the Easter weekend with
relatives in Nuevo, near Perris, California.

Riverside County Sheriff's deputies theorized that the Cooks had collided
with another automobile as evidenced by heavy damage to their car.
Fresh tire tracks nearby showed that the other vehicle had headed east
on Cajalco Road. Later that day, around 4:00 p.m., police officers located a
tan Oldsmobile parked in a service station in the city of Riverside that had
severe damage to its right front bumper. Upon searching the vehicle's trunk,
officers found a handgun stashed inside a bag of clothing.

The officers went to a nearby diner in search of the owner of the vehicle.
As they approached the diner, a young black man bolted from the establishment.
Officers gave chase and quickly apprehended the suspect. The young man,
Lawrence Walker, twenty, an Air Force sergeant stationed at nearby March
airfield, was taken to the service station where he admitted that the damaged
Oldsmobile and the handgun belonged to him. He told officers that he had
left the car there to be repaired. When asked about the damage to the car,
he stated that it had been in an accident in Hollywood a few days earlier.

When asked about the Cook murder, he denied any involvement.
Confronted with the fact that parts of his car were found at the scene of the
crime, he continued to deny that he had been in the area.

Walker was arrested and taken to jail for further questioning. The following
day, he changed his story, telling detectives that he had left the airfield around
10:00 a.m. the previous morning and went for a drive on Cajalco Road. He
stated that he had collided with another vehicle as he rounded a sharp turn
and didn't stop because he felt the damage was minor and there were no
injuries. He said he continued driving to Riverside where he found a service
station and stopped for a bite to eat. When asked why he had attempted to
flee from police, Walker commented that he did not like policemen.

On the morning of March 28, the battered body of Doris Cook was
found eleven miles east of the original crime location. Investigators noted
that there were signs of a great struggle and that the victim had been shot
once in the chest. In the brush a short distance away, a spent .45-caliber bullet
casing was found. Tire tracks were found near the body, which matched the
markings left by the tires of Lawrence Walker's Oldsmobile. Ballistics testing
later determined that the bullets that killed Richard and Doris Cook were
from Walker's handgun.

Walker was charged with the murders of Richard and Doris Cook. He
was also indicted for the February 23, 1951, assault and kidnapping of James
Hicks and Betty Maund near Fairmont Park in Riverside. Defense attorneys
wanted a change of venue for the trial, arguing that their client could not
receive a fair trial because of intense media coverage and that the police had

Gravesite of Richard and Doris Cook at Perris Valley Cemetery, Perris, California. *Courtesy of Kimberly Eazell.*

prejudiced the pool of prospective jurors because they had secretly leaked sensitive information about the case to the press. They also asserted that because the victims were white and the defendant was black, many people already considered him guilty before being tried. These motions were all denied and in late June 1951, Walker's trial began in Riverside County Superior Court before Judge Russell S. Waite. On August 3, 1951, after several weeks of testimony, a jury of eleven women and one man began deliberating Walker's fate, and two days later, they found him guilty on all counts. Throughout the whole proceedings he never admitted guilt and he was sentenced to life in prison on August 17, 1951. Following his conviction and imprisonment, there is no further information about Walker's life behind bars.

1953

BLOODY BABS

Burbank, California

Barbara Graham was a lovely, loveless girl, whose sordid, unthinking affairs led her to the depths of human evil and a final walk into San Quentin's gas chamber. Her tragic life is a casebook study in contrasts and shows how much power the news media wields in the American criminal justice system. She was found guilty of the murder of Mabel Monohan and was executed on June 3, 1955. After her death, she achieved pop-culture immortality through the anti-death penalty film *I Want to Live!* (1958), starring Susan Hayward for which she won an Academy Award. Conflicting newspapers accounts of the period described Graham as being streetwise, loyal, and innocent, as well as being cold-hearted and deceitful; reporters were her biggest supporters and harshest critics. Her sensational trial and subsequent execution would both occur at the beginning of an era of anti-death penalty activism, and, in the decades since her death, Barbara Graham has remained a fascinating and enigmatic figure.

The murder of sixty-two-year-old widow Mabel Monohan occurred at her home in the Mountain View district of Burbank, California, on the evening of March 9, 1953. Her body was discovered two days later by gardener Mitchell Truesdale, who noticed that the house appeared to have been vandalized. He immediately called police, who found Mrs. Monohan's body in a hallway closet. Her hands had been tied behind her back and she had been beaten and strangled to death. Even though the intruders had thoroughly ransacked the house, they had somehow overlooked Monohan's purse, which contained several hundred dollars in cash and other items of value. Investigators also found several dusty footprints and a smudged handprint on the wall of the crime scene.

Barbara Graham (1953). *Courtesy of the Los Angeles Public Library.*

A sizeable reward was offered by the victim's daughter, Iris Sowder, for information leading to an arrest. This provided incentive for an informer to come forward who led police to Baxter Shorter. After a period of intense questioning, Shorter provided a motive and the names of three of the alleged perpetrators, Emmett Perkins, John True, and Jack Santo, and a physical description of a fourth—a woman. Police quickly identified the unknown woman as Barbara Graham, who was the girlfriend of Emmett Perkins. John True was the first to be arrested and questioned. He claimed to have no knowledge of the murder and was released.

On April 14, 1953, Baxter Shorter was abducted from his home and never seen again. This gave John True doubts about his own safety, and when he

Mabel Monohan was murdered in her Burbank home on March 9, 1953. *Courtesy of Steve Goldstein (www.beneathlosangels.com).*

was rearrested, he eagerly agreed to testify against Santo, Perkins, and Graham in exchange for immunity. True's account of the motive and description of the crime was generally consistent with that of Baxter Shorter's, the only difference being that he pinned sole responsibility for Monohan's murder on Graham.

According to statements made by both men, the motive for the crime was robbery. There had been a rumor that Mrs. Monohan often stored hundreds of thousands of dollars in cash and jewels at her home for a relative who was an alleged gambler. They also stated that it was Graham who first approached the home of the victim and gained entry by falsely stating she had car trouble and needed to use the telephone. After Mrs. Monohan opened the door, True, Perkins, and Santo forced their way into the house. They demanded the stash of cash and jewels, but Monohan insisted that there wasn't any. Angered by her refusal to turn over the money, Graham struck the victim over the head with the butt of a handgun and strangled her to unconsciousness. The victim was tied-up and placed in a hallway closet. The gang then began to ransack the house. Finding nothing of value, they fled the scene and returned to their hideout at the La Bonita Motel in El Monte. True and Santo left for Northern California later that same day.

Under oath, John True told the Los Angeles County grand jury his account of the crime and indictments were issued for the arrest of Perkins, Santo, and Graham. Law enforcement officials were certain that they were still in the region, and an army of police officers searched throughout Southern California for the fugitive trio. Aware that they were being sought by police, Santo, Perkins, and Graham moved quietly from place to place.

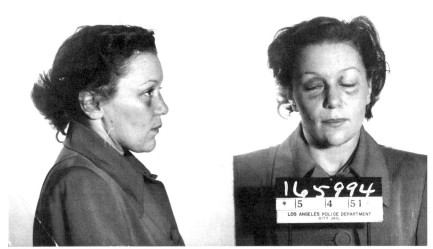

Mug shot of Barbara Graham taken by Los Angeles Police (1951). *Courtesy of the Los Angeles Public Library.*

In the end, it was Graham's drug addiction that got them caught. On the afternoon of May 4, 1953, a female undercover narcotics officer was present when Graham made a heroin purchase at a bus depot in Huntington Park. The undercover officer recognized Graham and sent out an urgent alert. The officer followed her to a Lynwood apartment, where heavily armed LAPD officers quickly surrounded the location. When they finally forced entry into the apartment, there was no resistance from the surprised fugitives, who were all found in various stages of undress. All three were handcuffed and led out to three separate patrol cars. No media was present at the scene of the arrest and the hunt for Mabel Monohan's killers was over.

Following her arrest, Graham became the center of a media frenzy in which newspapers sensationally described her arrest. They described her as being high on drugs, completely naked, and in bed with Santo at the time she was taken into custody. In the 1950s, Los Angeles' five daily newspapers were all fiercely competing for readership and crime stories were especially popular. As a woman accused of murder in the course of a robbery, Graham's case was particularly attention-grabbing.

She was born Barbara Elaine Wood on June 26, 1923, in a shabby rooming house in Oakland, California, to a troubled teen-aged mother. She had an unstable childhood and spent much of her youth in and out of various reform schools. When she reached the age of eighteen, she began traveling up and down the Pacific Coast of California, where she hung around the various naval shipyards. Graham would later admit that she had to prostitute herself to make ends meet. During this same time, she began to accumulate a record of petty criminal offenses but did not show signs of a violent temper. She was married four times and had three children.

Newspaper coverage of her murder trial was tilted toward guilt and tended to overemphasize her actual role in the crime. She was often named the key defendant in the case, but this was a description never used by the prosecution. Her personal life and sleazy past were continually over-dramatized. While both her codefendants had equally sordid pasts, as well as extensive criminal records, Graham's past and personal life received far more attention in the media. Her youth and attractiveness made her a tantalizing subject and she was often portrayed as a true-crime vamp: cold hearted and unemotional, who was more concerned about her appearance than the proceedings.

While awaiting trail, Graham, who was a known bisexual, became intimately involved with her cellmate. It was this cellmate, Donna Prow, who was approached by the Los Angeles district attorney's office with a deal that would shorten her vehicular manslaughter sentence in exchange for help in obtaining a taped confession from Graham. Prow agreed to the offer and approached Graham with the idea of establishing a false alibi to the murder, which would be provided by a friend of Prow's in exchange for $500. Faced with the reality of John True's testimony, Graham felt that she had no other choice but to accept Prow's offer of help. Prow's acquaintance was actually an undercover police officer named Sam Sirianni, who visited Graham three times to plan the false alibi and secretly tape record their conversations. They discussed the details of the alibi in which it was agreed that he would testify that on the night of the murder they had been together at an Encino motel. During these chats, Graham made several incriminating statements that were used by the prosecution to impeach her testimony during the trial.

Graham and her codefendants' joint trial began on August 14, 1953, before Superior Court Judge Charles W. Ficke. The prosecution's star witness would be John True, but the testimony of Sam Sirianni would prove to be the most damaging for Graham. The power of the tape-recorded conversations greatly harmed her credibility. Neither of Graham's codefendants took the stand in their own defense, but foolishly she elected to testify. On the witness stand, Graham admitted to knowing Santo and Perkins but denied being with them on the night of the murder. She told the court she was home with her husband on the night of the crime. However, the testimony of her fourth husband, Henry Graham, contradicted her statements. When asked about why she had gone along with Prow's false alibi plan, Graham said, "Oh, have you ever been desperate? Do you know what it means not to know what to do?"

On September 22, after five weeks of testimony and only five hours of deliberation, the jury of nine men and three women found all three defendants guilty of first-degree murder without a recommendation for life imprisonment. This automatically made the death penalty mandatory for all of the defendants.

After the trial, Graham and her codefendants appealed the verdicts and petitioned for a new trial, but the California Supreme Court upheld the

Codefendants from left to right: Jack Santo, Emmett Perkins, and Barbara Graham sitting in the courtroom of the Monohan murder trial. *Courtesy of the Los Angeles Public Library.*

convictions and sentences. The legal maneuvering would continue until the last hours of Graham's life. Initially, she was incarcerated at the women's prison in Corona, but because of concerns for her safety, she was transferred on November 11 to San Quentin Prison. The expense of housing Graham at San Quentin and providing security for her became a hot topic for the newspapers. During this period, her cell was inaccurately described as being luxurious, but in reality was just a small space in the prison hospital. Graham was returned to Corona in June 1954 but returned to San Quentin a day before her scheduled execution on June 2, 1955.

In the days prior to her execution, Graham told a reporter: "In a situation like this, you don't moan, you don't beg, you don't plead, you try to be a woman." Her execution was scheduled for 10:00 a.m., but California Governor Goodwin J. Knight delayed the proceedings twice, first setting the time back to 10:45 and then to 11:30. In the end, he found no basis for executive clemency and allowed the execution to proceed. During this time, Graham was quoted as saying, "Why do they torture me? I was ready to go at 10 o'clock." She requested to wear a blindfold and did not make eye contact with any of the witnesses as she was being strapped into the gas chamber. At least sixteen reporters were present at the execution, and some depicted her physical appearance in detail: "The brashly attractive thirty-two-year-old

convicted murderer, her bleached blond hair turned to its natural brown…
walked to her death as if dressed for a shopping trip." Her last words were
"Good people are always so sure they're right." The lethal gas pellets dropped
at 11:34 a.m. and Graham was pronounced dead eight minutes later. Her
body was claimed by her husband, and she was buried at Mount Olivet
Cemetery in San Rafael. Graham's two codefendants were executed together
three hours later.

1953-1970
CHILD KILLER
MACK RAY EDWARDS
Los Angeles County

By 1970, Mack Ray Edwards was living a respectable
life in Sylmar, California, a quiet suburb of Los
Angeles. He was married with two children, and no
one would have ever imagined the horrible secrets
that he had been harboring for decades. In early
March 1970, he freely confessed to the kidnap-murders
of six children dating from the early 1950s through
the late 1960s. Although he was only convicted of
three of these slayings, law enforcement officials
believed he was responsible for nearly a dozen child
disappearances during the period.

Born in Arkansas, Edwards moved to Los Angeles in the early 1940s and
eventually found employment with the California Department of
Transportation as a heavy machine operator building the freeways of
Southern California.

On Friday afternoon, March 5, 1970, Edwards, along with a fifteen-year-
old companion, approached Deputy George Rock at the Foothill substation
of the Los Angeles County Sheriff's department, handed the officer a handgun and said that he had a guilty conscience. He then confessed to the
kidnapping of three Sylmar girls, which had occurred earlier that same
morning. Edwards told detectives that he and his teenage accomplice had
secretly entered the Sylmar home of Edgar Cohen around 5:00 a.m. and that
they had waited undetected until Mr. and Mrs. Cohen left the house. They
then began to burglarize the residence and kidnapped the Cohen's three

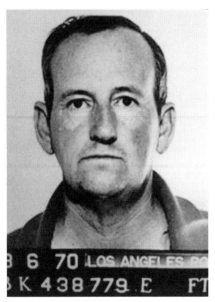

Police booking photo of Mack Ray Edwards.
Photo credit LAPD.

teenage daughters, Jan, Cindy, and Valarie. After leaving the home, he drove the three girls to Boquet Canyon in the Angeles National Forest, north of Newhall. However, two of the girls were able to escape, and a third was left unharmed on the side of the road.

Later that same day, after speaking with the father of his accomplice, Edwards decided it was time to turn himself into law enforcement and clear his conscience of his horrendous crimes.

Edwards confessed to the murder of six children dating back to 1953. He went on to detail these crimes stating that his first victim, eight-year-old Stella Darlene Nolan was abducted and killed on June 20, 1953, after the young girl had wandered away from her mother's Norwalk area food stand. His second crime occurred on August 6, 1956, when he kidnapped and murdered Don Baker, thirteen, and Brenda Howell, eleven, as they were riding their bikes in the foothills near Azusa. Edwards then told police he stopped killing for a dozen years but was eventually overwhelmed with renewed homicidal urges in the fall of 1968. His fourth victim, sixteen-year-old Gary Rochet was shot and killed at his Granada Hills home on November 26. Three weeks later, on December 16, he kidnapped and murdered sixteen-year-old Roger Madison. Edwards had been an acquaintance of the Madison family and was an occasional dinner guest at their home. His sixth and last documented victim was thirteen-year-old Donald Allen Todd, who was abducted on May 16, 1969, near his Pacoima home. The boy's parents had reported their son missing after he did not return home from mowing neighbors' lawns. His bullet-riddled body was discovered a few days later under a footbridge a mile away from his home.

On March 7, 1970, two days after turning himself in to police, Edwards led detectives into the San Gabriel Mountains, north of Claremont where he thought he had dumped the bodies of Baker and Howell. Unfortunately, altered terrain thwarted the effort to locate the remains. Edwards had better luck four days later, when he directed investigators to a section of the Santa Ana Freeway in Norwalk, where the skeletal remains of Stella Nolan were uncovered buried in an embankment one half mile south of the Florence Avenue off-ramp. Edwards told detectives that he had been working on that stretch of the freeway during the time of the kidnapping and took the young girl's body there, and using earth-moving equipment, dug a grave on the evening of June 20, 1953. He also told investigators that he buried the body of Roger Madison in the same fashion beneath the Ventura Freeway, but authorities declined to dig up the freeway to retrieve the body.

With Edwards safely imprisoned, police voiced skepticism at Edwards self-confessed twelve-year gap in his murderous rampage, suggesting that there might be countless other victims. Responding from his cell, Edwards steadfastly denied that there were any more victims. He was officially charged with the murders of Nolan, Todd, and Rochet because the bodies of the other three victims were never found. He pleaded guilty to three counts of first-degree murder and was sentenced to death by Superior Court Judge Thaxton Hanson on May 22, 1970. Edwards later commented that he knew he deserved to die for his crimes and wanted to be executed as soon as possible. On October 30, 1971, with the appeals process bogged down and aware of the fact that no one in California had been put to death since 1967, Edwards committed suicide by hanging himself with an electrical cord in his cell at San Quentin.

Law enforcement officials have always believed that Edwards most likely committed other murders. While imprisoned he claimed to have abducted and murdered eighteen children but later recanted these statements. He is still considered to be a prime suspect in the disappearances of Thomas Eldon Bowman, eight, of Redondo Beach, who vanished on March 23, 1957; Bruce Kremen, six, of Granada Hills, who disappeared from a YMCA camp in the Angeles National Forest on July 12, 1960; Lynn Tomkins, eleven, who was reported missing on August 18, 1961; Dorothy Gale Brown, eleven, who disappeared on July 3, 1962, and whose body was later recovered off the coast of Newport Beach; and Ramona Price, seven, who disappeared in August 1961, near Santa Barbara. All of these cases remain open and unsolved.

1954

MURDER AT STINSON BEACH

Marin County

Bart Luis Caritativo was forty years old when he came to the exclusive resort town of Stinson Beach, California, in 1954. An itinerant worker, his life had been full of odd jobs and hard luck. This appeared

```
to change at Stinson Beach, where he secured steady
employment—but ultimately found his demise.
```

At first, Caritativo went to work as a cook and house servant for wealthy San Francisco attorney Laz Lansburgh. He ingratiated himself to the point where the Lansburghs became protective, if not possessive, of their most-obedient Filipino employee. The Lansburgh house was located next to a sprawling ten-acre resort known as Sea Downs, the owner a wealthy fifty-two-year-old widow named Camille Banks. She had arrived in the area three years before Caritativo, then equally unemployed. After working briefly as a housekeeper for Theodore Malmgren, the elderly owner of Sea Downs, she married him. He promptly died, leaving all of his estate to his new bride.

Several years later, Camille married Joseph Banks, fifty-six, and also remained good friends with Bart Caritativo. The trouble in this paradise was Mr. Banks. He was seldom seen in public and was a known alcoholic. His drinking became so acute that his wife divorced him in 1954. Oddly, the couple continued to live together at Sea Downs and Caritativo also continued to enjoy Mrs. Banks's company.

On the morning of September 17, 1954, only days before Camille was scheduled to depart on a trip to the South Pacific, a neighbor, Mrs. Grunert, went to the Banks's home. There she found a grisly scene, Joseph Banks was dead on the living room couch with a large knife protruding from his stomach, his limp hand still gripping the handle, and Camille Banks's lifeless body was found in a bedroom with her skull split open. On a nearby dresser was found a bloody hammer and a half-empty bottle of gin.

After a thorough search of the crime scene, police detectives uncovered three suspicious-looking documents. One was a note written in pencil, allegedly scribbled by Mr. Banks that read:

> I had been pushed long enough, this is the end. Am responsible to what you
> see and find. Joseph Banks.

The note's grammatical errors puzzled investigators. Also alarming were two more documents, a letter and a typed will, in which Camille Banks left her entire estate to her Filipino friend Bart Caritativo. They too, were filled with misspellings and grammatical errors.

Police learned that both Camille and Joseph Banks were well-educated and the gross errors found in the documents could not have been made by them. Caritativo was brought to the Marin County Sheriff's office for questioning and he denied any knowledge of why Camille Banks had included him in her will. Detectives then obtained several samples of Caritativo's handwriting and experts concluded that all of the documents had been written by him. He was immediately arrested and charged with two counts of first-degree murder.

Throughout his trial, which began in late December 1954, Caritativo acted in a bewildered fashion. He pleaded not guilty, and his defense tried to pin the murder on Joseph Banks, pointing out that Camille had twice committed him to an insane asylum. The prosecution eliminated Banks as a suspect by reading reports from the asylum stating that Banks was merely an alcoholic drying out there; he was not insane. Prosecutors also called experts to the witness stand that testified that Banks was so drunk at the time of his death, that he could not have committed suicide, let alone have killed his wife. Caritativo's defense team tried to destroy the prosecution's case but was ultimately unsuccessful. The jury deliberated for only four hours before returning a verdict: guilty of two counts of murder in the first degree. Caritativo was sentenced to death in the gas chamber. On October 24, 1958, after several years of unsuccessful appeals, Bart Caritativo was strapped into the gas chamber at San Quentin. As the fumes rose about him, he cried out sobbing over and over again until he died, "God bless you all…God bless you all."

1955

THE MURDER OF STEPHANIE BRYAN

Alameda and Trinity County

The 1955 murder of teenager Stephanie Bryan and the sensational trial of her accused killer generated a media frenzy in the San Francisco Bay area. The public followed the progress of the case fanatically. There were dozens of reporters covering the trial. The aloof defendant never admitted guilt, the murder weapon was never found, and there were no eyewitnesses to the crime. Most believed that sex was most certainly a factor in the case, but there was no direct evidence of that occurring. In the end, the prosecution was forced to rely entirely on circumstantial and scientific evidence to convict the killer in a trial that would become one of the longest in Alameda County history.

Claremont Hotel, Berkeley, California. It was near here where fourteen-year-old Stephanie Bryan was abducted by Burton Abbott on April 28, 1955.

Stephanie Bryan was a fourteen-year-old student at Willard Junior High School in Berkeley. She vanished on the afternoon of April 28, 1955. On the day of her disappearance, Bryan and a schoolmate walked from school, stopping briefly at a local library, before parting ways near the Berkeley Tennis Club adjacent to the historic Claremont Hotel. Bryan often cut through the grounds of the hotel to get to her home located on Alvarado Street. On the day she vanished, Bryan was carrying several school books, including a French textbook and a purse that contained a wallet and a pair of glasses. She was wearing a navy-blue cardigan sweater over a white slip-on blouse with a blue cotton skirt.

Bryan lived in the affluent neighborhood above Berkeley with her younger sister, her mother Mary, and her father Charles, a successful Bay Area radiologist. Among Dr. Bryan's friends was Stanley Norton, the assistant managing editor of the *Oakland Tribune*. When Stephanie disappeared, her parents asked Norton to persuade police to search for their daughter. During this time, the failure of a teenager to come home was generally treated as a runaway case. Because of the stature of the Bryan family in the community and media attention, hundreds of people volunteered to search the hills in and around Berkeley, but no trace of the missing teenager was found.

During this period, several witnesses came forward who described seeing a man struggling with a young girl in a car a few miles north of the Claremont Hotel. They stated that the girl appeared to be scared and was screaming. She was in the back seat of the car and the man driving the car appeared to be leaning over the front seat and was beating the girl. The description of the young girl in the car appeared to match that of Stephanie Bryan.

For the next ten days no new evidence or trace of the missing girl was uncovered. Then on May 2, police found Bryan's French textbook on the side of a road in rural Contra Costa County. After this, the case went cold for another two months. A miraculous break came on the evening of July 15, when Bryan's purse and wallet were found at the Alameda home of twenty-seven-year-old Burton W. Abbott, a mild-mannered accounting student at the University of California, Berkeley. Abbott's wife, Georgia, had discovered the belongings in a box in the basement of their home. She had been searching for some costumes when she came upon the girl's wallet. Realizing immediately what she had found, she rushed upstairs to confront her husband. She held up the wallet and stated "Isn't this the girl who disappeared?" Burton Abbott appeared confused by the discovery, said very little, and remained calm. Mrs. Abbott phoned police. The next morning, after thoroughly searching the Abbotts' home, police found additional objects that belonged to the missing girl buried in the basement.

When questioned by police, Burton Abbott claimed to have no knowledge of how the missing girl's belongings had ended up in his home. He told detectives that anyone could have planted the evidence in his basement. In May of that year, he explained that his garage was used as a polling place and dozens of people would have had access to his house. He claimed to have an alibi, stating that on the morning of April 28, he had left Alameda and driven to his cabin in Trinity County. He told detectives that he arrived there sometime in the early evening, and remained there with his brother and sister-in-law until May 1, after which they all returned home in separate cars. Police discovered that on May 2, Abbott had purchased gasoline near the same area where Bryan's French textbook was found on the side of the road. When confronted with this information, Abbott admitted to being in the vicinity but stated that he had gone there to purchase used tires, which was never substantiated.

On July 20, a police search party discovered Stephanie Bryan's remains in a shallow grave near the Abbotts' cabin in Trinity County. An autopsy later determined that she had died from blunt force trauma to the head, but decomposition of the body had made it impossible to determine whether she had been sexually assaulted. A subsequent search of Abbott's car led police to discover hair and clothing fibers that appeared to resemble those of the victim. Police also found traces of blood on the floor mat of the car, the surface of which indicated it had been recently washed. It was also determined that Abbott's boots were encrusted with red mud, similar in composition to a sample of soil taken from the area where Bryan's body was discovered. Additionally, it was learned that Abbott was a regular customer

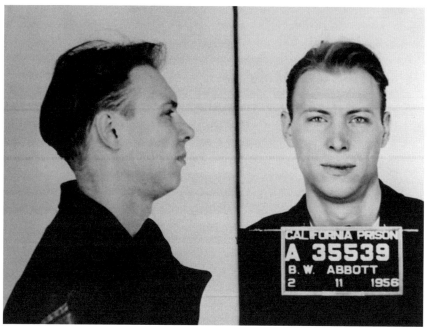

Prison booking photo of Burton Abbott.

at a doughnut shop located less than a block from Willard Junior High School that was frequented by students, and a witness also testified that he saw Abbott at this same donut shop on the afternoon of Bryan's disappearance.

Even though there was no direct evidence tying him to the crimes, prosecutors moved forward with a purely circumstantial case, charging Abbott with the kidnap and murder of Stephanie Bryan. During the trial, which began at the Alameda County courthouse on November 8, 1955, Abbott remained stoic, never showing any hint that he was overly concerned with the proceedings. When he took the stand in his own defense, he appeared confident and condescending towards the prosecution going so far as to claim that he had been framed. During the trial, the prosecution and defense lawyers presented over 100 witnesses. The jury of seven men and five women deliberated for seven days, eventually reaching a verdict of guilty on January 25, 1956. As the judgment was being read, Abbott showed no emotion. On February 3, 1956, Superior Court Judge Charles Wade Snook sentenced him to death in the gas chamber.

On March 15, 1957 at 11:15 a.m., Abbott was led from his cell at San Quentin Prison and taken to the death chamber. In a last ditch effort to stay their client's execution, defense attorneys hurriedly attempted to contact California Governor Goodwin J. Knight, who was aboard the aircraft carrier USS *Hancock*. When they finally reached him, he agreed to grant a one-hour stay of execution. He then placed a call to his clemency secretary, Joseph G.

Babich, who phoned San Quentin and spoke with the prison warden. He asked if the execution had already begun and the warden replied that it had. When asked if it could be halted, Babich was informed that it was too late. The executioner had already released the lethal gas pellets. Burton W. Abbott was pronounced dead at 11:25 a.m.

1955

THE LADY VANISHES

Los Angeles

Leonard Ewing Scott was convicted of murdering his wife, and his eventual conviction was the first successful prosecution in which the victim's body was never discovered.

Very little is known about Scott's early life other than he was born on September 27, 1896, in St. Louis, Missouri. In his early twenties, Scott began working as a bookkeeper for a stockbroker, where he studied the mannerism and dress of other successful salesmen. Over time, the handsome and well-tailored Scott was promoted to stock salesman and thrived in his new position. In 1934, he moved west to Los Angeles and met and married his first wife, Alva Gagnier Brewer, an heiress to a family mining fortune. Their marriage was less than idyllic, and after five stormy years, they were divorced. Scott received a substantial settlement from the divorce and moved to Washington, DC, but returned to Southern California after a few years. He then proceeded to squander his remaining funds on unwise real-estate ventures. A handsome, older bachelor in his early fifties, Scott managed, through sheer force of personality, to move within the wealthy circles of Los Angeles's high society while working as a paint salesman. But by the summer of 1949, he had quit his job and boasted to coworkers about the biggest sale of his life. He was marrying a rich widow, and was going to manage her money as his own.

On May 16, 1955, Evelyn Throsby-Mumper, sixty-three, vanished from her mansion in Bel-Air, a wealthy neighborhood on the west side of Los Angeles, and was never seen again. She had been twice divorced and twice widowed and was married to her fifth husband, L. Ewing Scott, at the time of her disappearance. An investigation into her disappearance showed no signs of foul play, but further evidence suggested that she might have been killed by her husband for financial gain. The couple had met in the summer of 1949, and on September 3, after a whirlwind romance were married in Mexico.

At an early age Scott began to believe that marriage was no more than a sales contract: goods ordered, goods delivered. All it took, he believed, was a shrewd salesman who knew how to package whatever his prospects could be sold. He had been waiting a lifetime for an opportunity like this, and at age fifty-three, he knew he had found her. Soon after returning from their honeymoon, Scott began to assert control over his wife's finances.

In the years following their marriage, Evelyn began to find herself more and more isolated from her friends and family. Then, in the months leading up to her disappearance, Scott hinted that his wife was quite ill, telling friends that her alcohol abuse was becoming more problematic and that she needed to be hospitalized. She was always very particular about her appearance and had a long-standing appointment at a local beauty salon. On May 17, 1955, the day after her disappearance, Scott called the salon and canceled all of his wife's upcoming appointments. Two days after that, he forged his wife's signature on a bank card giving him access to her safe deposit box. At that time, the bank was reluctant to give him access but, after claiming she was sick, was granted access to the box. That same day, he opened several bank accounts around the city in which he deposited large amounts of cash, presumably from the safe deposit box that he had just emptied.

Two weeks later, on May 30, Scott terminated all of the household staff, telling them that his wife had gone east because of illness and he was going to close-up the house and follow her. After months of trying to contact his sister, Raymond Throsby became suspicious and unsatisfied with his brother-in-law's explanations about her whereabouts and reported his sister missing on March 5, 1956. Los Angeles police opened a missing persons investigation and three days later, searched the Scott's residence and discovered evidence that Evelyn was most likely dead. In the bushes behind the house, buried in several inches of dirt, they found her dentures and two pairs of eyeglasses. In an interview with police, Ewing Scott said his wife had abandoned him and he was unaware of where she had gone. Although police were suspicious of his story, they had no evidence to arrest him at the time.

A year after Evelyn's disappearance, Ewing Scott was indicted on forgery and theft charges and was arrested on April 25, 1956. Soon after posting bail, he fled to Canada, where he remained a fugitive for a year. He was arrested on April 9, 1957, after attempting to cross back into the United States. Scott was extradited back to Los Angeles and during his time on the run, police had built a murder case against him.

His trial began in October 1957, during which the prosecution relied mainly on circumstantial evidence. Scott did not take the witness stand in

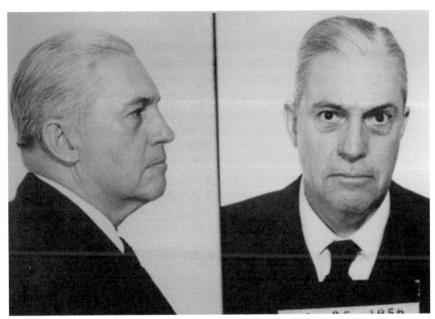

Los Angeles Police Department booking photo of L. Ewing Scott, April 25, 1956. *Photo credit LAPD.*

his own defense and his lawyers always contended that Evelyn had left voluntarily and would return someday. On December 21, 1957, after three days of deliberation, the jury convicted him of first-degree murder. Upon hearing the verdict, Scott looked at his attorneys and in a flat tone stated, "Well, I guess some people like Lincolns and some people like Fords." He was later spared the gas chamber and sentenced to life in prison. In subsequent appeals, Scott's attorneys cited the circumstantial evidence and lack of a body as grounds for reversal of the verdict, but these assertions were all denied. From his prison cell, Scott continued to assert his innocence and publicized his efforts to find his missing wife. He also bitterly fought against the settlement of her estate, which was finalized in 1963. His portion of his wife's estate was awarded to Raymond Throsby.

For Ewing Scott, prison was only a temporary inconvenience, and he waged his own single-minded war for release. As the years passed, the maximum security prison system had little time to care for an elderly infirm inmate such as Scott. In November 1974, he was given a release date, but adamantly and angrily turned it down. To accept parole, he said, was tantamount to admitting guilt for the crime. Authorities had no choice but to keep him in custody.

Two years later, he refused another attempt at release on the same grounds. In reality, as bleak as prison was, Scott had nowhere else to go, and with no friends, no resources, and no options, he was determined to stay in prison.

Then on March 26, 1978, after spending nineteen years behind bars and to his unhappy surprise, eighty-one-year-old Ewing Scott was awarded the unconditional discharge he had wanted, time served, no parole.

After his release, he moved back to Los Angeles where he lived in a series of shabby apartments. He continued to deny involvement in his wife's death, but a guilty conscience must have overwhelmed him by the summer of 1984, when he called author Diane Wagner and asked to talk. At the time, Wagner was writing a book about the case.

On August 5, 1984, Wagner met Scott at his shabby mid-Wilshire district apartment and there he confessed to murdering his wife. He stated matter-of-factly that he struck her once on the head with a mallet in the bedroom of their home. Then wrapped her body in a garden tarp, placed it into the trunk of his car and drove to Las Vegas. After dusk, he drove six miles due east of the Sands Hotel, where he dug a shallow grave, dumped the body in, and drove back to Los Angeles that same night. Asked why he had killed her and whether he was remorseful, he gruffly replied that she had tried to poison him and had gotten what she deserved. Wagner then asked whether he thought he'd ever be convicted because the body was never found, Scott replied that he didn't care whether he did or didn't. He never repeated the confession to any other reporter, and three years later in late August 1987, he died at the age of 91, at the Skyline Convalescent Hospital in Silver Lake. He had no survivors and was penniless. His body laid unclaimed at the Los Angeles County Morgue for more than a week after his death.

1955-1956

SELF-PROFESSED KING OF THE KILLERS

San Francisco, Sacramento, and Los Angeles

Serial killers are a tiny minority of murderers, but they often kill with pulverizing panache. They kill for the sexual pleasure and the sheer evil urge to cause pain. In the mid-1950s, the term had not even been coined yet when Stephen A. Nash began his homicidal rampage.

On November 16, 1956, thirty-three-year-old Stephen Nash met twenty-four-year-old Dennis Butler on Los Angeles' Skid Row. They went to a nearby bar and talked for an hour. Nash it seemed, harbored a deep resentment against society that had begun the day he was born in 1923.

As a baby, he had been abandoned by his mother and adopted by a Bronx, New York, couple. They changed his name to Vincent Patrick Michael Farrell, which was only the first of many indignations that caused him to hate his foster parents. He was forced to attend parochial schools and was punished often. He considered himself to be smarter than other kids but failed to finish high school. After a brief stint in the Army, during which he went AWOL several times, he informed his superior officers that he had homosexual tendencies and was immediately discharged from the service. He then drifted to California, where he began his criminal career and spent five years in prison for burglary.

As Nash and Butler slowly walked up Third Street, Nash became extremely agitated. When they entered the Third Street tunnel, he glared at Butler and without a word, thrust a knife into his abdomen. Butler screamed and began to run away with Nash in close pursuit. Finding refuge in the lobby of a hotel on Hill Street, Butler collapsed. His knife-wielding attacker followed him, but for some unknown reason, Nash did not kill his victim, and instead kicked him in the head and fled the scene. Although seriously injured, Butler managed to survive the attack and at the hospital gave police the name of his attacker.

For the next ten days, Nash wandered around Los Angeles and, on November 26, 1956, he befriended twenty-seven-year-old John Berg, a

Santa Monica Pier (modern day). It was near here where Stephen Nash murdered ten-year-old Larry Rice on November 29, 1956.

beauty school student on a street corner in Long Beach. Berg invited Nash back to his Atlantic Avenue apartment for sex. The next morning in a fit of rage, Nash viciously stabbed Berg to death, then calmly washed, dressed in some of his victim's clothing, and fled the scene.

He then traveled to San Diego but returned to Los Angeles on November 29, 1956, and continued his murderous rampage. Near Venice pier, Nash approached ten-year-old Larry George Rice, who was riding his bike. He struck up a conversation with the boy and offered to buy him a hot dog and soft drink at a muscle beach food stand. They then walked to Santa Monica pier, where they played some arcade games. Eventually, Nash lured the young boy beneath the pier where he viciously attacked him with a knife, stabbing the youth twenty-nine times. After killing Rice, Nash calmly hopped on a bus to Los Angeles' Skid Row, where later that same day he was arrested during a mass round-up of vagrants by Los Angeles police.

Two days later, in a police line-up, several witnesses identified Nash as the gaunt, toothless man who had been seen with Larry Rice on the afternoon of the boy's murder. An hour later, detectives listened as Nash confessed to the murders of Larry Rice and John Berg. When asked about the boy, Nash smugly replied:

> He was a kid; it was there in front of him—sex, fun, all of it. Why should he have it, when I never did, so I took it all away from him. Besides, I'd never killed a kid before and wanted to see how it felt.

Then, for the next two weeks, police investigators with tape recorders by their sides, listened with astonishment as Nash bragged and ranted about his hatred for humanity and detailed countless other crimes. He confessed to three other murders: Floyd Leroy Barnett, twenty-seven, a Sacramento area transient, who he'd beat to death around October 3, 1956, and whose body was dumped into the Sacramento River; William Burns, an Oakland area merchant seaman, whom he had befriended and then beat to death with a lead pipe in December 1955, and whose body was stuffed into a duffel bag and tossed into San Francisco Bay near Richmond. He also took responsibility for the August 1956 murder of Robert Eche, twenty-three, who he'd stabbed to death in San Francisco, after which he placed the victim's body into the trunk of a car and rolled it into San Francisco Bay near pier 52. When asked by detectives if he had abstained from murder during the eight-month period between December 1955 and August 1956, Nash arrogantly replied that there were another half dozen killings he could talk about if he wanted to, but they'd have to pay him for that information. Detectives refused the offer.

Because the bodies of Floyd Barnett, William Burns, and Robert Eche were never recovered, Nash was never charged with their murders but was only indicted for the slayings of John Berg and Larry Rice, and the assault on Dennis Butler. His trial began on February 6, 1957, before Los Angeles

Serial killer Stephen Nash talks with Los Angeles police detectives on December 1, 1956. *Courtesy of Bettmann/ Corbis.*

Superior Court Judge Burton Noble. During the trial, prosecutors asked Nash whether he ever planned to obey the laws and rules of society, Nash proudly replied:

I don't have to, with a knife in my hand.

After three weeks of testimony that included the taped confessions, a jury of ten men and two women found him guilty of two counts of first-degree murder. At his sentencing on April 2, 1957, Judge Noble stated that Nash was the most evil person who had ever appeared in his court and sentenced him to death in the gas chamber. On April 5, 1957, as he was being transferred from Los Angeles County jail to San Quentin, reporters asked him how he was feeling, a smug Nash with hands raised above his head replied:

I'm the winner, like any champion should feel, King of the Killers. Like any king should feel. I should hold up like a champion because I am the champ. 'Course they're gonna dethrone the champ.

Because of danger from other inmates and his endless bragging about his crimes, Nash was kept in solitary confinement at San Quentin until his sentence could be carried out on August 21, 1959. On the morning of his execution, he walked calmly and confidently into the gas chamber and while being strapped into the chair, looked around the room, finally fixating on Los Angeles District Attorney J. Miller Leavy and looking directly at him said:

I've never been able to live like a man, however, I expect to die like a man.

Then at 10:03 a.m., the toxic gas pellets were dropped and nine minutes later, one of California's most notorious serial killers was dead, unrepentant to his last breath.

1955–1956
THE SLEEPING LADY KILLER
Los Angeles

In the early morning hours of February 18, 1955, the Los Angeles area apartment of Louise Winkle, Dorothy Cowan, and Marcolla Drew was burglarized as they slept, and the sum of $87 was taken from their purses. On the same night, in an apartment a few blocks away on the same street, divorced art school registrar Karil Rogers Graham, thirty-nine, was beaten to death; her home had been ransacked and burglarized.

Karil Graham was murdered at her mid-Wilshire district apartment on the night of February 18, 1955.

Laura Lindsay was murdered by Donald Bashor on May 24, 1956, at her home on West 5th Avenue in Los Angeles.

Fifteen months later, on May 24, 1956, legal secretary Laura Lindsay, sixty-two, was found bludgeoned to death in her apartment several blocks from the site of Graham's murder. Her home had been ransacked and burglarized. At the scene, police found a bloody palm print on an open firewood box that was used to gain entry to the victim's home. Two weeks later, on the night of June 9, 1956, Los Angeles Police Officer Donald C. Wesley observed a suspicious man prowling the walkway between several apartment buildings on South Occidental Boulevard. When confronted by the officer, the suspect attempted to flee. Wesley fired several shots at him, hitting him twice in the left arm, but this failed to slow the suspect. He was apprehended a short time later after injuring his foot on a pile of lumber in a nearby alleyway. The suspected prowler was twenty-nine-year-old Donald Keith Bashor, a part-time house painter who lived in South Pasadena.

Detectives determined that the bloody palm print found at the Lindsay murder scene matched that of Bashor. Initially, he denied involvement in the murder and refused to take a lie detector test but after hours of intense questioning confessed to the slaying of Graham and Lindsay, as well as a dozen other burglaries in and around the city.

Donald Keith Bashor awaiting questioning on June 14, 1956, in connection with the murder of Laura Lindsay. His arm is in a sling from a police bullet that was inflicted during his capture. *Courtesy of Bettmann/Corbis.*

He was born in Glendale, California, in 1927 to a wealthy family. In his teens, Bashor began to amass an extensive criminal record. Following high school, he briefly attended the University of Southern California where he studied psychology but dropped out and joined the Navy. He was dishonorably discharged from the service in 1947 for desertion, after which he bummed around with no purpose and began to commit petty crimes.

Bashor told detectives that he'd entered Karil Graham's apartment through an unlocked door around 5:00 a.m. on February 18, 1955, and began searching for things of value. When the victim awoke and began yelling for help, he was forced to bludgeon her with a hammer until she stopped screaming. He then searched the apartment until he found the victim's purse, which contained $20. The next day he drove to Santa Monica, wrapped the murder weapon in his blood-splashed clothing and dropped it over the edge of the pier.

He then confessed to the May 25, 1956 murder of Laura Lindsay, the details of which were almost identical to that of the slaying of Karil Graham.

It had been the same time of night and Lindsay lived only a few blocks away from his previous victim. Armed with a ball-peen hammer, he entered Lindsay's apartment through an open firewood box on the west side of her apartment. The victim was asleep when he entered but awoke when she heard him prowling around. When she began to scream, he struck her on the head, but unlike Graham who died instantly, Lindsay attempted to fight back. He was forced to hit her multiple times before she fell to the floor unconscious. He told detectives that when he turned on his flashlight to search for the victim's purse, the light fell upon the semi-nude body of his victim and because of the blood, became nauseous and placed a blanket over the lifeless body. He then located the victim's purse, found another $20 and quickly fled the scene. The following afternoon, he drove to Santa Monica pier and disposed of the murder weapon and clothing as he had before. He told detectives that it was not his intention to murder these women; all he wanted was money but was forced to kill them when they awoke and began to scream for help.

On June 20, 1956, Bashor was indicted for the murders of Graham and Lindsay. His trial began on October 4, 1956, before Los Angeles Superior Court Judge Allen T. Lynch. Four days later, he interrupted the proceedings and plead guilty to all of the charges. On October 16, 1956, he was sentenced to death.

One year later, on October 11, 1957, he was led to the gas chamber at San Quentin Prison and prior to his execution, expressed remorse for his crimes stating:

> I'm glad my crimes are coming to an end. I am sorry I cannot undo the horrible things I did.

1956-1966

THE INSULIN MURDERS

Los Angeles

From an early age, William Dale Archerd was fascinated with medicine, but because of limited finances and a lack of self-discipline, he was forced to seek employment as a nursing assistant. It was during this time that he became familiar with the administration of all kinds of drugs. He was eventually convicted of the murder of his nephew and two of his seven

wives, but it is believed there may have been many
more victims. His weapon of choice was insulin, and
although his crime spree is thought to have begun in
the late 1940s, it took law enforcement twenty years
to bring him to justice.

Archerd was born on May 5, 1912, in Dardanelle, Arkansas, and very little
is known about his childhood. He married the first of his seven wives,
Eleanor Russell, on June 8, 1935, in Yuma, Arizona. They would have
two children and be divorced at an unknown date prior to 1949.

During this period, he held various jobs, and for one year, beginning in
1940, he was employed as a nursing assistant at the Camarillo State Mental
Hospital, where he assisted in insulin shock therapy, a form of psychiatric
treatment in which patients were repeatedly injected with large doses of
drugs to produce daily comas over several weeks. He first ran afoul of the
law in 1950, when he pleaded guilty to illegal possession of morphine and
was sentenced to five years of probation. After a second offense, probation
was revoked and he was sent to a minimum-security prison from which he
was paroled in October 1953. Archerd and his second wife, Dorthea (whom
he had married in 1949 prior to his arrest) divorced on May 14, 1956. A day
after his divorce was finalized, he married Zella Winders.

On July 24, 1956, Archerd phoned police to report a home invasion
robbery at his Covina residence. He told investigators that several intruders
had forced their way into his house and bound himself and his wife. They
placed pillowcases over their heads and injected them both with an unknown
substance. The attackers made off with several hundred dollars in cash but
left behind jewelry and other valuables. When police arrived on the scene,
Zella was still conscious and corroborated her husband's statement. She then
went into convulsions and lost consciousness. She was transported to a local
hospital where she died the next night, never having gained consciousness.
During a search of the house and surrounding area, police located a hypodermic
needle in a bathroom drawer and a half-used vial of insulin in a nearby field.

Police were unable to locate any puncture wounds on William's body,
who appeared to be suffering no ill effects from the alleged injection. The
coroner's office was alerted to the vial of insulin found at the scene, but
because no poisonous substances were found in Zella's bloodstream, her
official cause of death was ruled to be pneumonia. As there was no method
of measuring insulin at the time, there was no evidence pointing to insulin
poisoning as the cause of her death.

On October 4, 1957, Archerd married his fourth wife, Gladys Stewart.
The pair divorced in early 1958 but remarried in May 1959. The pair's second
attempt at wedded bliss ended less than a year later. In between these
unsuccessful nuptials, Archerd met and married a wealthy forty-six-year-old

woman named Juanita Plum. They were married on March 10, 1958, in Las Vegas, Nevada, and two days after the wedding, Plum was found unconscious in their hotel room. She was taken to Southern Nevada Memorial Hospital, where she remained unconscious and died the next day. An autopsy revealed that she had ingested a large amount of barbiturates. Medical personnel at the hospital also noted that she was suffering from very low blood sugar for which they could find no obvious medical explanation. Because her death appeared to be accidental, the case was closed.

On the evening of March 16, 1960, in a strange turn of events, Gladys Stewart's ex-husband Frank Stewart and Archerd hatched a plan to commit insurance fraud. They decided to take a flight from Los Angeles to Las Vegas and, prior to boarding the plane, Stewart, with the assistance of Archerd, took out two airline insurance policies. One of the policies named Gladys as a beneficiary and the second named Archerd's mother as the benefactor. The policy covered accidents that occurred in the plane as well as the airport terminal. Upon arrival in Las Vegas, Stewart faked a slip and fall in the airport's restroom. He was taken to Southern Nevada Memorial Hospital for treatment but unexpectedly died the next evening after suffering severe convulsions. Following Stewart's death, Archerd filed suit to collect the insurance money, but the claim was dismissed without his collecting anything. Despite strong circumstantial evidence of insurance fraud, Nevada police declined to pursue criminal charges against Archerd.

A year and half later, on August 21, 1961, Archerd's name again came to the attention of law enforcement when his fifteen-year-old nephew, Burney Archerd, was involved in an apparent hit-and-run traffic accident in Long Beach. The teenager was admitted to Long Beach Memorial Hospital, but police were unable to confirm an auto accident had actually occurred. He remained in the hospital until September 2 when he died. His uncle, William Archerd had been a constant visitor at the youth's bedside. An autopsy revealed that the boy had been injected with insulin and died from hypoglycemia, or low blood sugar. A search of hospital records showed that no such injection was administered by hospital staff. The incident was quickly forgotten and no further action was taken on the case.

In February 1965, Archerd (who had changed his last name to Arden) met his seventh wife, Mary Brinker Post, a well-known novelist who had written the bestseller *Annie Jordan* (1948). They were married on April 18, and six months later she was involved in a minor traffic accident in Montclair.

Although the accident did not appear to cause any injuries, in the early morning hours of November 2, she was found unconscious and taken to Pomona Valley Hospital. She died there the next day, never regaining consciousness. An autopsy revealed that she had very low blood sugar levels and barbiturates in her bloodstream at the time of her death. This aroused suspicion and a police investigation was opened. During the investigation, it was learned that William and Mary had been estranged and living apart for a while. He had moved in with his ex-wife Gladys Stewart at the time of Mary's car accident. He returned to Mary's home after she had the accident, and five days later she was dead.

Police interviewed several hundred people in connection with the suspicious death of Mary Brinker Post. Among those questioned was Archerd's second wife Dorthea, who told investigators about the death of William Jones in October 1947. He had been involved in a money-making scam with her ex-husband and had died under suspicious circumstances. Jones had apparently agreed to let Archerd inject him with insulin as a cover-up for their illegal activities, which involved a fake car accident. Although he was never charged with Jones' death, this information would be used against him at his trial as knowledge of insulin poisoning.

Police also determined that Archerd was motivated to kill because of greed. His wife Zella had been comparatively well off when he married her and he stood to gain from her death. Juanita had also left a sizable estate, but unbeknownst to him, she had altered her will shortly before her death and he got nothing. Mary Brinker Post was a successful author and, as her next of kin, Archerd stood to inherit her entire estate, whatever it was worth, despite her recent bankruptcy. It was also learned that prior to Burney Archerd's death, he had been awarded $8,000 from his father's estate and his uncle William was named the trustee. After Burney's death, none of the inheritance money could be found or accounted for.

On July 27, 1967, Los Angeles County Sheriff's detectives arrested Archerd at his home and charged him with the murders of Zella Winders, Burney Archerd, and Mary Brinker Post. He waived his right to a trial by jury and was eventually found guilty of three counts of first-degree murder. On March 6, 1968, he was sentenced to death in the gas chamber. His sentence was commuted to life in prison in 1972, after the US Supreme Court abolished the death penalty. On October 29, 1977, after serving only nine years of his sentence, William Dale Archerd died from pneumonia at Vacaville State Prison.

1957

THE GHOST OF EL SEGUNDO

Los Angeles County

Gerald Fiten Mason was a model citizen, kindly and well-liked, who had lived in an affluent suburb of

Columbia, South Carolina, since 1957. He owned and
operated a local gas station, was married, had two
children and several grandchildren. He golfed twice
a week and was quick to lend a helping hand to
neighbors in need. On the surface, life looked quite
normal, but as often is the case, looks can be
deceiving. Gerald Mason harbored a dark secret; for
over forty-five years he had gotten away with murder.

Mason's crime spree began in the early morning hours of July 22, 1957,
on an unpaved lovers' lane in Hawthorne, California. Four teenagers,
two boys, ages sixteen and seventeen, and two girls, aged fifteen, were
approached by Mason, who flashed a gun and demanded they hand over all
of their money. He then ordered the boys and one of the girls to strip. He
tied-up three of the victims and sexually assaulted one of the girls before
fleeing in the teens' 1949 Ford. A short time later, around 1:30 a.m., El
Segundo police officers Milton Curtis, twenty-five, and Richard Phillips,
twenty-eight, were on routine patrol near Rosecrans Road, when they
stopped Mason after he'd run a red light. As the officers approached the
vehicle, six shots rang out, mortally wounding both officers. One of the
officers managed to return fire, superficially wounding Mason in the back,
but he was able to escape. Mason then drove several blocks, abandoned the
stolen vehicle on the side of the road, and vanished on foot into the pre-dawn
darkness.

Only scant evidence was retrieved from the scene of the crime, which
included one dusty fingerprint from the door of the stolen vehicle. Although
an intensive manhunt was undertaken, no one was ever arrested and the case
went cold.

In 1960, a Manhattan Beach resident found two watches and a chrome-
plated .22-caliber handgun behind his house. The watches were later identified
as belonging to the Hawthorne victims. The handgun was later tied to the
murders of the El Segundo officers by ballistics tests. The gun had been
purchased at a Sears department store in Shreveport, Louisiana, four days
before the killings. The buyer gave the name G. D. Wilson and a fictitious
Miami, Florida, address. A day earlier at a YMCA across the street, the registry
had been signed by George Wilson. Armed with this new evidence, police
were still unable to locate a suspect in the slayings.

Forty-five years after the crimes, in February 2002, two chance developments
occurred that blew the case wide open: El Segundo police received an
anonymous tip about a possible suspect in the case, which turned out to be
false, but this caught the interest of two sheriff's homicide detectives. At this
same time, Los Angeles County became part of the national FBI fingerprint
database. Detectives ran the fingerprint found at the 1957 crime scene and

it matched Gerald Fiten Mason. As it turned out, Mason had been arrested in South Carolina in 1956 for burglary and had been routinely fingerprinted. In 2002, his prints had been added to the national database.

Armed with a name, law enforcement found it easy to track down Mason, now sixty-eight, who was retired and living in a suburb of Columbia, South Carolina. Detectives were also able to tie the murder weapon to Mason through handwriting analysis of the YMCA registry and gun permit. They were also able to locate several witnesses who identified Mason from a 1956 photo as the man they saw fleeing the area on the night of the murders. On Wednesday morning, January 29, 2003, detectives arrived at Mason's home and he was placed under arrest. He was extradited back to California to stand trial.

Faced with overwhelming evidence, Mason confessed to the murders and waived his right to a jury trial. At his sentencing hearing, he expressed remorse for the crimes and apologized to the victims' families. He was sentenced on March 24, 2003, to two life terms. The 1957 law under which he was convicted allowed him to be considered for parole after a minimum of seven years in prison. A search of the California Department of Corrections was unable to locate Mason's current incarceration status, and it is assumed that he has either been paroled or died in prison.

1957-1958

THE LONELY HEARTS KILLER

Los Angeles, Riverside, San Diego, and Orange County

Harvey Murray Glatman resembled a mild-mannered everyman, but behind the gentle façade hid the mind of a sadistic sexual predator.

He was born on December 10, 1927, in The Bronx, New York but raised in Colorado. Although he was an intelligent child, he displayed sociopathic tendencies and an obsession with ropes from an early age. In his teenage years, he began to experiment with deviant sexual activities and committed numerous petty crimes. His parents were concerned with his behavior, but medical professionals believed it was only a stage and that he'd eventually grow out of it. In his late teens, his criminal activities took a more twisted turn, when he began to break into women's apartments just to scare them.

Judy Ann Dull lived in this apartment building on North Sweetzer Avenue in West Hollywood, California.

This activity continued to escalate, when in 1945, he tried to molest a young girl, but when she began to scream he stopped and fled the scene. The girl was able to identify Glatman in a police lineup. He was convicted of assault and served eight months in prison.

After his release, Glatman moved to Albany, New York, where his deviant behavior became more violent. He continued to assault women, for which he was arrested and convicted. While serving his sentence at Sing Sing Prison, he was diagnosed by psychiatrists as a sociopath. After he was paroled in 1951, Glatman moved back to Colorado where he found work as a television repairmen. It was during this period that he became interested in photography and, on the surface, appeared to have put his criminal ways in the past, but in reality he was ready to explode into a sexually charged homicidal rampage.

In 1957, he moved to Los Angeles, where he continued to work as a television repairman. He also hoped to photograph young woman who flocked to Hollywood in search of stardom. These girls were looking for their big breaks and many of them would do anything to be discovered. Some of these women let sleazy photographers pose them in suggestive positions for true crime magazines that were popular in the 1950s. Glatman began hanging around modeling agencies looking for women who might be willing to pose for him, but even by the tawdry standards of the pulp magazines of the time, his photos were extreme. He wanted his models to reflect real fear in their eyes and expressions.

In late July 1957, using the alias of Johnny Glynn, Glatman was ready to move from sleazy photography to murder. He made a routine service call at the West Hollywood apartment of nineteen-year-old Judy Ann Dull, who was recently separated from her husband and the mother of a small child. After chatting with the young woman, Glatman learned that she was an

Harvey Glatman lived in this apartment building on Melrose Avenue, Los Angeles, and it was here, on the evening of August 1, 1957, that Judy Ann Dull was photographed and abducted.

aspiring model. He told her that he was a part-time photographer who freelanced for several true crime magazines and asked if she'd be willing to pose for some women-in-jeopardy photos. Dull agreed and, several days later, on August 1, Glatman picked her up at her home and drove back to his Melrose Avenue apartment, where for the next twelve hours he photographed Dull in every imaginable position. Finally, he had enough and, with a bound-and-gagged Dull, drove to the desert near Indio, where he continued to photograph, sexually assault, and eventually strangle her to death. He dug a shallow grave for his victim and then returned to Los Angeles where he excitedly developed his photographs.

He would kill two more times in much the same fashion and, in early March 1958, using the alias George Williams, Glatman joined a lonely hearts dating service. He was introduced to Shirley Ann Bridgeford, a twenty-four-year-old divorcée, and they seemed to hit it off. On March 8, 1958, Bridgeford agreed to another date with Glatman. He picked her up at her Sun Valley apartment and once she was in his car, he pulled a gun and ordered her to do as he asked. They drove to rural San Diego County, near Escondido, where Bridgeford was bound, photographed, sexually assaulted, and then strangled to death. She was buried in a shallow grave and, like before, he eagerly returned home to develop his prized photographs.

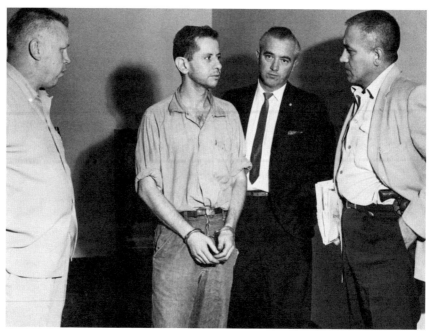

Lonely Hearts Killer Harvey Glatman with Orange County Sheriff's detectives Dan Rios (right), John Baker (center), and James Sands (left), after his arrest (October 31, 1958). *Courtesy of Bettmann/Corbis.*

Three months later, his sexual and homicidal urges still not satiated, Glatman met Ruth Rita Mercado, twenty-four, a part-time model and stripper. On July 23, 1958, he arrived at Mercado's East Los Angeles apartment under the false pretenses of going back to his studio to take photographs. Instead, he drove to the same area of San Diego County where he had murdered Shirley Bridgeford and, like before, his victim was bound, photographed, sexually assaulted, strangled to death, and buried in a shallow grave.

Glatman's killing spree had gone smoothly until he encountered his fourth potential victim, twenty-eight-year-old Lorraine Vigil. Much like his other victims, Vigil did not initially suspect any evil intentions when she agreed to pose for Glatman. But unlike his other targets, she would be the only one to fight back and survive. On the morning of October 27, 1958, she received a call from her modeling agency that they had a photo shoot assignment for Glatman, who was using the alias Frank Johnson. Early that same evening, Glatman arrived at her apartment and they got into his car with the intention of going to his photography studio. When Glatman abruptly turned onto the Santa Ana freeway instead of heading to Hollywood, Virgil began to get concerned. Driving south towards Orange County, Glatman eventually pulled off the freeway near Tustin. He parked on the shoulder of the highway and informed Virgil that he thought he had a flat tire. He then reached into the backseat and pulled out a gun. He told her that he wouldn't harm her if she listened to his instructions. She later told police that she instinctively knew he was going to kill her and that she had to do something to protect herself. Without thinking, she lunged for the weapon and a violent struggle ensued. Somehow the passenger door of the car opened and they both tumbled out onto the road. They continued to fight for the gun and a single shot rang out, which struck Virgil in the right thigh. At this very moment a highway patrol officer happened upon the scene and arrested Glatman without a fight.

After two days of questioning, Glatman confessed to the murders of Dull, Bridgeford, and Mercado. He then took detectives to the burial locations of his victims. On December 4, 1958, he pleaded guilty to the murders in San Diego County Superior Court and stated that he thought "the guilty plea was proper," and that he deserved to be executed for the crimes rather than spend the rest of his life in prison. On December 18, 1958, he got his wish when Judge John A. Hewicker sentenced him to death. As Glatman was being led out of the courtroom, he told reporters:

> I knew this is the way it would be. I decided to admit everything at the time of my arrest. If I had wanted to, I could have killed that highway patrol man who arrested me, but I gave up the ghost.

On September 18, 1959 at 10:12 a.m., Harvey Glatman "The Lonely Hearts Killer" was executed in the gas chamber at San Quentin Prison.

1957 and 1975
BORN TO KILL
Los Angeles County

Some people are just born bad and one such person was John Laurence Miller. He was born in 1942 in Long Beach, California, to Harold and Lela Miller and had a very troubled childhood. His first brush with the law came at age thirteen, when he was arrested for burglary. Two years later, he was arrested for stealing a car and was sent to the Fred C. Nelles School for Delinquent Boys in Whittier, California. While at the facility, Miller received a ten-hour weekend pass for good behavior. His parents picked him up on the late afternoon of November 10, 1957, and stopped at a local café for dinner. During the meal, John ran away and the next day found his way to the home of Stafford Thurmond, a family friend who lived in Rolling Hills Estates.

The teen's plan was to steal cash and a weapon from Thurmond's gun collection. When he got to the house, Miller discovered that the family was not home, but in the front yard he found twenty-two-month-old Laura Joan Wetzel playing. Miller lured the toddler into the house where he beat and smothered her to death. He fled the scene after being confronted by a neighbor who had come looking for the missing girl. Following a desperate search, Wetzel's body was discovered under a pile of blankets in a bedroom of the Thurmond's home.

After fleeing the scene, Miller stole a bike and rode to Redondo Beach, where he proceeded to steal a car. On November 15, after a four-day, multistate odyssey in which he stole three cars and robbed a San Mateo market, Miller was captured in Reno, Nevada. He had been identified from radio reports by Lloyd Defani, a hitchhiker, who called police with Miller's license plate number. Around 2:00 a.m., a taxi driver spotted the stolen car and trailed it to a gas station where Miller was arrested without incident. He was extradited back to California to stand trial. When interviewed by police, he showed no remorse for the murder but acknowledged he had messed up his life. He told investigators that he had harbored a strong urge to kill since he was a young child and smothered the toddler to see how it would feel.

On December 27, 1957, in Long Beach Superior Court, Miller was found guilty of first-degree murder and sentenced to life in prison. At his sentencing hearing, Charles Wetzel, the slain girl's father, made a prophetic statement in which he denounced the death penalty:

> We don't want revenge; all we want, is to see him put behind bars for the rest of his life, so he can never do it again.

In August 1975, after serving only eighteen years in prison, Miller was paroled. Two months later, on the evening of October 21, 1975, he went to the Long Beach home of his elderly parents, Harold and Lela Miller, and shot them to death. After fleeing the scene, he stole a neighbor's car and vanished. He was captured a week later, on October 30, after a failed robbery of a Bank of America in Downey, California. After his arrest, Miller told detectives that he shot his parents because they had been abusive to him since he was a child and they had ruined his life. He held his father responsible for his conviction in the murder of Laura Wetzel. He also stated that he was unable to cope with the real world after his release from prison.

His murder trial began in Long Beach Superior Court in March 1976, and Miller foolishly acted as his own attorney. In his defense, he told the court that there was no factual basis for finding him innocent or insane at the time of the murders. He confessed to the crime and that he was rational when he did it. Miller later told a probation officer that he wanted to be executed because he lacked the courage to commit suicide. On April 19, Miller was found guilty of two counts of first-degree murder and sentenced to death by Judge Carroll M. Dunnum. This sentence was later reduced to life in prison and he is currently incarcerated at the California State Prison in Lancaster.

1958

A MOTHER'S DEADLY LOVE

Santa Barbara and Ventura County

Elizabeth Ann Duncan was not simply a mother-in-law who resented losing her son to another woman; she was a con-artist and cold-blooded killer who would be the last woman executed in the state of California. Very little is known about Duncan's early life other than she was born in 1904 and allegedly, at one time, owned and operated a brothel in San Francisco. She was a drifter and scammer who preyed on men and had purportedly been married nearly a dozen times. Most of these marriages had been shams and were simply arrangements to swindle money, either through outright theft or alimony. Despite so many relationships, she had only one known child: a son named Frank, who was born in 1929 and was the center of her world.

In 1956, she and Frank moved to Santa Barbara, California, where he began a career as an attorney. Their relationship was incredibly unhealthy but not incestuous; Elizabeth was simply overprotective in her motherly love. Her fixation was so suffocating that she often spent days on end following Frank from courtroom to courtroom. Despite this intense scrutiny, Frank was a skilled lawyer whose friends believed would thrive once he was able to rid himself of his mother's repression.

By 1957, Frank began to assert his independence and decided to move out of the apartment he shared with his mother. In desperation, Elizabeth attempted suicide by taking an overdose of sleeping pills. She was rushed to a local hospital, where her stomach was pumped and she slowly recovered. During her recuperation, she was aided by Olga Kupczyk, a pretty twenty-nine-year-old nurse. While visiting his mother, Frank became infatuated with the young nurse and began spending a lot of time with her. This did not fail to get Elizabeth's attention, whose anxiety over Frank's new woman and an overriding fear of abandonment began to mount.

Over the next three months, Elizabeth clearly objected to her son's dating and threatened Olga. She told her that if she did not leave her son alone, she'd kill her. Olga refused to believe Elizabeth's threats and she and Frank were secretly married on June 20, 1958. When Elizabeth learned of the nuptials, she angrily declared that she'd never allow them to live together. Frank, the ever obedient son, remained at his mother's house until the end of June, visiting his wife at her apartment. Tiring of this double life, he eventually decided to move in with Olga but kept the address a secret from his mother.

In July 1958, Olga became pregnant and once Elizabeth learned of this, she became angry and homicidal. She approached friend Barbara Reed and asked her if she'd assist in killing her daughter-in-law. Elizabeth told Reed that Olga's baby wasn't Frank's, and that Olga was attempting to trap her son. Reed listened and pretended to be of help but immediately informed Frank of the deadly plot. In desperation, he moved back into his mother's home to forestall any notion of murder.

Undeterred, in early August, Elizabeth met with ex-convict Ralph Wintersteint, who agreed to assist in a scheme to secretly annul her son's marriage. On August 8, she and Winterstein appeared as Frank and Olga in Ventura County court and applied for annulment of marriage. The request was granted, but this did not fully satisfy Elizabeth's desire to murder.

On November 12, 1958, Elizabeth met with Esperanza Esquivel at the Tropical Café in Santa Barbara. She was the wife of one of her son's clients. Elizabeth asked Esquivel if she knew anyone who could help get rid of Olga. The next day, Elizabeth returned to the café and was introduced to twenty-one-year-old Luis Moya and twenty-six-year-old Gus Baldonado. Both were petty criminals with bad reputations. Elizabeth told the men that her son was being blackmailed by her daughter-in-law and that she wanted her dead. They agreed to do the deed for $6,000 and planned to kidnap Olga, take her across the border into Mexico, and kill her.

On the evening of November 17, 1958, Moya and Baldonado rented a car and drove to Olga's Santa Barbara apartment. When she came to the door, Moya informed her that her husband was in their car, he was drunk, and needed help. She went outside to investigate and as she opened the rear passenger door, Moya hit her on the back of the head with a handgun and she was pushed into the back seat. They then drove south on Highway 101 with Olga screaming the entire way. Failing to silence her, they pulled off the road near Cabrillo Beach, where they beat her until she lost consciousness. They continued driving south on the 101 until car trouble forced them to

Elizabeth Duncan (center), fifty-four, stands between attorney S. Ward Sullivan (left) and her son, attorney Frank Duncan (right), as she hears Judge Charles F. Blackstock sentence her to death in the gas chamber for hiring two men to kill her daughter-in-law, Olga Duncan. *Courtesy of Bettmann/Corbis.*

change plans. At the Ojai junction, they drove into the mountains and found a secluded location near the Casitas Pass. After pulling to the side of the road, they dragged Olga from the car and began to beat her with a handgun. When the handle of the weapon broke, they were forced to take turns strangling her to death. When she appeared to be dead, they dug a shallow grave, placed her in it, and fled the scene.

Returning to Santa Barbara the next day, Moya contacted Elizabeth Duncan and informed her that they had performed their part of the bargain. She told him that she had not been able to withdraw their money from the bank as planned because police had been inquiring about Olga's disappearance. That same day, Elizabeth cashed a check that Frank had given her to pay for a typewriter. She then met with Moya and gave him an envelope containing $150. When Frank became suspicious and questioned his mother about the check, she made up a story about being blackmailed. Frank believed his mother was somehow connected with his wife's disappearance and went to police. She was brought in for questioning on December 13, and two days later, Moya and Baldonado were arrested. Olga's body was discovered on December 21, and that same day Luis Moya confessed to the murder and implicated both Baldonado and Elizabeth Duncan as accomplices in the crime.

On February 17, 1959, the murder trial of Elizabeth Duncan, Luis Moya, and Augustine Baldonado began in Ventura County Superior Court before Judge Charles F. Blackstock. Taking the stand in her own defense, Elizabeth denied any knowledge or involvement in her daughter-in-law's murder. She stated that she had made the cash payment to Moya and Baldonado because Esperanza Esquivel had threatened her. She testified that Esquivel was unsatisfied with legal advice her son had given her husband. On March 16, unmoved by Elizabeth's testimony, a jury of eight men and four women found all three defendants guilty of first-degree murder. Two and half weeks later, Judge Blackstone sentenced them all to death in the gas chamber.

On August 8, 1962, at 10:00 a.m., Elizabeth Ann Duncan was led into the gas chamber at San Quentin Prison. Pausing at the door of the death chamber, she turned to Warden Frank Dickson and said, "I'm innocent, where's Frank?" Her son was not present at the execution because he was attempting to have the proceedings halted by the governor. Twelve minutes later, she was pronounced dead. Three hours later, it was Moya and Baldonado's turn and, at 1:05 p.m., sitting side by side and showing no remorse for their crimes, they were both executed. This was the first triple execution at San Quentin since 1955, when Barbara Graham and her accomplices had been put to death on the same day.

1958

THE ACTRESS AND THE MOBSTER

Los Angeles

The crime committed here was eventually determined to be largely the victim's fault: Johnny Stompanato's uncontrollable temper made his violent death on the night of April 4, 1958, not only a thing to be expected but was also determined to be justified. Still, Stompanato wasn't the real star of this drama; his girlfriend, Lana Turner, the eight-times-married Hollywood actress who paused between husbands five and six for an ill-advised romance with a hot-headed mobster, was the main event.

Actress Lana Turner, studio publicity photograph.

Lana Turner was no stranger to violent crime. She was born Julia Jean Turner on February 8, 1921, in Wallace, Idaho. The financial hardships of the Great Depression forced her family to relocate to San Francisco in the early 1930s. Her father often supplemented his meager income by gambling, and on the night of December 14, 1930, after a successful run at the poker tables, John Turner was robbed and murdered in the Potrero Hill section of the city. His slaying was never solved and deeply affected his young daughter. Shortly after the murder, Mrs. Turner and her daughter relocated to Los Angeles, where they lived a nondescript life until sixteen-year-old Lana was discovered by Hollywood talent scout Billy Wilkerson at the Top Hat Malt Shop in Hollywood. Her first movie *They Won't Forget* (1937), earned her the nickname "The Sweater Girl" from the form-fitting attire she often wore in that film and others to come. She would reach her peak of stardom during the 1940s and 1950s, and would eventually appear in over fifty feature films and television series.

The tall, dark, and handsome Johnny Stompanato had already lived a life of adventure by the time he got to Hollywood in 1948. Born on October 10, 1925, in Woodstock, Illinois, Stompanato's childhood was filled with trouble. He joined the Marine Corps during World War II and served in the Pacific theater with distinction. After the war, he drifted to various places but eventually found himself in Southern California. There he found employment as a bouncer at one of gangster Mickey Cohen's nightclubs. His size, personality, and style got the crime boss's attention and before long he was hired as Cohen's personal bodyguard. Always a charmer, Stompanato was often photographed on the arm of beautiful, older women whose financial

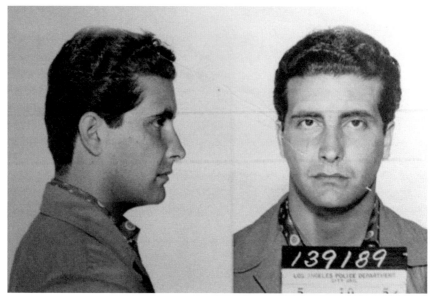

Johhny Stompanato's mug shot (1952). *Photo credit LAPD.*

generosity helped supplement his paltry income. Before meeting Lana Turner, he was married three times.

Turner said she first met Stompanato in 1957, while still married to her fifth husband, Lex Barker. Stompanato called himself John Steele and, for some reason, told Lana that he was five years her senior, when in fact it was the other way around. Things moved quickly between the pair. Turner later wrote:

> His wooing was gentle, persistent, and finally persuasive. By the time I found out his real name, we were already having an affair.

She had mixed feelings about dating a man who was a known gangster, yet the danger factor was quite appealing. It was in England during the filming of *Another Time, Another Place* that Stompanato first became physically violent with Turner. He was bored and complaining bitterly about Lana's reluctance to be seen in public with him when an argument escalated into a shoving match. After the incident, Turner decided that she needed space from the relationship and traveled to Acapulco, Mexico. She tried to keep her arrival a secret, but when her plane landed at the airport, Stompanato and a group of reporters met her. No studio publicity agent was present, leading her to believe Johnny had set up the press conference. His physically abusive behavior continued to escalate. While vacationing in Mexico, Lana learned she had been nominated for a best actress Academy Award for her work in *Peyton Place*. Stompanato was equally excited until Lana made it clear he wasn't going to be accompanying her to the ceremony. She couldn't

Newsmen and the coroner's van outside the Beverly Hills home of actress Lana Turner, where Johnny Stompanato was stabbed to death on April 4, 1958. *Courtesy of Bettmann/ Corbis.*

be seen in public with a known gangster and no amount of pleading would change her mind.

The evening of March 26, 1958, began blissfully for Lana Turner but ended in a nightmare. At Turner's Beverly Hills mansion, Stompanato sat home alone, watching the Academy Awards ceremony on television and was growing angrier by the minute. By the time Turner returned home from several post-Oscar parties, Johnny was drunk and raging. He berated her for not winning and slapped her face. Witnessing all of this was fourteen-year-old Cheryl Crane, Turner's daughter from her second marriage to Joseph Crane. The incident obviously loomed large in the teen's mind one week later when Stompanato was again berating her mother. On the evening of April 4, during yet another argument between Turner and Stompanato, Crane decided her mother had suffered enough abuse. She ran to the kitchen, grabbed an eight-inch knife, and made her way to her mother's second-floor master bedroom. Crane later testified that she walked into the room, and said, "You don't have to take that, Mother," and without warning plunged the knife into Stompanato's stomach.

Within minutes, a doctor was at the scene, who attempted to revive Stompanato with a shot of adrenaline, but it was useless. He was already dead. It was inevitable that the news media would be tipped to the story by police sources, so Turner called her lawyer, Jerry Geisler, who was on the scene before law enforcement officials arrived. The next morning, lurid photos of

Johnny Stompanato's lifeless body were splashed across the front page of every newspaper in Los Angeles. Turner and her daughter were taken to the Beverly Hills Police Station for questioning, where Cheryl recounted the events surrounding Stompanato's death.

Mickey Cohen identified Johnny Stompanato's body at the city morgue. He knew all about Turner and Stompanato, and he intended to get some cash out of the situation. Weeks after the slaying, a mysterious package was delivered to Turner's attorney's office. Inside was a series of photographs of a naked Lana Turner. When she failed to be swayed by Cohen's blackmail threats, he leaked Turner and Stompanato's love letters to the press. If he wasn't going to make any money from the situation, he was going to make sure she was finished in Hollywood. The *Los Angeles Herald Examiner* was the first to break the story, and two days before the inquest into Stompanato's death was to convene, they printed every word from the letters. Cohen freely admitted that it was he who had leaked the titillating correspondence.

After the killing, Cheryl Crane escaped the immediate glare of the media by being detained in the Beverly Hills city jail, then at a Los Angeles County juvenile detention center. On April 11, 1958, exactly one week after Stompananto's slaying, a coroner's inquest hearing was convened. While live television broadcasted the proceedings, millions of viewers watched as a flawlessly and impeccably dressed Lana Turner sobbed on the witness stand, recalling the abuse she had suffered at the hands of Stompanato. Two weeks later, the jury declared that Crane had committed justifiable homicide and the district attorney's office declined any further prosecution in the case.

After the inquest, Stompanato's family brought a wrongful death civil lawsuit against Turner. The case was eventually settled out of court and financial damages were never disclosed. Cheryl Crane went to live with her maternal grandmother and later reconciled with her mother. Today, she is a successful businesswoman living in the San Francisco Bay area. In 1988, she wrote a memoir in which she discussed not only the killing but also the sexual abuse that she had suffered at the hands of Turner's fifth husband, Lex Barker. After the death of Stompanato, Lana Turner went on to more men, movies, and tabloid headlines. She also starred in the successful 1980s television drama *Falcon Crest,* and until her death from lung cancer in 1995, remained one of Hollywood's legendary actresses.

1959

A TERRIBLE URGE TO KILL

San Mateo County

Rosemarie Diane "Penny" Bjorkland wasn't a serial slayer or mass murderer, but she was a cold-blooded thrill killer. At the age of eighteen, the pretty young blonde lived with her religiously strict parents and siblings in Daly City, California, and worked as a file clerk at a publisher's service bureau in downtown San Francisco. She was conscientious in her work habits and considered an asset to the firm. A loner, she secretly harbored a deep-seeded hatred for her mother. For many years, Penny daydreamed about how it would feel to kill someone—anyone. She stole a .38 caliber handgun from a friend and began target shooting with it in the hills near her home.

On Sunday morning, February 1, 1959, Penny awoke abruptly and said to herself: "This is the day I will kill someone. If I meet anyone, that will be it." After a contemptuous breakfast with her mother, Penny went into her room, got dressed, and, after taking out her gun, went hunting for someone to kill. Later that same day, twenty-nine-year-old August Norry came across the young woman as she was hiking in the hills above Daly City. He pulled off the road and offered her a ride. Once inside the truck, Bjorkland pulled out a handgun and began to fire it out the open passenger window. Norry abruptly stopped the car and asked her to put the gun away. She complied momentarily and they sat and spoke casually for several minutes. She then, nonchalantly and without a word, pulled the gun out and shot Norry in the side of the head, killing him instantly. Bjorkland exited the truck, walked to the driver's side and emptied the gun's remaining rounds into his body. She then reloaded the gun and pushed the dead man over to the passenger side. After driving a short distance, she pulled off the road and drove through a fence. Her blood lust not yet satisfied, she pulled Norry's body out of the truck and shot him until the ammunition was again expelled. Now fully satiated, she left her victim's body in the bushes and drove his truck a short distance to Christmas Tree Hill, where she had parked her own car. She then got into her vehicle and drove home to have dinner with her family. The next day, she disposed of the murder weapon and unused ammunition in a sewer drain.

Norry's truck and body were found later that same day, and because he had sustained eighteen bullet wounds, seventeen of which had been committed after he died, police assumed the killing must have been a crime of passion. A witness later came forward and stated he saw a freckle-faced blonde woman driving the truck on the day of the murder. Over the next two months, police investigators dug into Norry's background, hoping to uncover a motive or suspect in the slaying. They discovered he was married with a pregnant wife and had been a Korean War veteran. After leaving the military, he attended landscape architecture school. At the time of his death, he was employed at the Lake Merced Country Club as a gardener. Detectives interviewed his fellow coworkers and found out that he might have been involved in several extramarital affairs.

Investigators initially believed the murder was most likely revenge related, perpetrated by either a jilted lover, angry boyfriend, or husband. After ballistic testing on the bullets used to kill Norry were concluded, it was determined that the ammunition was unusual and easily traced. Detectives were able to track down the manufacturer of the ammo and learned that it was sold in a San Francisco gun shop owned by Lawrence Schultze. The proprietor admitted to selling fifty rounds of "woodcutters" to a teenage blonde. He had her name on his receipt files: Penny Bjorkland of Daly City.

On April 15, 1959, San Mateo County Sheriff's detectives went to Bjorkland's house. Penny appeared calm and answered all of their questions. She also gave them permission to search her room where they found newspaper clippings of the Norry murder. Convinced that she was connected to the slaying in some way, investigators asked her to accompany them to sheriff's headquarters for further questioning. After hours of intense interrogation, she confessed to the murder of August Norry. She told them she had a terrible urge to kill for over a year and that the crime had been random and it had satiated her curiosity. At no time in the process did she ever show remorse for the killing.

On July 20, 1959, Bjorkland threw herself on the mercy of the San Mateo County court and pleaded guilty to second-degree murder. In exchange for the plea arrangement, she received a sentence of life in prison with the possibility of parole in seven years. Prior to her sentencing on August 6, she underwent several weeks of psychological examinations in which no diagnosable mental deficiency was detected. Bjorkland was paroled from prison in the late-1960s and her whereabouts since her release are not known. There are some unverifiable claims that place her in Thousand Oaks, California, where she allegedly works as a volunteer at a local hospital.

1959

FATAL LOVE TRIANGLE

Los Angeles County

"I know he will kill me," the attractive thirty-six-year-old blonde said to her lawyer. "I know exactly how it will happen. He will take me to the desert or the mountains in my car and kill me and make it look like an accident." This was Mrs. Barbara Finch speaking to her lawyer Joseph T. Farno on the morning of May 1, 1959. She went on to relate how her husband had pistol-whipped her and threatened to strangle her to death the night before. This prophesy would become a reality two-and-a-half months later.

By the summer of 1959, wealthy Los Angeles area physician Bernard Finch, forty-two, yearned to marry his twenty-two-year-old mistress Carole Tregoff. Standing directly in the path of their happily-ever-after was Barbara Jean Finch, thirty-three, the doctor's wife—and the formidable California community property laws. Divorce would have entitled Mrs. Finch to half of her husband's sizable fortune. Furthermore, if she could prove infidelity, her husband could face financial ruin, since the court could allocate any percentage of the community property it deemed fit to the distressed party.

Bernard was introduced to Tregoff in 1955, when she began working as a receptionist at his West Covina medical office. The doctor was immediately infatuated with the beautiful redhead, but they did not consummate their sexual relationship until two years later. Finch's womanizing behavior was common knowledge around the office, and it was well-known that he had carried on numerous office romances over the years.

At the time Dr. Finch began the affair with Tregoff, she was still married to James Pappa. When Barbara Finch became aware of her husband's infidelity during the summer of 1958, she immediately asked her husband to move out of their West Covina home and filed for divorce. On September 9, 1958, Mrs. Finch telephoned James Pappa and told him of their spouses' affair. A furious Pappa confronted his wife when she came home from work. The next day, Carole moved out of their La Puente home and also filed for divorce. Two contentious months would pass, before Tregoff and Finch agreed that it would be better if she got out of town until the divorce actions were settled. She moved to Las Vegas and found work as a cocktail waitress. (In an interesting

Finch home in West Covina. *Courtesy of Gary Cliser.*

twist to the case, Barbara Finch was the ex-wife of Lyle Daugherty, who was the husband of Frances Daugherty, Bernard Finch's first wife.)

Unwilling to accept financial ruin, Dr. Finch and Tregoff secretly began to plot a way to end his marriage. In early July 1959, Finch drove to Las Vegas and they hatched a scheme in which they would hire a hit man to kill Barbara. It was Tregoff who suggested they ask John Patrick Cody, a friend and ex-convict, if he'd be willing to help. On July 1, Cody met with Tregoff and agreed to kill Mrs. Finch for $1,400. After accepting an initial down payment, he departed for Los Angeles but never intended to carry out the plan. Instead of killing Barbara Finch, he spent the weekend with one of his many girlfriends. Returning to Las Vegas a few days later, he lied to Tregoff telling her he had taken care of the situation. She paid him the balance of the money owed, only to learn later that Mrs. Finch was still very much alive. When she confronted Cody, he again lied stating he must have killed the wrong woman but for another $200 he'd rectify the mistake. With additional cash in hand, Cody then disappeared without fulfilling the deadly plan. Finch and Tregoff now became more desperate and decided to take the matter into their own hands.

Around 10:00 p.m. on July 18, 1959, Dr. Finch and Carole Tregoff arrived at his West Covina home to confront Mrs. Finch. She wasn't home but an hour later, arrived and was immediately confronted by her husband in the driveway. At some point, a struggle broke out and Barbara Finch was shot and killed. For reasons that have never been fully explained, Dr. Finch and Tregoff became separated during the altercation. He fled the scene, stealing several cars along the way and, the next morning, joined Tregoff in Las Vegas. That afternoon, he was taken into custody by Las Vegas police and charged with the murder of his wife. Eleven days later, Tregoff was similarly charged.

Their murder trial began in Los Angeles Superior Court on January 4, 1960. Prosecutors called their first witness, nineteen-year-old Marie Anne Lindholm, a Swedish exchange student and maid who was living at the

Finch's home. Lindholm testified that on the night of the slaying she heard Mrs. Finch scream for help in the garage of their home. Alarmed, she entered the garage and saw Mrs. Finch on the floor bleeding from a wound to her forehead with Dr. Finch standing directly over his estranged wife. She then testified that the doctor rushed at her and threw her against the garage wall. He ordered both women to get into his car shouting, "I'll kill you if you don't listen." At that same moment, Mrs. Finch attempted to flee the scene with her husband in pursuit. Seconds later, Lindholm stated she heard a gunshot and retreated into the house to call police. Barbara Finch's body was discovered about 100 feet from the house on an embankment under a small tree.

This testimony was extremely damaging to the defense's case, but equally harmful was the fact that Lindholm testified that she had witnessed Dr. Finch regularly abuse and threaten his wife. When John Cody took the witness stand, he admitted to every form of reprehensible conduct imaginable, but by far the most damning testimony came when he detailed the conversation he had with Tregoff, in which she allegedly stated:

Jack, you can back out. But if you don't kill her, the doctor will; and if he doesn't, I will.

When defense attorneys called Dr. Finch to the witness stand in his own defense, he described in great detail how his wife, and not he, was the aggressor the night of her death. He stated that he and Carole had approached his wife as she exited her car in an attempt to persuade her to get a quickie Nevada divorce. He stated that Barbara became belligerent and refused to talk, reached back into the front seat of her car and produced a hand gun that she pointed directly at Tregoff. Fearing for his life, he attempted to take the gun away and in the ensuing struggle, Mrs. Finch was inadvertently pushed into the wall of the garage and injured her head. She began to scream for help and that was when Miss Lindholm saw him standing over his wife in the garage. He also testified that Lindholm had misinterpreted his attempts to calm her obvious distress, when he grabbed and roughly shoved her against the wall. He also denied threatening either woman. He acknowledged that he did chase his wife down the driveway, but only because he wanted to take the gun from her and that during the struggle to disarm her, the weapon accidentally discharged striking her in the back. He also testified that because of the shock of what had just happened, he ill-advisedly fled the scene in a state of panic, and somehow ended up at Carole Tregoff's Las Vegas apartment the next morning.

When Carole Tregoff took the stand, her account of the events were also quite farfetched. She told of silently watching the scene unfold, then cowering for five or six hours behind some shrubs, paralyzed with fear, while police turned the house upside down. Later, she had driven back to Las Vegas, alone.

Carole Tregoff and Dr. R. Bernard Finch at their first murder trial (1960). *Courtesy of the Los Angeles Public Library.*

Allegedly, her first knowledge of Barbara Finch's death came via the car radio. Prosecutors succeeded in discrediting much of her testimony in which they highlighted her leading role in the solicitation of Cody, and her conflicting statements as to why the couple had gone to the Finch's home the night of the killing.

After eight days of deliberation, the jury announced that they were unable to agree on a verdict and a mistrial was declared. A second trial convened on June 27, 1960, and it too ended in a mistrial. A third trial opened on January 3, 1961, before Superior Court Judge David Coleman. By now, much of the news media coverage had dissipated and, on March 27, 1961, Raymond Bernard Finch was convicted of first-degree murder and Carole Tregoff was found guilty of second-degree murder. Both escaped the gas chamber and were sentenced to life imprisonment. In 1969, Tregoff was paroled, changed her name, and moved back to the Pasadena area. Dr. Finch was released two years later, practiced medicine in Missouri for a decade, remarried and moved back to Southern California. He died in 1995.

1959

THE SEX CLUB SLAYING

Marin County

On the morning of November 16, 1959, twelve-year-old Lorna Jane Lax was found dead near her Kentfield, California, home. Her body was discovered in her secret tree house hideaway by a neighborhood friend. She was dressed in a pajama top, her legs were stuffed into a sleeping bag, and her torso was held erect by a rope that was tied around her neck and lashed to a tree branch. She had been beaten, sexually assaulted, and stabbed to death with a steak knife, which was found nearby. The young girl was shy and reserved. She suffered from a cleft palate that caused a slight speech impediment. Because of the disability and its stigma, she suffered psychological issues that caused her to withdraw and commit self-destructive behavior. In search of attention, she allegedly created a "sex club" with area boys who visited her at her secret hideaway and sometimes paid her small amounts of cash for sexual favors.

On Saturday November 14, Lax was having a particularly bad day. She left a note for her parents saying she was "mad at the world" and would return the next day. Since this wasn't unusual behavior for the young girl, her parents weren't overly concerned. That evening she attended a local high school football game at the College of Marin where she rendezvoused with a neighborhood boy, fifteen-year-old Clifford Fortner. He and his family had moved to Kentfield six years earlier from Jasper, Alabama. When Lorna did not return the next day, her parent's became concerned and reported her missing. The girl's body was discovered on Monday morning by thirteen-year-old Norman Fortner, the younger brother of Clifford.

Over the next several weeks, Marin County Sheriff's investigators questioned numerous suspects about the murder. On the morning of December 2, they arrived at Kentfield Elementary School and asked to speak with Clifford Fortner. After several hours of interrogation in the principal's office, the boy confessed to killing Lax. He told police that he had met the girl at the high school football game and around midnight they went back to her secret hideout to have sex. Lorna's hideaway was in a wooded section along Ross Valley Creek, several hundred yards from her house and a short walk from the College of Marin football stadium. The teen also told investigators that after having sexual intercourse with the girl, he flew into a sudden fit of rage and hit her on the head with a flashlight. When he saw that she wasn't dead, he hung her from a tree limb and stabbed her twice in the stomach with a knife. When asked why he had killed the girl, Fortner replied, "I don't know why I did it, something just came over me." The girl had been a playmate of the Fortner children and had visited their home the day before she was murdered.

Clifford Fortner was taken to Marin County Juvenile Hall to await arraignment. While in custody he underwent extensive psychological testing that showed him to have significant sociopathic tendencies. Court-appointed psychiatrists went on to state that his character and emotional difficulties were such that it was probable that his psychological state of mind would deteriorate if left in jail without intensive mental health care. On January 8, 1960, Marin County Superior Court Judge Thomas Keating declared Fortner a ward of the state and mentally unfit to stand trial. The proceedings were indefinitely suspended and he was remanded to the custody of the Langley Porter Psychiatric Clinic in San Francisco. He remained at the facility until March 1961, when he was transferred to a Marin County foster home. Fortner was never officially charged with the murder of Lorna Lax and what happened to him after reaching adulthood is not known.

1959

THE REAL HOUSE ON HAUNTED HILL

Los Angeles

In February 1959, William Castle's classic horror movie *House on Haunted Hill* premiered. The exterior scenes of the film were shot at the historic Ennis House in the affluent and picturesque neighborhood of Los Feliz, which is nestled in the foothills of Griffith Park in Los Angeles. The plot of the movie revolves around an eccentric millionaire, played by Vincent Price, who invites a group of guests to a rented mansion. The house is supposedly haunted and if any of them manages to survive the night, they each would receive a large sum of cash. Throughout the night, each of the hapless guests is subjected to a multitude of frights and tormented by ghosts and murders. As is often the case, real life oftentimes imitates art, and ten months after the release of the film, a true-life horror occurred in the same area.

Today, not far from the Ennis House, stands another mansion that sits abandoned and frozen in time. The grounds of the once-beautiful estate are chocked with overgrown weeds and, through its filthy soot-covered windows, one can still see the personal belongings of its long-gone former inhabitants. The home on Glendower Place, near the famed Greek Theatre,

On December 6, 1959, Dr. Harold Perelson murdered his wife and committed suicide at this mansion in the Los Feliz section of Los Angeles.

still harbors many secrets and unanswered questions: Why has the home remained exactly as it appeared on the frightful night of December 6, 1959?

On that evening, Harold N. Perelson, fifty, a well-liked physician associated with the Inglewood Medical Clinic, used a ball-peen hammer to bludgeon to death his forty-two-year-old wife Lillian as she slept. He also attacked and severely injured his eighteen-year-old daughter, Judye. When the Perelson's two younger children, Debbie, eleven, and Joel, thirteen, were awoken by the commotion and screams of their older sister, their father entered their bedroom and told them to go back to bed; they were just having a nightmare.

After being savagely attacked by her father, Judye, with a severe wound to her head, managed to stumble to a neighbor's home for help. The neighbor, Marshall Ross, immediately called police and then went to the Perelson's home to investigate what had happened. At the door, he was greeted by Dr. Perelson, who appeared to be very agitated. Ross told Perelson to lie down on a couch and that police were on the way.

When Los Angeles police officers arrived at the scene, they found Dr. Perelson and his wife dead in the master bedroom of the house. Lillian was lying on the bed in a pool of blood with massive head wounds and Harold was found on the floor. He had apparently ingested a bottle of acid (although some accounts point to overdose of pills) and beside him on the floor was the alleged murder weapon. On the night stand next to the bed, detectives found a copy of *Dante's Divine Comedy*, which was open to a prophetic passage, which read: "Midway upon the journey of our life I found myself within a forest dark, for the straightforward pathway had been lost." Detectives speculated that Perelson had committed the murder because he was distraught over financial difficulties. This theory was further reinforced by a note that was found in Judye Perelson's sports car that also pointed to possible money issues within the family, but the real reason for the killing died with Harold Perelson.

Following the attack, Judye Perelson was transported to a local hospital and successfully recovered from her wounds. The younger children were taken to live with relatives on the East Coast and, today, the whereabouts of the three children are unknown. Harold and Lillian Perelson were buried beside one another at Home of Peace Cemetery in East Los Angeles. In December 1960, the Perelson's home was sold to Julian and Emily Enriquez, and for some reason they never moved into the home and never removed any of the Perelson's belongings. Since 1959, the house has fallen into major disrepair and it's no surprise that rumors persist of its possible haunting. Current owner Rudy Enriquez inherited the home in 1994, after his mother's death. He has been asked to sell the property but has refused all offers. So, why does the home remain a time capsule to the tragedy that took place there in 1959? No one really knows the answer to that question, but if the home is not inhabited by restless spirits, then it is truly haunted by the horrific events that occurred within its walls.

CHAPTER TWO

The Sensational Crimes of the 1960s

"Crime and bad lives are the
measure of a State's failure,
all crime in the end is the
crime of the community."

-H. G. Wells
Author (1866-1946) from *A Modern Utopia*

1961

THE DOWNFALL OF THE KING OF WESTERN SWING

Kern County

Donnell Clyde "Spade" Cooley was an actor and big band leader of the 1940s and 1950s and rose to become the King of Western Swing music. His rise to fame and fortune was cut short after he murdered his second wife in a fit of jealous rage on April 3, 1961.

Cooley was born on December 17, 1910, in Oklahoma, and being of Cherokee descent was educated at the Chemawa Indian Boarding School in Oregon. He began playing violin with Western bands while in high school and got his nickname "Spade" during a poker game in which he won several straight hands with spade flushes. In 1931, at the age of twenty-one, tired of farm work, Cooley headed to Hollywood to become a singing cowboy. There he joined The Jimmy Wakely Trio, who performed at the Venice Pier Ballroom. After Wakely left the band to pursue a movie career in the early 1940s, Cooley took over the band, changing its name to Spade Cooley & His Western Band. They would have several hits that included "Shame on You," which was number one on the country charts for several weeks in 1944. Riding the wave of success, Cooley became friends with actor and singer Roy Rogers, and appeared in over thirty-eight films as a stand-in or stunt double for the singing cowboy. Contrary to popular belief, Cooley was never a member of the Sons of the Pioneers. In 1948, he became a local Los Angeles television personality, hosting a variety show for five years.

Though Cooley was a talented musician and actor who was well-liked, he had a darker side that often came out when drinking. During drunken binges, he would often become violent and start fights with friends and fellow band members. He was also a known womanizer, who in 1945 began an affair with twenty-year-old Ella Mae Evans, a pretty back-up singer in his band. That same year he divorced his first wife Ann, and on December 9, married his mistress in Las Vegas. Cooley and Evans would have two children together. After the wedding, he bought a sprawling ranch estate in Willow Springs, near the foothills of the Tehachapi Mountains in Kern County, north of Los Angeles.

Spade Cooley and his wife Ella Mae in 1954. *Courtesy of AP/Corbis.*

In the 1950s, country swing music began to decline in popularity with the rise of rock 'n' roll, and Cooley's music career declined. He retired from show business, had a beautiful wife and family, and had millions of dollars in his bank account, but there wouldn't be a happily ever after ending. As he got older, his drinking got worse, his temper became more violent, and paranoia began to overwhelm him. He began to imagine his wife was having an affair with Roy Rogers, even though she rarely left the secluded ranch and was never allowed visitors. Even on the rare occasion when she was allowed to go out, Cooley would grill her about every detail.

By March 1961, Cooley's paranoia had reached such a level that he filed for divorce and Ella Mae moved out of the family home. On April 3, 1961, the situation turned deadly. In a fit of jealous rage, Cooley beat his wife to death. In the days leading up to the murder, Cooley and his wife had made an attempt at reconciliation. The tragedy was partially witnessed by the couple's fourteen-year-old daughter Melody, who told investigators that she had gone to the ranch house after speaking with her mother by phone. Melody and her younger brother had been living with Mrs. W. P. McWhorter in Rosamond. The young girl stated that when she arrived at the house in the early evening, she found her mother unconscious in the family bathroom. She witnessed her father drag her mother's body out of the shower and beat her head on the floor and stomp on her stomach. She was then ordered to put her mother into bed. Her father threatened to kill her if she told anyone about the incident. At that point, Melody ran from the house and encountered Mrs. McWhorter, who was waiting outside. Knowing the domestic violence history of the family, McWhorter phoned Cooley's daughter-in-law. When

Dorothy Cooley arrived at the ranch around 7:00 p.m., she was met at the front door of the residence by her father-in-law. He had a blank stare on his face and his clothing was blood-spattered. When he asked her to look in on Ella Mae, because he feared she was dead, Dorothy refused and left the scene. Later that night, Cooley's longtime business manager Barbara Bennett arrived at the ranch. She found Ella Mae unconscious on the bed. Cooley told her that she had fallen in the shower and hit her head. He insisted that he thought she'd be okay. An ambulance was called and Ella Mae was transported to a local hospital where she was pronounced dead on arrival. Cooley was arrested and charged with murder.

His trial began on July 10, 1961, in Kern County Superior Court in Bakersfield. During the proceedings, Cooley suffered numerous health ailments that included a heart attack, which delayed the trial. The prosecution described Cooley as the aggressor and that he basically tortured his wife to death. They relied primarily on the eyewitness testimony of Melody Cooley and forensic evidence. Spade Cooley eventually took the stand in his own defense and told the court that he struck his wife in a fit of rage after she gloated about several recent affairs and that she was going to join a free-love colony. He told the court that after striking his wife, he helped her into the shower where she fell and struck her head. He did not recall seeing his daughter at the home that evening. The jury of ten men and two women did not believe the defense's allegations of temporary insanity and that Ella Mae was a contributor in her own death. They found Cooley guilty of first-degree murder on August 19, 1961. Three days later, Cooley unexpectedly withdrew his insanity plea and waived a jury hearing on the penalty phase and threw himself on the mercy of the court. On August 22, 1961, Superior Court Judge William L. Bradshaw sentenced Cooley to life in prison. During his time in prison, Cooley became a model prisoner and eventually confessed to the murder of his wife. On November 23, 1969, eight years into his life sentence, Cooley, fifty-nine, collapsed while performing at a benefit concert for the Deputy Sheriff's Association of Alameda County at the Oakland Auditorium. He had received a seventy-two-hour furlough to perform and, during intermission of the concert, in which he received a standing ovation from the crowd of over 2,000, he suffered a fatal heart attack backstage. His last words were allegedly, "I have the feeling that today is the first day of the rest of my life." Ironically, he was scheduled to be released on parole only a few months later in February 1970. Cooley was buried at the Chapel of the Chimes Memorial Park in Hayward, California.

1962

ESCAPE FROM ALCATRAZ

San Francisco

At its peak of operation, Alcatraz was considered to be the definitive maximum security prison in the United States. Located on an island in the middle of San Francisco Bay, it was nicknamed "The Rock" and had held prisoners since the Civil War. In 1775, Spanish explorer Juan Manuel de Ayala was the first to sail into San Francisco Bay. His expedition mapped the bay and named one of the three islands Alcatraces. Over time, the name was changed to Alcatraz. While the exact meaning is still disputed, Alcatraz is usually defined as meaning pelican or strange bird. Beginning in 1934, Alcatraz was rebuilt to house some of the twentieth century's most notorious criminals, such as Al Capone, George "Machine Gun" Kelly, Alvin Karpis, Arthur "Doc" Barker, Mickey Cohen, and "The Birdman of Alcatraz," Robert Stroud. The convicts who passed through its gates were considered to be the worst of the worst, hardened felons with no hope of rehabilitation, or considered to be extreme escape risks.

Prior to its renovation during the Great Depression, Alcatraz was already a bleak and depressing place, surrounded by the icy and treacherous waters of San Francisco Bay. The reconstruction plans included installing stronger bars, more guard towers, and stringent guidelines. Because of the natural barriers and these structural and procedural improvements, "The Rock" was considered to be escape-proof. Despite the safeguards, between 1934 and its closing in 1963, thirty-six men made fourteen different attempts to escape. Almost all of them failed. However, the fate of three fugitive convicts remains unsolved to this day.

John and Clarence Anglin were convicted of the 1958 robbery of a Columbia, Alabama, bank for which they both received thirty-year prison sentences. After a failed escape attempt from an Alabama prison, John was sent to Alcatraz on October 21, 1960. His brother Clarence followed on January 10, 1961. Frank Morris was a hardened criminal with a long history of violent crimes that included burglary, armed robbery, assault, and drug possession. He was born in Washington, DC, in 1926, where he was abandoned by his mother. He spent almost his entire childhood in and out of juvenile

Alcatraz Island, San Francisco Bay.

detention centers. He arrived at Alcatraz on January 3, 1960, and almost immediately began plans to escape.

At 7:15 a.m., on June 12, 1962, a routine head check turned out to be anything but ordinary. Three prisoners were not in their cells: John Anglin, his brother Clarence, and Frank Morris. In their beds, guards found lifelike dummy heads with real hair that were so realistic they had fooled the overnight watch. After the discovery, the prison was put into lockdown mode and an intensive manhunt began. Federal, state, and local law enforcement agencies were immediately notified. The FBI began checking records on the missing prisoners and their previous escape attempts. They interviewed relatives and asked boat operators in and around San Francisco Bay to be on the lookout for debris. Several days later, a pack of letters, pieces of wood, a homemade life vest, and portions of a rubber inner tube were found on a local beach, but no other items were ever found.

As the days and weeks went by, law enforcement began to piece together the escape plan. There had been a fourth conspirator, Allen West, who wasn't able to get out of his cell in time. He helped piece together vital information on the escape plan. Investigators learned that the group had begun planning the escape in December 1961. Using crude tools, they each loosened the air vents in the back of their cells. Behind the cells was an unguarded service corridor, through which the escapees made their way to the roof of the cell block. Once there, they took turns watching for guards until after the last

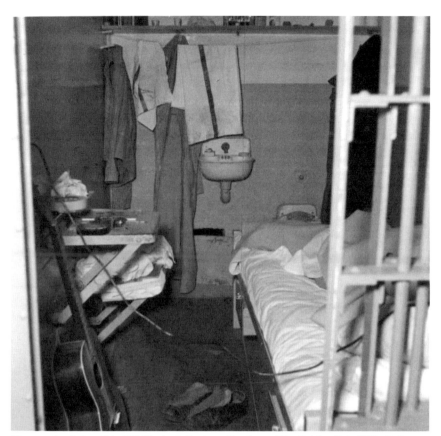

Clarence Anglin's cell in "B" Block at Alcatraz. *Courtesy of the Golden Gate NRA, Park Archives, GOGA-17975-21.*

head count. Leading up to the escape, they collected a variety of materials that would aid them in the escape.

They stole more than fifty raincoats, which were turned into makeshift life preservers and a small rubber raft. They also built wooden paddles and converted a musical instrument into a tool to inflate the raft. All of these supplies were stored in the utility corridor. One stumbling block to the escape was how to get off the thirty-foot-high roof. Using a network of pipes, each of them shimmied down the rear of the cell house, climbed over the fence, and snuck to the northeast shore of the island to launch their raft.

Did they make it across the Bay to Angel Island, and then into Marin County as planned? Plenty of people have gone to great lengths to prove that they could have survived, but the question remains: did they? The FBI concluded they could not have made it for the following reasons: the mile-long swim from Alcatraz to Angel Island had very strong currents, frigid water temperatures, and was shark infested. The plan, according to Allen West, was to steal a car and some clothes once in Marin County, but in the days

WANTED BY THE FBI

ESCAPED FEDERAL PRISONER — BANK ROBBER
CLARENCE ANGLIN

FBI No. 4,731,702

Photograph taken 1960   Photographs taken 1958

DESCRIPTION

Age: 31, born May 11, 1931, Donalsonville, Georgia (not supported by birth records)
Height: 5'11"   **Complexion:** Light

FBI wanted poster for Clarence Anglin. *Courtesy of the Golden Gate NRA, Park Archives, GOGA-231684-c-46b.*

after the escape, there were no reported auto thefts. If they had received outside assistance, it was never proven. The families of the three escapees appeared unlikely to have provided any real financial support. For the past five decades since the escape, no credible evidence has ever arisen to suggest that these men were still alive, either in the US or any other place. On December 31, 1979, the FBI officially closed its case, and turned over responsibility to the US Marshals Service, which continues to investigate leads in the unlikely event the trio is still alive.

On March 21, 1963, Alcatraz closed after nearly three decades of operation. Contrary to popular belief, it was not closed because of the escape. The decision to close the prison was made long before the three disappeared; and, because the institution was too expensive to continue operating, the Department of Justice found that it was more cost-effective to build a new institution than to keep it open. In 1969, Alcatraz again made news headlines when a group of Native American protestors took over the island. In 1972, Congress created the Golden Gate National Recreation Area, and Alcatraz Island was included as part of the new park. The prison and grounds opened to the public in the fall of 1973 and has since become one of the most popular tourist attractions in San Francisco.

WANTED BY THE FBI

ESCAPED FEDERAL PRISONER — BANK ROBBER
JOHN WILLIAM ANGLIN

FBI No. 4,745,119

Photographs taken 1960

DESCRIPTION

Age: 32, born May 2, 1930, Donalsonville, Georgia (not supported by birth records)
Height: 5'10"   **Complexion:** Ruddy
Weight: 140 pounds   **Race:** White
Build: Medium   **Nationality:** American

FBI wanted poster for John Anglin. *Courtesy of the Golden Gate NRA, Park Archives, GOGA-231684-c-46b.*

1964

PACIFIC AIRLINES FLIGHT 773

Contra Costa County

In the 1960s, getting on board a commercial airplane was much simpler than it is today. As a customer, you paid your fare, walked through a gate or across a tarmac, and simply boarded the aircraft. There were no x-ray screeners, security checkpoints, or TSA guards. The peak of political hijackings to Cuba was still several years away, only to be followed by more radical terrorist hijackings in the 1970s and 1980s. The first documented hijacking of an aircraft came on February 21, 1931, in Peru. After that, the number of accounts of air piracy continued to climb with

each passing year. Even with the rising statistics,
people still generally believed it was safe to fly
and no one thought a person was foolish enough to
bring a handgun on an airplane and threaten to kill,
let alone actually carry out the threats, but that's
exactly what happened in the spring of 1964.

Francisco Paula Gonzales, twenty-seven, of San Francisco, was a troubled soul, severely depressed and on the verge of a psychiatric breakdown when he boarded a commuter flight in Reno, Nevada, on May 7, 1964. He had been a member of the Philippine sailing team at the 1960 Summer Olympics in Rome. However, since then his life had been in a steady decline. He was having marital issues and suffering tremendous financial distress. On the evening of May 6, in a state of severe depression, Gonzales purchased a .357-magnum handgun and, according to later reports, told friends and relatives that he planned to commit suicide and referred to his impending death on a daily basis. The same night he purchased the gun, he arrived at San Francisco International Airport, purchased a round-trip ticket to Reno, and took out two insurance policies totaling over $100,000.

At the airport, Gonzales showed his gun to numerous people and told them he intended to commit suicide. He then boarded the flight to Reno, with a ticket to return the next day aboard Pacific Airlines Flight 773. Sadly, no one bothered to report the bizarre behavior to authorities. Once in Reno, Gonzales spent the night drinking and gambling at various downtown casinos. Early the next morning, he arrived at the airport and boarded flight 773, which was headed to San Francisco with one stop in Stockton. According to witnesses who had departed the flight in Stockton, Gonzales was seated directly behind the cockpit door. The Fairchild F-27, twin-engine turbo prop commuter plane took off at 5:54 a.m., with thirty-three passengers and three crew members. A half hour later, the plane landed in Stockton. Two passengers deplaned and ten more got on board. One of the passengers who boarded the ill-fated plane in Stockton was famed gospel music singer Polly Johnson.

At 6:38 a.m., the plane took off for San Francisco. Several minutes into the next leg of the flight, Gonzales pulled out his gun and stormed the cockpit. He immediately shot and killed fifty-two-year-old pilot Ernest Clark. At 6:48 the aircraft radioed its last message: copilot Raymond Andress, thirty-one, was heard to say, "Skipper's shot. We've been shot. Trying to help. Oh my God, help." Gonzales also shot the copilot and then himself. The plane went into a nose dive and crashed into a hillside near San Ramon killing all forty-four people on board. The wreckage of the aircraft was strewn over a large area and in the debris, along with personal belongings, investigators

Photograph of the doomed Pacific Airlines plane, N2770R taken December 29, 1962, at San Francisco International Airport. *Courtesy and Copyright © Jon Proctor.*

recovered Gonzales's .357 handgun. All of its ammunition had been expelled. In the aftermath of the tragedy, the federal government enacted laws that required cockpit doors to aircraft be locked from the inside.

1964, 1985

A FATHER'S DESPAIR

Sacramento

Robert Henry Nicolaus would become one of only a handful of men with the dubious distinction of being sentenced to death twice, for two different crimes that were committed two decades apart. He was a twice-married father of three young children, a graduate of Sacramento State University with a degree in child psychology, and an analyst for the California Department of Highways. In the late spring of 1964, his life appeared to be normal, but beneath the calm exterior lurked a man on the edge of a psychotic breakdown. His second marriage was falling apart and he dreamed of a better life for his children.

On Sunday morning, May 24, 1964, the bodies of Roberta Nicolaus, seven, Donald Nicolaus, five, and Heidi Nicolaus, two, were found shot to death and stuffed inside the trunk of a car in north Sacramento. The previous morning, Robert Nicolaus' second wife, twenty-one-year-old Charlyce, mother of the youngest child, told her husband that their marriage was over and walked out. That same day, a distraught Nicolaus, with his youngest child, drove to the home of his first wife, Norma Lara, in north Sacramento, California, to pick-up his two oldest children. He told Lara that he planned to take all three of the kids to have their portraits taken. There was no indication in Nicholas' demeanor that indicated something was terribly wrong.

After picking up the children, they drove around, stopping to buy toys and have lunch at a local drive-in. After finishing eating, Nicolaus drove to an apartment complex on Arcade Street and parked the car. He told the children that he had lost a key in the trunk and wanted them to help find it. The children eagerly got into the trunk and began searching for the lost key. Then without a word, Nicholas methodically shot each of the children in the back of the head with a .38 caliber revolver. He then walked to a local bus station and headed to Lake Tahoe for a night of gambling and drinking.

Early the next morning, he walked into a Lake Tahoe Sheriff's substation and confessed to killing his children. He told investigators that he shot his children because he believed they'd be better off in heaven than living in a broken home. On September 14, 1964, a Sacramento jury of four men and eight women deliberated for only two hours before finding him guilty of three counts of first-degree murder and he was sentenced to death. Three years later, on appeal, the sentence was overturned by the California Supreme Court and reduced to second-degree murder. The court ruled that although Nicolaus was sane at the time of the murders, he lacked the ability to understand the enormity of the act. He was resentenced to three concurrent terms of five years to life in prison. In 1977, after serving only thirteen years, he was paroled and released from prison.

For the next seven years, Nicolaus harassed and stalked his second ex-wife, Charlyce Robinson, whom he secretly blamed for all of his troubles. By early 1985, he was on the verge of another psychotic breakdown. On February 22, Nicolaus lured Robinson into a Sacramento alley and shot her twice in the head with a small caliber revolver. But before she died, she was able to identify her ex-husband as the attacker. Nicolaus fled the scene and for the next five months, remained a fugitive from justice and was placed on the FBI's Ten Most Wanted list. On July 20, 1985, his luck ran out when a citizen recognized him from a wanted poster at a York, Pennsylvania, post office and phoned local police. He was arrested that same day without incident at his YMCA apartment and was extradited back to California to stand trial for the murder of his ex-wife.

His second murder trial began in early 1987 and was moved to Santa Clara County because of excessive pre-trial media publicity. On June 24, 1987, Nicolaus was found guilty of first-degree murder and sentenced to death. He was incarcerated at San Quentin Prison for the next sixteen years awaiting appeals and an execution that would never come. On April 12, 2003, at the age of sixty two, Robert Henry Nicolaus, a convicted quadruple murderer, who was twice condemned to death, died in prison from natural causes.

1964, 1972-1973

THE CO-ED KILLER

Alameda and Santa Cruz County

It was the early 1970s; peace, love, and 'rock n' roll had come to Santa Cruz. But along with the counterculture and good times came an unimaginable terror. Young California co-eds were disappearing. Today, Edmund Emil Kemper III is remembered as one of the most deviant serial killers in California history. He was nicknamed "The Co-ed Killer" by the media because of the six female college students he abducted, mutilated, and killed between 1972 and 1973. He was also responsible for the murders of four other people, including his mother and paternal grandparents. His childhood is eerily similar to that of many other psychopathic killers. His parents were divorced when he was very young, he was bullied by classmates, and had a difficult time sustaining friendships. As a teenager, he tortured animals and began fantasizing about violent sexual acts against women.

Kemper was born on December 18, 1948, in Burbank, California, the middle child of Clarnell and Edmund Kemper Jr., a decorated World War II veteran and successful electrician. Marital friction made for a stormy home life, and, in 1957, Kemper's parents divorced. He, along with his two sisters and mother, then relocated to Montana. His relationship with his mother was always contemptuous, as she was an alcoholic who constantly belittled and verbally abused her son. As a teenager, Kemper began acting bizarrely and started killing small animals. Alarmed by her son's behavior,

Edmund Kemper, towering above police officers, is escorted into Judge Donald May's courtroom on April 30, 1973, to be arraigned on eight counts of first-degree murder. *Courtesy of Bettmann/Corbis.*

Clarnell forced him to sleep in the basement away from the family out of fear he might harm them.

Life for Kemper was becoming unbearable, and at the age of fifteen, he ran away from home to live with his father in Los Angeles, whom he idolized. His father had a new wife and stepson, and when Kemper realized that he'd have to share his father's attention, he became jealous and hostile. After only a month, he asked to return home to live with his mother, but she did not want a difficult teenager and he was sent to live with his paternal grandparents, Edmund and Maude Kemper, at their secluded ranch in North Fork, California. His grandmother was a freelance writer and his grandfather worked for the highway department. His grandfather was kindhearted but was suffering from the early stages of Alzheimer's disease. His grandmother on the other hand was difficult, domineering, and easily angered. Although the move did not make Kemper happy, he appeared to adjust to his new surroundings. At school, he didn't cause trouble and was an average student, but he was becoming extremely self-conscious about his size and weight for which he endured a tremendous amount of teasing. In adulthood, he would reach an imposing height of six-foot-nine and weigh over 300 pounds.

While things at school appeared to be okay, home life was becoming tense. During the summer of 1964, Kemper was becoming more menacing in his behavior and the situation came to a boiling point on the morning of August 27, 1964. While sitting with his grandmother at the kitchen table, where she was editing proofs from a children's book, Edmund became visibly upset. After a few moments, he abruptly picked up his .22-caliber hunting rifle and headed out the back door of the house. After exiting, he silently watched his grandmother through the screen door. With her back to him, he raised his rifle and fired, striking her in the head and back. He then dragged her body into a bedroom. Within a few minutes, his grandfather returned home, and as he unloaded groceries from his car, he was approached by his grandson and shot in the back of the head and killed.

Kemper then phoned his mother and told her what he had done. She advised him to call the sheriff's department and he waited calmly on the front porch for them to arrive. After being taken into custody, he told investigators that in the days leading up to the killings, he had thoughts about killing his grandmother and shot her because he just wanted to know how it felt to kill someone. He also stated that he killed his grandfather (who he viewed as being senile), because he knew he'd be mad. While in custody, he was diagnosed by psychiatrists as being both paranoid and psychotic.

On December 6, 1964, he was committed to the Atascadero State Hospital instead of the California Youth Authority. While at Atascadero, he would begin to gain insight into the nature of his own crimes but never fully accepted responsibility. He was also beginning to experience more violent sexual thoughts, which he did not share with doctors. In 1969, on the outside he appeared to be healthy, well adjusted, and reformed. Because of this, he was released from custody but doctors warned that he was not to live with or associate with his mother. The California Youth Authority disregarded this advice and sent him directly back to his mother, who had since relocated to Santa Cruz and was employed at the University of California. Upon her son's arrival, she immediately began to belittle him and they argued constantly.

During Kemper's four years of incarceration, the world had changed. Sex, drugs, and rebellion became the new norm for young people. Santa Cruz teemed with rebellious students and Kemper bristled at his peers' disrespect for the establishment. Longing to put the world right, he dreamed of a career in law enforcement. His juvenile records had been sealed, so his earlier crimes would not disqualify him but his size exceeded police regulations. He eventually took a job with the highway department. Although he could not become a police officer, he found a way to be close to them by hanging out with them at local bars. Kemper saved his money and, with his parole officer's permission, moved to an apartment in Alameda, ninety minutes from Santa Cruz. Free from his mother, his dark past was now a seemingly distant memory. Though he had persuaded doctors that he had been cured, his demons lingered beneath the surface. Soon, his disturbing desires would control him and no woman would be safe.

Violence was Kemper's response to anger, especially his intense hatred of his mother. His stormy relationship with her set a pattern for his life. At age twenty-three, he feared women and felt lonely, awkward, and began having violent sexual fantasies that overwhelmed him. By the spring of 1972, the pull to act on these thoughts was growing stronger. Over the previous few years, he'd spent hours cruising the highways of Northern California looking for co-eds. He observed them patiently and picked up over 150 female hitchhikers, noting their strengths and weaknesses. On the evening of May 7, 1972, Kemper was ready to kill and, in Berkeley, he picked-up two eighteen-year-old Fresno State University co-eds: Mary Ann Pesce and Anita Luchessa, who were hitchhiking to visit friends at Stanford. Kemper drove the girls to a secluded area near Alameda, where he forced Luchessa into the trunk at gunpoint. He then returned to the car and stabbed Pesce to death. When through with Pesce, Kemper opened the trunk and killed Luchessa. After that, he returned to his apartment, where he sexually assaulted the corpses, dismembered their bodies, and dumped the remains in nearby ravines around Livermore. Portions of Pesce's body were discovered three months later but Luchessa's remains were never found.

While the citizens of Santa Cruz were reeling at the horrors of the recent abduction slayings, Kemper prepared to strike again. On the evening of September 14, 1972, he picked-up another hitchhiker, fifteen-year-old ballet dancer Aiko Koo, at a Santa Cruz bus stop. He drove the young girl into the nearby hills, where he raped and strangled her to death with her own scarf. As he had done previously, Kemper returned to his apartment, dismembered the body, and disposed of the remains in different locations. Four months would pass before he would strike again.

With the murder of Koo, Kemper had stepped over a line. Now more than ever he needed to conceal his true nature. His split personality allowed him to deal with feelings of worthlessness and self-loathing—feelings he blamed on his mother. Even after moving out of her home, she still dominated him. There was only one thing that made him feel powerful and that was killing women. He had now struck three times and had a taste for blood.

More dead bodies were showing up and the public was beginning to panic. Strapped for cash, Kemper moved back to his mother's house, and one day after a series of heated arguments with her, he became extremely agitated and was overwhelmed with the urge to kill again. On January 8, 1973, he picked-up another female hitchhiker while driving through Cabrillo College in Watsonville. He offered a ride to nineteen-year-old Cindy Schall, drove to a secluded location, and shot her once in the head. He took his fourth victim's body back to his mother's house and, like the others, raped the corpse and dismembered the body. He buried the head in the backyard as an insult to his mother and then scattered the rest of the remains in the Pacific Ocean. Less than twenty-four-hours later, portions of Schall's body began washing ashore on area beaches.

One month later, on the night of February 5, 1973, after another argument with his mother, Kemper went out looking for a new victim. He found two hitchhikers, Rosalind Thorpe, twenty-four, and Alice Liu, twenty-three, near the University of California Santa Cruz campus. With rage seething inside him, he shot and killed both girls and, like his previous victim, returned to his mother's house where he acted out his usual ghoulish behavior. The body parts of these victims were dumped throughout the area.

Surprisingly, Mrs. Kemper never seemed to show any suspicion that her son was committing such heinous acts. But he began to worry that she would become aware of his crimes. He didn't want her to suffer the embarrassment of what he had done, so he resolved to commit the crime he had always fantasized about since his childhood. Roughly a month after the twin slayings of Thorpe and Liu, Kemper decided that it was time for his mother to die.

In the early morning hours of Good Friday, April 21, 1973, he retrieved a claw hammer from the kitchen, went to his mother's bedroom, and beat her to death. In his mind he had now exorcised his biggest demon and she would never trouble him again. He dismembered the body and tried to dispose of the vocal cords in the kitchen sink. Fearing the murder would be discovered, Kemper phoned his mother's best friend Sally Hallet, fifty-nine, and invited her to dinner. Immediately upon her arrival, he strangled her to death. He hoped that when the two bodies were found, the killings would be blamed on an intruder. Kemper then fled the scene and drove to Pueblo, Colorado, where on April 24, 1973, after three days of no sleep, he phoned Santa Cruz Police and confessed to the murders.

He was arrested by Pueblo police without incident. On the drive back to California with Santa Cruz police detectives, Kemper confessed to all of the co-ed murders and related the crimes in minute detail. On April 30, he was formally charged with eight counts of murder. While in custody, he tried and failed to commit suicide four times.

His trial began on October 23, 1973, in Santa Cruz Superior Court before Judge Harry F. Brauer. During the three-week proceedings in which Kemper testified on his own defense, he calmly detailed the grisly murders and stated that for most of his life he had fantasized about killing and beheading women. Although the defense tried to prove that he was insane at the time of the slayings, they were ultimately unable to persuade the jury. On November 8, the jury of six men and six woman took only five hours and forty minutes of deliberation to decide Kemper's fate. They found him guilty of all eight counts and determined that he was sane at the time of the crimes. Upon hearing the verdict, Judge Bauer stated:

> If I seem a bit excited, I had some fear that you [the jury] might possibly have arrived at a different verdict, and I just want to say I agree with your verdict entirely.

The next day, because the death penalty had been suspended in 1972, he was sentenced to eight concurrent life sentences. As he was being led from the courtroom, Kemper stopped and thanked the judge for his help. He was sent to the Vacaville Prison Medical Facility, where he is still incarcerated today. Since his conviction, he has been a model prisoner and has been instrumental in helping to build the FBI's serial killer profiling program.

1964-1975

THE SKID ROW SLASHER

Los Angeles

Vaughn Orrin Greenwood, the original "Skid Row Slasher," was convicted of murdering nine men, all of whom were primarily transients near downtown Los Angeles' Skid Row District and Hollywood between 1964 and 1975. He has also been considered a suspect in the killing of an additional thirteen people. Most of his victims were slashed to death, with their wounds surrounded by markings that have been considered satanic in nature.

Stymied in apprehending the killer, Los Angeles police detectives recruited psychiatric experts to create a profile of the killer and published assorted sketches of the suspect, erroneously described as being a white male in his late twenties or early thirties, six feet tall, and 190 pounds, with shoulder-length stringy blond hair. Unfortunately for police, Greenwood was actually a thirty-two-year-old black man. The case was ultimately solved by accident, which further embarrassed authorities whose profiles of the murderer were way off mark. Greenwood's first known victim was David Russell, sixty, a transient who was murdered on November 13, 1964. His body was found on the patio of the main branch of the Los Angeles Public Library with his throat slashed. The following day, sixty-seven-year-old Benjamin Hornberg was killed in the second-floor restroom of a skid row hotel. His throat had also been slashed. Although detectives saw a pattern developing, they were unsuccessful in finding a suspect.

Greenwood then drifted to Chicago, where, in 1966, he was arrested and convicted of the aggravated assault of Mance Porter, for which he received a five-and-a-half-year prison sentence. Upon his release from jail, Greenwood returned to Los Angeles but did not immediately return to killing.

Los Angeles Public Library circa 1971, scene of the murders of David Russell (1964), Charles Jackson, and David Perez (both December 1974). *Courtesy of the Library of Congress Prints and Photographs Division, HABS Cal, 19-LOSAN, 65-9.*

Greenwood's rampage began again in the early morning hours of October 19, 1974, when he broke into the apartment of Joseph Arnold Nolan. There he attempted to rob and slash his victim with a kitchen knife, but Nolan was able to flee the scene and alerted a passing patrol car. Greenwood was arrested and eventually pleaded guilty to one misdemeanor count of assault and served only ten days in jail. One month later, he would begin a homicidal killing frenzy that extended from Los Angeles skid row to Hollywood and would claim the lives of an additional nine people. His victims included:

1. Charles Jackson, forty-six, killed on December 1, 1974, on the steps of the Los Angeles Public Library
2. Moses Yakanac, forty-seven, whose body was found on December 8, in an alley off Broadway
3. Arthur Dahlstedt, fifty-four, found dead on December 11, on the steps of a vacant building near the intersection of 5th and Towne Avenues
4. David Perez, forty-two, found slain on December 22, in some bushes near the Los Angeles Public Library
5. Casimir Strawinski, fifty-eight, found dead on January 9, 1975, by a maid at the Pickwick Hotel on Grand Avenue
6. Robert Shannahan, forty-six, found slain on January 17, in his room at the MacDonald Apartment Hotel on Valencia Street

Hotel Barclay, downtown Los Angeles, scene of the murder of Samuel Suarez in January 1975.

7. Samuel Suarez, forty-nine, found dead several days later in his fifth-floor apartment at the Barclay Hotel on 4th Avenue
8. George Frias, forty-five, an employee of the Los Angeles Hilton, found slain on January 29, in the bedroom of his Hollywood apartment
9. Clyde Hays, thirty-four, a mechanic for the National Cash Register Company found dead, nearly decapitated at his apartment in Hollywood on January 31

Then, in the predawn hours of February 2, 1975, Greenwood attempted to burglarize the Hollywood Hills home of William Graham, who he attacked with a hatchet before being chased off by house guest Kenneth Richer. That same night, Greenwood attempted to burglarize the home of actor Burt Reynolds, where he carelessly dropped a letter that was addressed to himself from the Department of Social Services in the driveway. This led police to his apartment on Jefferson Boulevard, where he was arrested and charged with attempted murder and burglary. After searching the apartment, police found a pair of cuff links stolen from victim George Frias.

On January 23, 1976, he was indicted on eleven counts of murder in the Skid Row Slasher case to which he pleaded not guilty. Prior to the murder trial, which began on November 3, Greenwood was convicted of assaulting William Graham and Kenneth Richer, and burglarizing Burt Reynolds' home for which he received a prison term of thirty-two years to life. During the murder trial, prosecutors relied primarily upon circumstantial evidence to tie him to the slayings with the strongest evidence being a bloody shoe print that was found at the scene of the Shannahan murder. On December 30, 1976, a jury of seven men and five women convicted Greenwood of nine

George Frias was murdered by Vaughn Greenwood, the Skid Row Slasher, at this Hollywood apartment on January 29, 1975.

counts of first-degree murder but failed to reach a verdict in the case involving victims David Russell and Charles Jackson. He was subsequently sentenced to nine life sentences by Los Angeles County Superior Court Judge Earl E. Broady and is currently incarcerated at the California Men's Colony in San Luis Obispo.

1964

THE MYSTERIOUS DEATH OF THE KING OF SOUL

Los Angeles

Sam Cooke is generally considered to be one of the greatest R & B singer-songwriters of all-time. In the late 1950s and early 1960s, he would record over thirty Top 40 hits. His stellar recording career was tragically and mysteriously cut short on December 11, 1964, when he was shot to death at a seedy motel in Los Angeles, California.

Sam Cooke, *Billboard Magazine* photograph, 1966.

Samuel "Sam" Cook (he later changed the spelling to Cooke) was born on January 22, 1931, in Clarksdale, Mississippi. His family moved to Chicago two years later and, as a young child, he began singing in his father's Baptist church. In 1950, he became the lead singer of the legendary gospel group "The Soul Stirrers." After several successful years, he left the group to focus on a solo career. His first hit "You Send Me," would reach number one on the Billboard Music Chart in 1957. He would go on to have a succession of chart topping hits that included "Cupid," "Chain Gang," and "Twistin' the Night Away."

In 1959, Cooke married his childhood sweetheart Barbara and they would have three children. Cooke moved his family into a beautiful mansion in the Hollywood Hills. Their bliss was cut short, when their eighteen-month old son Vincent drowned in the family pool. The marriage then became strained and the pair were separated. Over the next several years, Cooke immersed himself in his recording career and other business ventures.

On the evening of December 11, 1964, he met a beautiful twenty-two-year-old Asian woman named Elisa Boyer at Martoni's Italian Restaurant on Sunset Boulevard in Hollywood. The pair would eventually end up at PJ's nightclub on Santa Monica Boulevard. As the night came to a conclusion, Cooke offered to drive Boyer home but instead drove to the Hacienda Motel on South Figueroa Street in Downtown Los Angeles. There he allegedly tried to rape the woman, but she was able to break free. Clad in only a sport jacket and shoes, the semi-naked Cooke pursued Boyer and suddenly entered the motel's front lobby. There he encountered the night manager Bertha Lee Franklin. Frightened by the site of Cooke, who was agitated and yelling, Franklin fearing for her safety pulled out a .22-caliber handgun and shot him once in the chest. His last words were, "Lady, you shot me," then collapsed and died.

At a coroner's inquest that was held on December 17, 1964, Cooke's death was deemed to be justifiable homicide. Not satisfied with the results of the hearing, Cooke's family hired a private investigator and, although the events surrounding Cooke's death have been deemed by some to be suspicious, no concrete evidence has ever been presented supporting a criminal conspiracy.

In a side note to the tragedy, one month after Cooke's death, Elisa Boyer was arrested for prostitution and, in 1979, was found guilty of second-degree murder in the shooting death of a boyfriend. Her whereabouts today are unknown. After her exoneration, Bertha Franklin is alleged to have moved to Michigan and died in June 1966, but this information is not verified. Sam Cooke's funeral was held in Chicago and a second in Los Angeles and was attended by thousands of mourners. He was buried at Forest Lawn Memorial Park in Glendale, California.

1965 and 1979

THE STRANGE CASE OF ROBERT LEE MASSIE

San Gabriel and San Francisco

Robert Lee Massie would spend two separate stints on California's death row and would gain notoriety while pursuing his own demise for more than three decades. He killed in 1965 and again in 1979, and his case was one of the most bizarre in state history. Massie was born on December 24, 1941, in Virginia and, after a childhood filled with neglect and abuse, drifted to California by 1965. By the age of twenty-four, he had already amassed a long rap sheet of violent crimes and had spent years in prison.

On January 7, 1965, his crimes turned homicidal when he attempted to rob Mildred and Morris Weiss, the owners of a successful furniture store, in the garage of their San Gabriel apartment. The couple had just returned home around 10:00 p.m. and were exiting their car when Massie approached them with a .22-caliber rifle. He mumbled something, shot

Mildred Weiss in the stomach, and fled the scene without any money. Mrs. Weiss died in surgery at San Gabriel Hospital two hours after the altercation.

Massie, who was suspected of several other robbery assaults in the area, was arrested on January 20, in Los Angeles. After his arrest, he identified Robert Vetter, thirty-five, as the driver of the getaway car. The pair had met while they were both in jail in Massachusetts. Vetter was apprehended on January 21, in West Peabody, Massachusetts. Massie and Vetter were charged with the murder of Weiss, attempted murder, robbery of thirty-five-year-old Frank Boller of West Covina, and the robbery of Frank Maccia and Harold Bolivar, both of West Covina. On April 13, Massie pleaded guilty to one count of first-degree murder, one count of attempted murder, and three counts of robbery in San Gabriel Superior Court. Vetter pleaded not guilty to the charges and waived a trial by jury. On April 30, Superior Court Judge found Vetter guilty of all charges. On May 5, Massie was sentenced to death and Vetter to life in prison.

During his time on death row, Massie denounced his confinement as harsh and cruel, and he repeatedly told state officials he did not want to be kept alive. By the early 1970s, he was dubbed the "Prisoner Who Wants to Die" by the press. He wrote magazine articles making the case for his own execution and was quoted frequently. When the California State Supreme Court banned the death penalty in 1972, his sentence was reduced to life in prison with the possibility of parole. A model prisoner who immersed himself in the law and became an advisor to many inmates, Massie was given a second chance when the state's parole board released him in the summer of 1978. Vetter was eventually released on parole, and his life and whereabouts after his release are not known.

Several months after Massie was released from prison, he committed another murder. On January 3, 1979, during an attempted robbery, he killed sixty-one-year-old Boris "Bob" Naumoff and wounded a clerk at Naumoff's Liquor Store in San Francisco. Two days later, on January 5, after a high-speed police pursuit through the Haight-Ashbury district of the city, Massie was taken into custody and charged with Naumoff's slaying.

Like the previous case, Massie pleaded guilty to all of the charges and was again sentenced to death. He welcomed the verdict and openly fought the automatic appeals process that followed, but the state's high court, led by then-Chief Justice Rose Elizabeth Bird, overturned Massie's conviction because he had plead guilty against the advice of his attorney. The court ordered a retrial and, in 1989, Massie was again convicted of murder and for a third time was sentenced to death. For a brief period after this third conviction, Massie sought freedom through state and federal appeals, but eventually returned to saying he wanted to die and requested that all appeals be dropped.

On March 27, 2001, he finally got his wish when he was executed by lethal injection at San Quentin Prison. His rambling last words were: "Forgiveness: giving up all hope for a better past."

1965-1977

THE TRASH BAG MURDERS

Southern California

In April 1975, police found a bulky, plastic trash bag discarded along the highway between Los Angeles and Mexico. Inside was the naked and dismembered remains of a young man. Police were mystified, and it emerged that the man had been a member of Los Angeles's large gay community, but they knew little more than that and the case remained unsolved. By the end of the next year, five more dismembered bodies were found in trash bags along the highways of Southern California. All were naked and had been shot once in the head. After painstaking police work, each of the bodies were identified. They were all gay men who were known to frequent the Los Angeles and Hollywood cruising areas. Yet police were no closer to finding the killer than before. They were, however, convinced the murders had been committed by the same person. During the first few months of 1977, the death toll mounted. Los Angeles's gay community was terrified. No one knew how or when the killer would strike again. Despite police efforts, at least twenty-eight young men and boys had disappeared by early summer. The media dubbed the crimes "The Trash Bag Murders."

Patrick Wayne Kearney was a mild-mannered electrical engineer who was born in Los Angeles in 1939 but raised in Texas. He came from a stable home but was shy and bullied as a child. During his teenage years, he began to experience sexual fantasies about murder. In the early 1960s, he moved back to Southern California and began working at Hughes Aircraft. He would later claim to have murdered his first victim, an unnamed male hitchhiker in Orange County, California, in 1965.

Over the next few years, he killed several more times, before moving to Culver City where he began living with longtime acquaintance David Douglas Hill. Hill was a high school dropout from Lubbock, Texas, who had met

Kearney in 1962 while the latter was stationed at a local air force base. Their sexual attraction to one another was mutual, and Hill divorced his wife in 1966 and moved to California. Their stormy relationship would often be the catalyst for Kearney's murderous rampages. He would primarily pick up his victims at local gay bars or on the street. He would shoot them in the head, have sex with their corpses, dismember the bodies, place the remains in trash bags, and then dump them along freeways. His murder spree officially began on April 13, 1975, when the body of twenty-one-year-old Alberto Rivera of Los Angeles was found near San Juan Capistrano. Over the next six months, a half-dozen bodies were discovered mutilated in several counties in Southern California. The discovery of two more victims in March 1977 raised the body count to nine.

In the late afternoon of March 13, 1977, seventeen-year-old John Lamay of El Segundo told his parents he was going to Redondo Beach to meet a man named "Dave" whom he had befriended at a local gym. Five days later, his dismembered remains were found in a trash bag beside the 91 freeway, south of Corona in Riverside County. Friends of the victim identified "Dave" as David Hill, and supplied police with an address. Arrest warrants were issued for Hill and Kearney, but the pair fled to Mexico. They remained at large until July 1, when they walked into a Riverside County Sheriff's office, pointed to a wanted poster and identified themselves. Police searched the men's home and found a hacksaw stained with blood. They also found hair and carpet fibers that matched those found on tape binding the victims' bodies.

Kearney would later confess to fifteen murders and led police to dumping sites throughout Southern California. Hill would be released for lack of evidence. On July 14, 1977, Kearney was formally indicted for the murders of Alberto Rivera, Arthur Marques, and John Lamay. On December 21, in Riverside Superior Court, he pleaded guilty to three counts of first-degree murder, with the stipulation he would not receive the death penalty. He was then sentenced to life imprisonment by Judge John Hews. The following year, Los Angeles County prosecutors charged Kearney with an additional eighteen counts of murder, two of whom were children, ages five and eight, along with four victims whose bodies were never recovered. On February 21, 1978, he pleaded guilty to those charges and received another life sentence.

The only reason he ever gave for the murders was that they excited him and left him with a feeling of dominance over his victims. Today, Kearney is incarcerated at the Mule Creek Penitentiary in Ione, California.

1966

MURDER IN BRENTWOOD

Los Angeles

Twenty-eight years before Nicole Brown Simpson and Ronald Goldman were brutally murdered in Brentwood, California, another high profile Hollywood-connected tragedy engulfed the affluent enclave.

On the morning of February 1, 1966, the bodies of twenty-nine-year-old Barbara Ann Thomason, the estranged fifth wife of film actor Mickey Rooney, and her boyfriend Milos Milosevic, twenty-five, were found shot to death at Rooney's mansion in an apparent murder-suicide. Mickey Rooney was a popular Hollywood film actor and, as a teenager, had appeared as Andy Hardy in the first of fifteen films featuring the character. He also co-starred with Judy Garland in a string of successful musicals. As an adult, he would star in many successful movies and television programs.

Barbara Ann Thomason was born on January 25, 1937, in Phoenix, Arizona. She and her family moved to Southern California in the early 1950s. Because of her good looks, Thomason won many local beauty pageants. In the mid-to-late 1950s, she appeared in several B-movies under the stage name Carolyn Mitchell. She met Rooney in 1958 at a Los Angeles area nightclub, and there was an immediate physical attraction. The pair soon began an affair and, at the time, Rooney was still married to Elaine Devry, his fourth wife. In the fall of 1958, infatuated with and pressured by his new girlfriend to end his marriage, Rooney traveled to Mexico with Thomason to obtain a quickie divorce. On December 1, they were secretly wed, but the legality of the nuptials would later be questioned. Thomason gave birth to the first of their four children in September 1959. Due to the dubious nature of their Mexican marriage, they officially remarried in 1960. Their relationship was volatile from the start, and Rooney's continuous philandering did not help the situation.

In the fall of 1964, French actor Alain Delon introduced his stunt double and bodyguard, Milos Milosevic to the Rooneys. The handsome and suave Yugoslavian was born on July 1, 1941, in Nis. He was a troubled young man with an explosive and erratic temper. He had been briefly married to Cynthia Krensky Bouron, but the relationship ended in divorce in 1964. Over the next several months, Milosevic and the Rooneys were inseparable. In mid-1965, Rooney naively asked Milosevic to check in on his wife while he was on location in the Philippines shooting a movie. Almost immediately,

Left to right: Milos Milosevic, Barbara Thomason, and Mickey Rooney. *Courtesy of Bettmann/ Corbis.*

Thomason and Milosevic began an affair. She accompanied her young lover to the Northern California set of his movie *The Russians Are Coming, The Russians Are Coming*, in which he had a small role. When Rooney returned home from filming in late 1965, be became aware of his wife's infidelity and filed for divorce. Once Rooney had moved out of his Brentwood home, Milosevic moved in.

Thomason soon began to have doubts about the divorce and began to fear she might lose custody of her children due to her adulterous affair. On Sunday, January 30, 1966, she visited Rooney at Saint John's Hospital in Santa Monica to discuss a possible reconciliation. He was recovering from an intestinal infection picked up while filming in the Philippines. The pair had a pleasant conversation and discussed getting back together. When she arrived home that night, Milosevic was furious when he learned she was considering returning to her husband.

The next evening, Thomason and Milosevic, along with a female friend, went to dinner in Beverly Hills. After they returned to their Brentwood home around 8:00 p.m., the couple retired to their master bedroom and began to argue. At some point during the night, Milosevic shot Thomason with a .38-caliber revolver that was owned by Rooney and then turned the gun on himself. The following morning, February 1, a maid and family friend forced their way into the locked bedroom and found the bodies of Thomason and Milosevic on the bathroom floor. She was lying on her back, shot through the jaw, Milosevic was beside her, face down, a bullet hole in the side of his head. At the time of the shooting, three of the Rooneys' children were asleep in their bedrooms in the house and no one had heard the gunshots. Barbara Thomason was buried at Forest Lawn Memorial Park in Glendale, and Milosevic's remains were returned to his native Yugoslavia.

Upon hearing the news of his estranged wife's death, Mickey Rooney was devastated and fell into a deep depression. In his grief, he ill-advisedly married Marge Lane, a good friend of Thomason's. The marriage would last a little over three months.

On April 6, 2014, at age ninety-three, Mickey Rooney died in his sleep at his home in Studio City, California, from natural causes. He was survived by his eighth wife, Jan Chamberlain, from whom he had been separated for two years.

> As a side note to the tragedy, on October 30, 1973, Milosevic's ex-wife, Cynthia Bouron was found bound and beaten to death in the trunk of a car in the parking lot of a supermarket in North Hollywood. In 1970, she had been embroiled in a paternity suit against film actor Cary Grant that was eventually dismissed. No one was ever arrested and the murder remains unsolved.

1966, 1970

THE CANDLELIGHT KILLER

Orange and San Diego County

Very little is known about the life of Robert Willard Liberty, other than the fact that he was born in 1947 and is assumed to have grown up in Southern California. He lived a troubled life and, in 1966, was hospitalized in Orange County for a failed suicide attempt. While in treatment, Liberty became acquainted with thirty-one-year-old Marcella Landis, a fellow patient who was also being treated for a suicide attempt. He was attracted to the woman, twelve years his senior and their relationship appeared to flourish. Upon release, they moved-in together sharing a tiny apartment in Westminster, California. Although things appeared to be going well and Liberty seemed to be happy, below the surface raged a homicidal maniac ready to kill.

On the evening of April 4, 1966, for some unknown reason, Liberty snapped and strangled Landis to death at their apartment. He called police and, when they arrived at the scene, they found Landis's body stretched out on a couch in the living room, candles burning at her head, a Bible on her chest and Liberty calmly sitting nearby strumming a guitar. He was arrested and charged with first-degree murder.

On August 26, Orange County Superior Court Judge Robert Gardner ruled that Liberty was insane and unable to assist in his own defense. His trial was vacated and he was remanded to Atascadero State Hospital for an indefinite period. Three years later, on September 15, 1969, he was released from custody and deemed no longer a threat to society. This vote of confidence would turn out to be quite premature.

Six months after his release, on March 12, 1970, Liberty shot and killed his roommate, Thomas C. Astorina, twenty-five, after an argument over a television set. The victim's body, with a gunshot wound to the stomach, was later discovered by a passing motorist dumped along Edinger Avenue near Sunset Aquatic Park in Seal Beach. Warrants were immediately issued for the arrest of Liberty and several other roommates.

For the next three months, Liberty was somehow able to avoid detection. On June 7, he and a female companion, Kendall Ann Bierly, twenty-four, robbed his mother of $45 at gunpoint at her Westminster home. They then made their way to Long Beach where they kidnapped seventeen-year-old Richard Greytak. The teen had picked up the hitchhiking pair and was forced to drive to the San Diego home of Robert J. Irion. Upon reaching Irion's uptown San Diego apartment, Greytak and Irion were bound with neckties. Liberty then beat and strangled Irion to death. He placed burning candles near the body and pinned a note to a nearby wall that read:"The candlelight killer strikes again. Catch me if you can."After murdering Irion, Liberty and his companion fled in their victim's car. They left Greytak unharmed, and the teen was eventually able to loosen his bindings and called police. Detectives quickly discovered that Irion and Liberty had been acquainted while incarcerated at Atascadero State Hospital and a second arrest warrant was issued.

Liberty and Bierly were able to evade capture for the next two days and found their way to Colorado Springs, Colorado, where on the evening of June 9, they attempted to rob a local motel. They tied up the manager, his wife, and a small child. The man was able to get free and ran to call police. When Liberty discovered what had happened he kidnapped the manager's wife and fled the scene. Police arrived at the motel moments later and gave chase. A high-speed pursuit ensued and shots rang out. A short time later, knowing escape was futile, Liberty pulled to the curb and surrendered. He and Bierly were married in jail prior to being extradited back to California to stand trial for the murder of Robert Irion.

Seven months later, on the morning of January 20, 1971, Liberty was found dead in his jail cell. He had been strangled with his own undershirt, and his body was found face down on his bunk with a blanket pulled up to his head. There were signs that a violent struggle had ensued prior to his death. Two fellow inmates were charged and eventually convicted of Liberty's murder.

On January 26, one week after her husband's death, Kendall Bierly pleaded guilty to voluntary manslaughter and robbery. On February 16, San Diego County Superior Court Judge Leland Nielsen sentenced her to fifteen years to life for manslaughter and one year to life for robbery. Today, her whereabouts are unknown.

1968

THE MURDER OF ACTOR RAMON NOVARRO

Los Angeles

Ramon Navarro (1934). *Courtesy of the Library of Congress, Prints and Photographs Division, Carl Van Vechten Collection.*

Some movie stars die at just the right time to fulfill their legendary status: James Dean will forever be remembered as the rebel; Marilyn Monroe as the ultimate blonde bombshell. Others, such as Greta Garbo, chose isolation to further their legends, but Ramon Novarro's legacy was unquestionably tarnished by his murder and the salacious details of his sex life that emerged after his death. Still, his name is synonymous with the silent film era, and his place among the pantheon of Hollywood's greatest film stars is secure. Beyond that, the repressive pressures that have kept actors closeted, even homophobic, gives new life and critical relevance to the tragic death of this movie icon.

Ramon Novarro was a swashbuckling star of silent films and early talkies who later became a television character actor. On October 20, 1968, he was beaten to death at his Laurel Canyon mansion.

Born Jose Ramon Samaniego on February 6, 1899, in Durango, Mexico, he, along with Rudolph Valentino, were Hollywood's top Latin male actors of the 1920s. He would appear in over fifty movies including *The Prisoner of Zelda* (1922), *Ben-Hur* (1925), *Student Prince* (1927), and *Mata Hari* (1931). Unable to find good roles after the advent of talking pictures, Novarro quit acting in 1934. He returned to Hollywood in the 1940s taking small roles that required an accent. In the late 1950s and until his death, Novarro made numerous appearances on television, mainly westerns, such as *Bonanza*, *Rawhide*, *Wild Wild West*, and *High Chaparral*. At the peak of his success, he was earning more than $100,000 per film and invested most of his income in real estate and his Hollywood Hills residence, which was designed by Lloyd Wright, the son of Frank Lloyd Wright. Because he had invested wisely, Novarro was able to maintain a comfortable lifestyle. But behind the glamorous Hollywood exterior loomed a troubled soul who wrestled with conflicted feelings toward religion and sex. These conflicts led to a lifelong struggle with alcoholism and dangerous sexual liaisons that could have severely tarnished his film image.

Novarro's badly beaten body was found by his personal assistant Edward Weber on the morning of October 31, 1968, in the actor's bedroom. There were signs of a violent struggle and blood stains were found on the furniture. He had massive upper body and head injuries. Police were unable to determine any clear motive for the crime; robbery was ruled out because nothing was missing from the house and revenge was excluded because he had no known enemies.

On November 6, less than a week after the slaying, two brothers, twenty-two-year-old Paul Robert Ferguson and seventeen-year-old Thomas Scott Ferguson, were arrested in connection with the crime. The brothers were linked to the slaying by physical evidence that included fingerprints, telephone records, and clothing.

Their trial began on August 5, 1969, in Los Angeles Superior Court before Judge Mark Brandler. Prosecutors alleged that on the day of the murder, Paul Ferguson, then in need of money, telephoned Novarro and introduced himself as a friend of a mutual acquaintance. He and his brother arrived at the actor's home later that evening and were offered cocktails and some food. At some point, the brothers demanded money from Novarro, and when he would not reveal where it was hidden, they bound, tortured, and beat him to death with a cane. The house was then ransacked to look like a robbery.

As a defense tactic, both brothers accused each other of committing the murder, but both agreed that they had gone to the house to hustle the actor, not to kill him. It was alleged that Thomas Ferguson had engaged in sex acts with Novarro at some time in the evening.

On September 17, the jury of seven men and five women deliberated for only two-and-a-half hours before convicting the brothers of first-degree murder. Eight days later, they were both sentenced to life in prison with the possibility of parole in seven years. Astonishingly, both brothers were released from prison, Thomas in 1976 and Paul in 1978, but both were later convicted of other crimes and spent additional time behind bars before fading into the lurid pages of Hollywood history.

1968

THE ASSASSINATION OF ROBERT F. KENNEDY

Los Angeles

Senator Robert F. Kennedy was shot in the kitchen pantry of the Ambassador Hotel in Los Angeles shortly after midnight on June 5, 1968. He had just finished giving a victory speech to supporters in the hotel's ballroom after winning the California Democratic Presidential Primary. As Sen. Kennedy was walking through the pantry area of the hotel, he was shot three times at point-blank range by Sirhan Sirhan. Kennedy's bodyguards, former NFL football great Rosey Grier, Olympic gold medalist Rafer Johnson, and others, subdued the shooter. Five other bystanders were also shot. They included Paul Schrade, head of the United Automobile Workers union; William Weisel, an ABC TV unit manager; Ira Goldstein, a *Continental News Service* reporter; Elizabeth Evans, a friend of Kennedy's press secretary Pierre Salinger; and Irwin Stroll, a teen-aged Kennedy volunteer. All five survived their injuries.

Robert Francis Kennedy was born on November 20, 1925, in Brookline, Massachusetts, the seventh child of businessman and former US Ambassador Joseph P. Kennedy and his wife Rose Fitzgerald. He was the younger brother of President John F. Kennedy. After managing his brother's successful 1960 presidential campaign, he was appointed US attorney general where

Sen. Robert Francis Kennedy, his wife Ethel standing behind him, at the Ambassador Hotel June 5, prior to making his victory speech after winning the California primary. A few minutes later, he was brought down by an assassin's bullets upon entering the hotel's pantry. *Courtesy of Bettmann/Corbis.*

he fought against organized crime and was a key supporter of the civil rights movement. After his brother's assassination in November 1963, Robert was elected to the US Senate from New York. On March 18, 1968, he announced his candidacy for the Democratic presidential nomination. His campaign brought hope to a troubled nation that had tired of protests at home and the Vietnam War. Kennedy spoke to enthusiastic crowds across the nation and had won crucial primaries in Indiana and Nebraska before heading to California for the last primary before the Democratic National Convention in August.

As Kennedy lay mortally wounded, Juan Romero, a busboy, comforted the senator and placed a rosary in his hand. Kennedy asked the young man, "Is everybody safe; OK?" and Romero told him, "Yes, yes, everything is going to be OK." Ethel Kennedy was soon led to her husband's side and knelt beside him. He turned his head and appeared to recognize her. After several minutes, emergency medical personnel arrived and lifted Kennedy onto a stretcher, prompting him to whisper, "Don't lift me," and lost consciousness. He was first transported to Central Receiving Hospital but was quickly transferred to Good Samaritan Hospital for surgery. Despite doctor's best efforts, Kennedy was pronounced dead at 1:44 a.m., on June 6, 1968.

Kennedy's assassin Sirhan Bishara Sirhan was born on March 19, 1944, in Jerusalem, Israel, to Palestinian-Christian parents but was raised a Maronite

Catholic. In his early teens, his family immigrated to the United States, first settling in New York, then in California. As a young adult, he frequently changed his religious beliefs and, in 1966, joined the Ancient Mystical Order of the Rose Cross, commonly referred to as Rosicrucians. Their theology is built around mysterious facts—hidden from the average person, which provide insight into nature, the physical universe, and the spiritual realm. During this same period, he worked as a stable boy at Santa Anita Race Track.

Sirhan's trial began on February 12, 1969, in Los Angeles County Superior Court. His defense attorneys relied primarily on the testimony of Bernard L. Diamond MD, who stated that the defendant was suffering from diminished capacity at the time of the assassination. Sirhan claimed he had no recollection of the crime, but did admit he felt betrayed by Kennedy for his support of Israel in the June 1967 Six-Day War, which had begun exactly one year before the assassination. This was contradicted by evidence found in Sirhan's personal journal and his infamous "RFK must die" entry, which was dated prior to any public acknowledgment of Kennedy's support for Israel. Most of these journal entries were rambling and illogical, though this one single item expressed a desire to kill Kennedy. When confronted with this evidence, Sirhan admitted the writing appeared to be his own, but he had no recollection of writing it.

On April 17, 1969, after two months of testimony, a jury of seven men and five women found Sirhan guilty of first-degree murder and six days later was sentenced to death. Moments after the sentence was read, Sirhan turned to his defense attorney and said, "Don't be concerned. Even Jesus Christ couldn't be saved." In 1972, his sentence was commuted to life in prison after the California Supreme Court banned the death penalty.

As with the assassination of his brother President John F. Kennedy, numerous conspiracy theories have developed that question the validity of the official account that casts Sirhan as the lone assassin. All of the witnesses in the kitchen pantry on that night placed Sirhan in front of Sen. Kennedy, at a distance no closer than three feet, and more significantly, most of them placed the tip of his gun no closer than a foot from Kennedy's head. Yet according to Dr. Thomas Noguchi, the Los Angeles County Coroner, who performed the autopsy, the fatal head wound was fired one inch behind the senator's right ear. According to Noguchi's book *Coroner*, published in 1983, the day after Kennedy's autopsy, a Los Angeles Police Department criminologist came to his office and stated he found gunpowder residue and soot in the hair samples taken from Kennedy's head prior to surgery. Thus, the gun must have been only inches away when the shots were fired and the angle was wrong.

In the years since his conviction, Sirhan has been routinely eligible for parole but has always been denied. On May 10, 1982, he told a parole board: "If Robert Kennedy were alive today, he would not countenance singling me out for this kind of treatment." Currently, he is confined at the California State Prison in Corcoran. The Ambassador Hotel, site of the assassination, was demolished in September 2005.

1966–1969

THE ZODIAC

Riverside, San Francisco, Vallejo, and Napa County

California's most notorious and elusive serial killer, the Zodiac claimed his first documented victim in Riverside, California, on October 30, 1966. That evening, eighteen-year-old Cheri Jo Bates, a Riverside Community College student, was stabbed to death in her car on the college campus. In November 1966, a letter from the killer was sent to the *Riverside-Press Enterprise* that declared that the young girl was not his first victim and wouldn't be his last.

Fourteen months after Bates's murder, he would strike again on the evening of December 20, 1968, in the hills above San Francisco Bay. A little after 11:00 p.m., a car sat in a lover's lane overlooking the Lake Herman Reservoir on the outskirts of Vallejo. Inside were high school students: seventeen-year-old David Farraday and sixteen-year-old Bettilou Jensen. As the teens sat and listened to the radio, a man approached the car from the rear. In his hand was a .22-caliber pistol. Suddenly, the man appeared at the driver's side window and Farraday found himself looking down the barrel of a handgun. As the boy attempted to open his car door, the gunman fired once striking the teen behind the left ear. Bettilou Jensen, now in a state of panic, also flung her door open and attempted to flee. In the bright moonlight, it was impossible for the gunman to miss her; five shots rang out striking Jensen in the back. She collapsed dead seventy-five yards from the car. When police arrived on the scene, Farraday was still alive but was unable to provide any description of the attacker. He died a short time later at a local hospital. There were no witnesses to the murders and police were unable to find a motive for the crime.

Seven months passed without any leads or further slayings, and it appeared as if the Farraday and Jensen murders were an isolated incident. But just

Location of the murders of David Farraday and Bettilou Jensen on December 20, 1968, at Lake Herman Reservoir.

before midnight on July 4, 1969, another young couple was brutally murdered. Darlene Elizabeth Ferrin, twenty-two, and Michael Mageau, nineteen, parked their car at Blue Rock Springs Park in Vallejo, several miles from the previous murders. As soon as the couple had pulled into the location, another car parked beside them. The second vehicle soon left but returned a few minutes later. A blinding beam of light shone through the window of Ferrin's car, which made the young couple think the other automobile was a patrol car. The man exited his vehicle and without a word approached the young couple. There was a sudden flash of gunfire and two shots struck Darlene Ferrin as she sat at the wheel of her car; another ploughed into Michael Mageau's neck. The gunman then abruptly turned and walked back to his own car. He paused briefly before turning back and firing an additional four shots into Ferrin's car and then drove away.

A few minutes after the shooting, a switchboard operator at the Vallejo Police Department received a call in which an unknown man stated:

> I want to report a double homicide. If you go one mile east on Columbus Parkway to a public park, you will find kids in a brown car. They are shot with a 9 mm Luger. I also killed those kids last year. Goodbye.

The call was traced to a pay phone just blocks from the police department, but when they arrived at the location the receiver was off the hook and the caller had vanished. No usable fingerprints were lifted from the phone. Police were immediately dispatched to the crime scene and discovered that the mysterious caller was wrong about one fact; it was not a double homicide, one of the victims was still alive. Michael Mageau slowly recovered from his wounds and was able to provide a detailed description of the attacker. Police had little doubt that the caller was also telling the truth when he admitted to killing David Farraday and Bettilou Jensen.

The unknown killer had now claimed four victims and injured one, and he wanted to boast about his crimes. On August 1, 1969, he sent three separate letters to the *Vallejo Times-Herald*, *San Francisco Chronicle,* and *San Francisco Examiner* claiming to be the Vallejo killer and offered intimate details of the crimes as proof. Each of the letters contained one third of a cryptic cipher that was eight lines long with seventeen symbols. The killer claimed his identity would be revealed if the ciphers were decoded. The code was eventually cracked by Donald Harden, a high school teacher from Salinas. The message began:

I like killing people because it is so much fun.

The letter-writer went on to explain that he was killing to collect slaves for the afterlife. Another letter mailed on August 7, 1969, was signed with a crossed circle, a zodiac symbol that would become synonymous with the killer.

The Zodiac's murderous rampage resumed on the afternoon of Saturday, September 27, 1969. Two students from Pacific Union College in Napa Valley went for a picnic on the shores of Lake Berryessa, north of Vallejo. Bryan Hartnell, twenty, and Cecelia Shepard, twenty-two, had just finished eating lunch around 4:30 p.m., when they were approached by a mysterious hooded man. The man asked Hartnell for money, and the young man complied. The man then told the couple that he was an escaped convict from Montana and needed their car to go to Mexico. He then bound both victims before drawing a long knife. He proceeded to stab Hartnell and Shepard multiple times in the back and chest. Fleeing the scene, the attacker paused at the couple's car and scribbled the dates of his previous two murders on the side door and drew the sign of the zodiac killer. A local fishermen heard the screams of the victims and summoned police. By the time they arrived, both victims were barely alive. Shepard died two days later from five stab wounds, but Hartnell survived and was able to give detectives a detailed description of the attacker. An hour after the killings, a call came into the Napa police department and a man stated he wanted to report a double homicide and that he was the killer. The call was traced to a pay phone less than five blocks from the police station in downtown Napa and detectives were able to retrieve a dusty palm print from the handle of the phone.

The Zodiac would commit his last confirmed murder two weeks later. Around 10:00 p.m., on October 11, 1969, twenty-nine-year-old cab driver Paul Stine picked up a passenger near the Fairmont Hotel on Nob Hill in San Francisco. A short time later, two people standing near the intersection of Washington and Cherry Streets heard a gunshot. It came from a taxi that was parked near the curb. They watched as a man exited the back seat of the

Corner of Washington and Cherry Streets in San Francisco. It was here where Paul Stine was murdered by the Zodiac Killer on October 11, 1969.

vehicle and briskly walked towards the Presidio park area. Police were alerted to the shooting and upon arrival found Stine dead with his wallet missing. The crime looked like a typical armed robbery, which happened regularly in the city, but the only difference was the sheer ruthlessness of it.

Initially, detectives did not connect Paul Stine's slaying to the Zodiac murders, until the killer launched a new barrage of letters three days later, part of which read:

> This is Zodiac speaking I am the murderer of the taxi driver over by Washington street…last night. To prove this here is a blood stained piece of his shirt. I am the same man who did in the people in the North Bay area.

He goes on to taunt the police:

> The San Francisco police could have caught me last night if they had searched the park properly instead of holding road races with their motorcycles.

He then shared his plans for the future increasing the quotation of terror exponentially:

> School children make fine targets and I shall wipe out a school bus one morning just shoot out the front tire and then pick off the kiddies as they come bouncing out.

Law enforcement took this threat very seriously and deployed officers on all area school buses. These precautions proved unnecessary, as the killer never fulfilled his promised threats, but the Zodiac was where he wanted to be, at the center of attention holding a major American city under his control.

WANTED

SAN FRANCISCO POLICE DEPARTMENT

NO. 90-69	WANTED FOR MURDER	OCTOBER 18, 1969

ORIGINAL DRAWING   AMENDED DRAWING

Supplementing our Bulletin 87-69 of October 13, 1969. Additional information has developed the above amended drawing of murder suspect known as "ZODIAC".

WMA, 35-45 Years, approximately 5'8", Heavy Build, Short Brown Hair, possibly with Red Tint, Wears Glasses. Armed with 9 mm Automatic.

Available for comparison: Slugs, Casings, Latents, Handwriting.

ANY INFORMATION:
Inspectors Armstrong & Toschi
Homicide Detail   THOMAS J. CAHILL
CASE NO. 696314   CHIEF OF POLICE

San Francisco Police wanted poster of the Zodiac killer, October 1969. *Courtesy of Bettmann/Corbis.*

Police from three jurisdictions were now vying for control of the investigation and they interviewed hundreds of suspects and fielded thousands of calls from an anxious public. All the while, Zodiac reveled in the publicity and continued sending taunting letters to newspapers and police. Before Christmas 1969, the Zodiac killer wrote to attorney Melvin Belli, in which he pleaded for help and stated he wouldn't be able to stay in control for much longer.

Three months later, on the evening of March 22, 1970, Kathleen Johns and her young daughter were driving near Modesto, California, when another motorist pulled her over, flashing his lights and honking his horn. The man told Johns that her rear tire seemed to be loose and offered to help secure it. When she tried to drive away, the tire came completely off and the "Good Sámaritan" offered her a ride to the nearest service station. He then took Johns on an aimless drive through the countryside, threatening her the whole way. At some point, she and her daughter managed to escape from the vehicle and hid in a ditch. A passing motorist took them to a local police station where Kathleen identified her kidnapper from a wanted poster of the Zodiac.

Between April 1970 and March 1971, nine more letters were received from the Zodiac, but police were unable to trace any further crimes to the killer. Then on January 30, 1974, after three years of no contact, a San Francisco newspaper received a letter from the killer in which he praises the film *The Exorcist* and signed off: "Me-37; SFPD-0." The letter taunted police with the fact that he had allegedly murdered thirty-seven victims and police had no suspect in custody. The Zodiac's final confirmed correspondence was received on April 24, 1978, in the letter the killer stated: "I am back with you," but no crimes were attributed to the killer...and he disappeared.

In the decades since the Zodiac murders, numerous theories have abounded in the case and despite various leads and other evidence, the killer's identity has remained unknown. Hundreds of suspects were questioned, their fingerprints compared to those on file, but all efforts have been in vain. A prime suspect, Arthur Lee Allen, was questioned repeatedly and circumstantial evidence pointed to his possible guilt, but he was never arrested.

Police took what may be their last attempt at solving the case in 2002, when they submitted envelopes from various Zodiac letters for DNA testing. If the killer had licked a stamp or envelope flap, saliva traces might contain enough genetic material to identify the killer. Unfortunately, the tests were inconclusive and the Zodiac remains unknown; either dead, in prison, or still at large.

1969, 1971

THE CARBON COPY KILLINGS

Santa Clara County

On Sunday afternoon, August 3, 1969, fourteen-year-old Deborah Furlong and her fifteen-year-old friend Kathy Snoozy set off for a bike ride and picnic near their home in Almaden Valley, an affluent neighborhood near San Jose. Neither girl knew that they were being stalked by a serial killer. After failing to come home for dinner that evening, they were reported missing by their parents. That same evening, off-road motorcyclists found the girls' bodies at the bottom of a hill in a grove of trees. They had been viciously beaten and stabbed hundreds of times. Since there was very little blood at the scene, police assumed the victims had been killed elsewhere and dumped. They also knew the girls must have been surprised and overwhelmed by their attacker because there were very few defensive wounds on their bodies.

Following the double homicide, panic swept San Jose as the public and law enforcement searched in vain for suspects and clues. One theory developed that linked the murders to a branch of the Manson family, while another concentrated on links to the Zodiac killer. Several suspects were detained, but no one was arrested and the case went cold. Twenty months would pass before the killer would strike again.

On Easter Sunday, April 11, 1971, eighteen-year-old Kathy Bilek told her parents that she was going to the Villa Montalvo Park in the foothills of Saratoga, near San Jose to hike and read. When she did not return home that night, her parents called police. Bilek's body was found the next morning in a shallow gully beneath a tree in the park. She had been stabbed forty-nine times. Like the previous victims, there was no sign of sexual molestation. Investigators immediately knew that the crime was connected to the previous murders, but unlike the earlier slayings, witnesses were able to provide a detailed description of a suspect who had been seen prowling the park on the day of the murder. A park ranger had also written down the license plate of a suspicious driver.

Police ran the license plate of the car and found it belonged to Karl Francis Werner, nineteen, of San Jose. Armed with this new evidence, police began to focus their attention on the young San Jose City College student. They found out that he was a former classmate of Furlong and Snoozy at Oak Grove High School and, at the age of sixteen, had committed a similar knife attack on a woman in Marlboro, Massachusetts. After the attack, he had been confined to the Westboro State Mental Hospital where he was diagnosed as having epileptic seizures that caused violent outbursts and aggression. In 1967, after his release, the Werner family had moved to San Jose to start a new life.

At 6:00 a.m. on April 29, eighteen days after the murder of Kathy Bilek, Santa Clara County Sheriff's detectives arrived at Werner's apartment with an arrest warrant. He was taken into custody without incident and charged with the murders of Furlong, Snoozy, and Bilek. A search of his apartment uncovered the possible murder weapon and other evidence. On September 1, 1971, to avoid a possible death sentence, Werner pleaded guilty to all of the murders. Three weeks later, on September 24, Santa Clara Superior Court Judge James B. Scott sentenced him to life in prison. Following his arrest, Werner was considered a prime suspect in the infamous Zodiac killings but was eventually eliminated because he was not living in California at the time of the slayings. Currently, he is incarcerated at the Vacaville State Prison medical facility.

1969

THE MANSON FAMILY MURDERS

Los Angeles

The canyons above Beverly Hills are quiet and isolated, just far enough away from the hustle and bustle of Hollywood to afford celebrities some privacy. Actress Sharon Tate and her film director husband Roman Polanski had found their dream house on Cielo Drive. Little did they know that the dream would soon become a nightmare. Saturday night, August 9, 1969, was unusually hot and muggy in the "City of Angels"—a perfect evening for demons to lurk. Tate, who was eight months pregnant and lonely, invited several close friends to stay overnight because her husband was away shooting a film. The house was secluded but not completely secure, although it had a locked gate. No one ever imagined anyone would want to break in and harm them. Around 12:30 a.m., neighbors were awoken by several faint gunshots coming from the direction of Tates' property but heard nothing else and went back to sleep. The next morning, they awoke to a scene of unimaginable horror and death.

Charles Milles Maddox was born in Cincinnati, Ohio, on November 12, 1934, to Kathleen Maddox, an unwed teenage mother. He received his notorious surname from his mother's brief marriage to William Manson. Charles had a horrible childhood and spent most of his youth in and out of reformatories. As an adult, his proclivity for petty crime and violent behav-

Sharon Tate, studio publicity photograph (unknown date).

ior did not fade, and he wound up in prisons in California and Washington State. As his most recent release date neared, in 1967, Manson had spent more than half of his thirty-three years in detention centers and asked officials if he could be allowed to stay. He later elaborated on his plea in a television interview with Tom Snyder:

> I said, I can't handle the maniacs outside; let me back in.

After his release from prison, Manson earned money by begging in Berkeley, California, and moved in with Mary Brunner, an assistant librarian

Charles Manson shown on his way to the courtroom to hear the jury's verdict on March 28, 1971. Later that day, Manson and three codefendants were sentenced to death for the murder of actress Sharon Tate and others. *Courtesy of the Los Angeles Public Library, Herald Examiner Collection.*

at the university. Brunner is considered to be the first female member of the so-called Manson Family, and she would later give birth to Charles's only child in the spring of 1968.

Traveling in a Volkswagen minivan and later a converted school bus, Manson and Brunner roamed the West Coast, recruiting followers. He set himself up as a guru of sorts and over two dozen people eventually joined Manson's "Family," and the group established its headquarters at the Spahn Ranch, north of Los Angeles. Manson, an aspiring musician, also began to assert himself into the music industry and, at one point, auditioned his singer-songwriter skills for producer Terry Melcher, who declined to work with him. This rejection would serve as a catalyst for murder.

During this same period, Manson became obsessed with two things: the Beatles and the approaching end of the world. He merged the two by using the name of a Beatles's song as a code word for the coming chaos, "Helter Skelter," then set it all into motion on August 8, 1969, telling his devotees:

Now is the time for Helter Skelter.

He instructed his second in command, twenty-four-year-old Charles "Tex" Watson to go to "that house where Melcher used to live and totally destroy everyone in it, as gruesome as you can." He also sent Susan Atkins, twenty-one, Linda Kasabian, twenty, and Patricia Krenwinkel, twenty-two, telling the women to "leave a sign…something witchy." Manson was aware that Terry Melcher had moved from the Benedict Canyon home, but the house represented his humiliating rebuff by the music establishment.

(Left to right) Susan Atkins, Patricia Krenwinkel, and Leslie Van Houten, shown at Los Angeles Superior Court on March 24, 1971. *Courtesy of the Los Angeles Public Library, Herald Examiner Collection.*

The four Family members arrived at the Benedict Canyon address around midnight. They were unaware that the new owners of the house were acclaimed film director Roman Polanski and his twenty-six-year-old film actress wife Sharon Tate. If they had known who they were about to kill, it mattered not. At the home that night, along with Tate, were Jay Sebring, thirty-six, a celebrity hairstylist; Wojciech Frykowski, thirty-three, an aspiring screenwriter; and his girlfriend Abigail Folger, twenty-six, heiress to the Folger Coffee fortune. Roman Polanski was not at the residence as he was filming in London.

The mayhem that followed was merciless. The Manson group crept onto the grounds and broke into the house. Victims fleeing outside were tracked down, screaming as they were stabbed or shot to death. Tate pleaded for her unborn baby's life but was stabbed sixteen times by Atkins and Watson. Atkins would write the word "PIG" on the front door of the house with Tate's blood. Five people were murdered that night, including eighteen-year-old Steven Parent, son of the caretaker, was shot four times and stabbed to death by Tex Watson after encountering the murderous foursome on the driveway prior to them breaking into the Tate's home. The next night, the Family continued their homicidal rampage at the Los Feliz home of Leno and Rosemary La Bianca.

Manson had been critical of the way in which the murders had been carried out and took personal charge to ensure the next victims would be easily restrained and that there would be no panic. The next night, Manson, accompanied by Watson, Krenwinkel, Atkins, Kasabian, eighteen-year-old Steve Grogan, and twenty-year-old Leslie Van Houten, drove to Los Angeles in search of new victims. The group stopped at several locations that were considered inappropriate, but Manson eventually remembered a house on Waverley Drive in Los Feliz, where he had attended several parties. Watson was told to drive there. Just after midnight, Manson and Watson broke into the house and subdued the owners Leno and Rosemary La Bianca, wealthy grocery store owners. Manson assured the couple that they would not be harmed and then went outside to the others and instructed Krenwinkel and Van Houten to go inside and follow Watson's instructions. Manson, along with Kasabian, Atkins, and Grogan then drove to Venice Beach, where he ordered the trio to murder actor Saladin Nader and hitchhike back to the Spahn Ranch. Fortunately for Nader, they could not find his apartment and abandoned the plan. Linda Kasabian would later state that she intentionally went to the wrong location to spare Nader's life.

Back at the La Bianca's, Van Houten and Krenwinkel took Mrs. La Bianca to a back bedroom and tied her up, while Watson remained in the living room with Mr. La Bianca. When Rosemary heard her husband being stabbed, she became hysterical and was attacked by Van Houten and Krenwinkel. Unable to kill their victim, Watson was summoned to finish her off. Before leaving the residence, the attackers carved "War" into the abdomen of Mr. La Bianca and scrawled numerous inflammatory phrases on the walls and painted in blood "Healter Skleter," (which was misspelled) on the refrigerator door.

In the months that followed, panic swept Los Angeles and police were unable to solve the crimes. A break in the case came on October 10, 1969, when dozens of Manson Family members were arrested at the Spahn Ranch in connection with an auto theft ring. Among those arrested were Leslie Van Houten and Susan Atkins. Under interrogation, Van Houten told investigators that Susan Atkins had been involved in the July 27 murder of musician Gary Hinman. Then in late November, Atkins began bragging to a cellmate that she had been responsible for the murder of Sharon Tate. Word leaked out and police detectives questioned Atkins about the Tate murder. She eventually admitted to being present at the scene of the slaying and named the other coconspirators, Manson, Watson, Krenwinkel, and Kasabian. Atkins also revealed that the La Bianca murders were committed by the same people and named Van Houten as an added participant. Arrest warrants were issued for all those who were not yet in custody.

On November 30, Watson was apprehended in Texas, while Manson and twenty-six other Family members were taken into custody on December 1, near Death Valley, California. The next day, Linda Kasabian turned herself in to authorities in Concord, New Hampshire, and on December 6, Patricia Krenwinkel was arrested in Mobile, Alabama.

The Manson Family murder trial began on June 15, 1970, in Los Angeles County Superior Court before Judge Charles H. Older. At the time, Tex Watson was still fighting extradition and his trial would be held separately. In exchange for immunity from prosecution, Linda Kasabian agreed to testify against the others. During the seven-month trial, which at times took on a circus-like atmosphere, prosecutors attempted to convince the jury that Manson and his followers were motived by hatred of the establishment and that they had committed the murders in an attempt to start a race war between blacks and whites. The defendants' attorneys offered no defense during the initial proceedings. On January 25, 1971, after nine days of deliberation, the jury of seven men and five women found all of the defendants guilty of seven counts of first-degree murder and conspiracy to commit murder. They were all sentenced to death on March 29, 1971, and as Manson was being led away from the courtroom after the sentencing, he shouted to the judge:

> Are you not allowed to put on a defense…you won't outlive that, old man.

Tex Watson was extradited back to California to stand trial and was eventually convicted of seven counts of first-degree murder. On October 21, 1971, he was sentenced to death. When California banned capital punishment in 1972, all of the Manson murder defendants' sentences were commuted to life terms.

In the years since their convictions, all of the defendants have routinely come up for parole and all have been denied. As of today, Charles Manson, who has become a distorted pop culture icon, is incarcerated at Corcoran State Prison, while Charles "Tex" Watson, who became a born-again Christian in 1975, married and has fathered four children. He is currently incarcerated at the Mule Creek Penitentiary. Since her conviction, Patricia Krenwinkel has been a model prisoner and attained a college degree. She has attempted to distance herself from Manson and has expressed remorse for the murders. Krenwinkel is presently serving her sentence at the California Institute for Women in Corona. Leslie Van Houten has also expressed remorse for the crimes, and she is also incarcerated at the California Institute for Women. Susan Atkins became a born-again Christian in 1974 and married twice. She expressed remorse for the slayings and advocated against the idolization of Charles Manson by misguided youths. She died at age sixty-one from complications related to brain cancer on September 24, 2009, at the Central California Women's Facility in Chowchilla.

"There are crimes
that, like frost
on flowers, in one
single night destroy
character and
reputation."

–Henry Ward Beecher
American clergyman and social reformer
(1813-1887)
from Proverbs from Plymouth Pulpit

CHAPTER THREE
The Infamous Crimes of the 1970s

1970

THE DEVIL'S OWN

Orange County

Steven Craig Hurd was a troubled soul and lived on the fringes of society. He was a habitual drug user and devil worshipper, who believed it was okay to "snuff people out," and had allegedly consulted with a mysterious San Francisco man who considered himself to be the Devil.

Very little is known about Hurd's early life other than he was born somewhere in Southern California in 1950 and, by the age of twenty, had organized a small group of homeless men and teenage boys in Santa Ana, California. They lived under highway overpasses and other places throughout the area, begged for money, took drugs, rummaged through garbage cans for scraps of food, and worshiped Satan. They were similar to but less cohesive than the Manson Family, who had committed the headline-grabbing Tate-LaBianca murders ten months earlier. When Hurd and his followers grew tired of chanting and dismembering small animals in their sacrificial demonic ceremonies, they began looking for larger game and found it in human form. On two consecutive nights, in June 1970, members of the group murdered twice in the name of Lucifer.

The homicidal rampage began on June 2, 1970, when Jerry Wayne Carlin, twenty-one, a Santa Ana service station attendant was robbed of $73 and bludgeoned to death with a hatchet by Hurd and two teenage accomplices, nineteen-year-old Herman Taylor and sixteen-year-old Arthur "Moose" Hulse. The trio had robbed and murdered Carlin because they needed cash to buy drugs. Early the next morning, Hurd, Taylor, and Christopher "Gypsy" Gibboney, seventeen, piled into a car owned by a fellow group member and headed to Scotsman's Cove in Laguna Beach. However, their car broke down a short time later on the Santa Ana Freeway in Irvine. Desperately in need of transportation, Hurd and the others decided to carjack another vehicle. Around 3:00 p.m., the group forced their way into the station wagon of thirty-one-year-old Florence Nancy Brown, an El Toro elementary school teacher and mother of five. She was on her way to a PTA meeting and had stopped on the northbound Sand Canyon Boulevard off ramp. The group forced their way into Brown's vehicle at knife point and ordered her to drive a few miles to a secluded orange grove near the University of California, Irvine. There she was repeatedly stabbed with a bayonet and her body was dismembered and mutilated in an apparent sacrificial offering to Satan. On June 17, her remains were found buried in a shallow grave off the Ortega Highway in Riverside County by several hikers.

Shortly after the slaying, Hurd and the others fled north to San Francisco in Brown's station wagon, allegedly to consult with the presiding "Head Devil." They abandoned Brown's station wagon near Santa Cruz and set it ablaze. The group's activities over the next several weeks is uncertain, but what is clear is that they began to split up.

On the evening of June 26, acting on information from an anonymous source, Riverside County Sheriff's deputies apprehended Hurd in Norco. He was found hiding in a barn after a short foot pursuit.

Three days later, Arthur Hulse was arrested in Garden Grove without incident. On July 1, Christopher Gibboney was arrested in Portland, Oregon, and Herman Taylor was taken into custody in Norwalk.

The murder trials of Hurd, Taylor, Hulse, and Gibboney were separated. Then in a surprising turn of events, Herman Taylor pleaded guilty to accessory charges and agreed to testify against Arthur Hulse in the Jerry Carlin murder case in exchange for time already served. Hulse, who was a minor at the time of the crimes, was tried as an adult and his trial began on February 8, 1971, in Orange County Superior Court. He was eventually convicted of first-degree murder and sentenced to life in prison.

On March 22, 1971, Steven Hurd was found to be mentally unfit to aid in his own defense and was ordered committed to the Atascadero State Mental Hospital for an indefinite period. Four years later, in May 1975, he was deemed sane enough to stand trial and on June 24, 1975, was convicted of the first-degree murders of Jerry Carlin and Florence Brown and sentenced to life in prison.

On May 19, 1972, Christopher Gibboney pleaded guilty to the second-degree murder of Florence Brown and was sentenced by Superior Court Judge William Murray to five years to life in prison. Because he was a minor at the time of the murder, he was remanded to the custody of the California Youth Authority and was eventually released at an unknown date. His whereabouts are unknown.

Today, Arthur Hulse remains in custody and is currently serving his life sentence at the Vacaville Prison medical facility. Steven Hurd died from a brain hemorrhage on May 28, 2005, at a hospital near Mule Creek State Prison. Notice of his death was not released to the public and went unnoticed in the news media.

1970

THE KILLER PROPHET

Santa Cruz County

Along with serial killers Edmund Kemper and Herbert Mullin, John Linley Frazier was the third component in the evil triumvirate that trolled Santa Cruz in the early 1970s. Frazier was a fairly normal person for the first twenty-three years of his life, but like Charles Manson, he was driven by paranoid delusions of the end of the world.

Unlike Manson, who suffered through a horrible early life, Frazier's adolescence was quite ordinary. He was born in Ohio in 1946 and by his teen years had begun to lose interest in school and started committing petty crimes. He dropped out of high school at age seventeen, moved to California, began working as an auto mechanic, and got married. On the surface, he appeared to have straightened out his life, but all of that changed in the spring of 1970, when he began experimenting with drugs, which included LSD, and his marriage broke up. He embraced the counterculture revolution and became an extreme advocate for environmental protection. He quit his job as a mechanic, telling his boss he refused to participate in the destruction of the planet and then joined a Santa Cruz hippie commune.

Because of increasing drug use, he became extremely paranoid, which didn't fit in with the laid-back style of the others in the hippie group. This exceedingly bizarre behavior caused the group to ask him to leave, and Frazier began living alone in a six-foot-square hut in the woods near Soquel in Santa Cruz County. Not far away in a hilltop mansion lived Dr. Victor Ohta and his family. Ohta was a successful Santa Cruz eye surgeon, and Frazier quickly became agitated by what he perceived to be the Ohtas' overly materialistic lifestyle. His paranoia came to a murderous boiling point on the afternoon of October 19, 1970, when he went to Ohtas's house to confront the owners.

At the front door of the home, Frazier encountered Virginia Ohta, the forty-three-year-old wife of Victor. Holding a gun to Ohta, he tied her hands with a scarf and waited for the rest of the family to come home. A short time later, Dr. Ohta's secretary Dorothy Cadwallader, thirty-eight, arrived with one of the children, eleven-year-old Taggart, and they were both bound and gagged. Then Dr. Ohta returned home with his other son, twelve-year-old Derrick, and they too were accosted and tied-up. Standing outside by the pool, Frazier lined-up his victims and began to lecture them on the evils of a greedy society and the ways in which it destroyed the environment.

Dr. Ohta began to argue with Frazier and was shoved into the pool. While he was trying to get out of the water, Frazier shot him three times. Then, one by one he methodically shot and killed the rest, went into the house, typed a rambling note about the coming apocalypse, and set the house on fire. The Ohtas' two daughters, eighteen-year-old Taura and fifteen-year-old Lark, were away at boarding school at the time of the murders. When firefighters arrived at the scene, they found five bodies floating in the backyard pool and discovered Frazier's typewritten note under the windshield wipers of Dr. Ohta's car in the driveway. The note read:

Halloween, 1970

Today World War III will begin as brought to you by the people of the free universe. From this day forward anyone and/or company of persons who misuses the natural environment or destroys same will suffer the penalty of death by the people of the free universe. I and my comrades from this day forth will fight until death or freedom, against anything or anyone who does not support natural life on this planet, materialism must die, or man-kind will.

Signed: KNIGHT OF WANDS, KNIGHT OF CUPS, KNIGHT OF PENTACLES, KNIGHT OF SWORDS

As a result of the ritualistic nature, randomness, and brutality of the slayings, the public was in a panic. People became suspicious of the local hippie communes, fearing another Manson Family-type crime spree. The note left by the killer was published in the local newspapers and its ideology was immediately recognized as belonging to John Linley Frazier. His former hippie friends thought that he had gone too far and gave police information on his whereabouts. Four days after the murders, Frazier was arrested by police at his cabin. His fingerprints were matched to those found on Dr. Ohta's car and a beer can found at the scene of the crime. He was charged with five counts of first-degree murder, to which he pleaded innocent by reason of insanity.

Because of news coverage and fear that Frazier could not receive a fair trial, the proceedings were eventually moved to San Mateo County. The trial began on October 18, 1971, and after several weeks of testimony, Frazier was found guilty of the murders. During his sanity hearing, Frazier did his best to look and sound crazy, shaving half his head and eyebrows. On December 15, 1971, despite his bizarre actions, he was found to be sane and sentenced to death. Frazier was spared the death penalty when California abolished capital punishment in 1972 and his sentence was automatically commuted to life imprisonment. On August 20, 2009, after serving thirty-eight years behind bars, Frazier carried out his own death sentence by hanging himself in his cell at the Mule Creek State Prison in Ione, California.

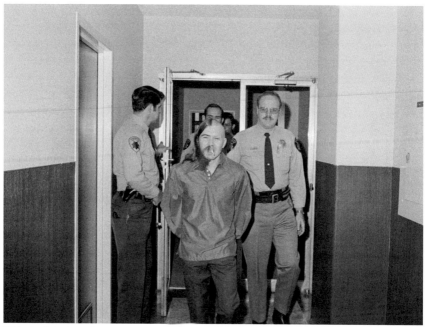

With the left side of his head and face shaved clean, John Linley Frazier returns to his cell during recess of his sanity hearing on December 2, 1971. *Courtesy of Bettmann/Corbis.*

In a tragic side note to the case, two years after the murders, Victor Ohta's mother committed suicide and the Ohta's oldest child, Taura took the same path seven years after the murders.

1971

THE MACHETE MURDERER

Sutter County

The year 1971 was a turbulent year for crime in the state of California. In Los Angeles, police had just learned about the twenty-year killing spree of Mack Ray Edwards, who confessed to murdering half a dozen children, and was just two years removed from the horror of the Manson Family slayings. The state would, unfortunately, take center stage once again in the world of serial killings and bear witness to the highest known murder count yet by one person.

Juan Vallejo Corona was born in Mexico in 1934. His life there is somewhat of a mystery, but what we do know started after he migrated to California in the 1950s and found work as a farm laborer in Yuba County. Unlike most itinerant laborers who traveled around the region, Corona stayed on after the harvest, married, and started a family. Because of his strong work ethic, he was eventually promoted from a picker to a labor contractor. By the mid-1960s, he was well-liked and his reputation as a supplier of good workers was second-to-none.

Things began to take a turn for the worse in 1970 when a young Mexican man named Jose Raya was viciously attacked with a machete at a gay bar in Maryville that was owned by Corona's brother Natividad. The man accused Natividad of the assault and filed a personal injury lawsuit for which he was eventually awarded over $250,000. Before the case could be settled, Natividad Corona fled to Mexico and disappeared. No one at the time suspected Juan Corona could have been involved in the crime.

On May 19, 1971, Goro Kagehiro, a Japanese farmer, found a large, freshly dug hole on his property near the Feather River in Sutter County. He asked several workers if they knew about the strange hole, but no one knew how it got there. Being a curious sort, Kagehiro returned to the location later that night only to find that it had been filled in. He called the local sheriff's office, and after a bit of digging, they found the remains of forty-year-old Kenneth Edward Whitacre, a local transient. He had been hacked to death with a machete. Police also discovered stacks of gay pornography in the shallow grave, which led detectives to speculate the murder was most likely sex related.

On May 23, 1971, in a nearby peach orchard owned by Jack Sullivan, workers discovered another grave. In it, police found the body of Charles Fleming, another transient. As investigators searched the area, they uncovered twenty-five more victims. All had been stabbed to death and had two slashes across the back of the head in the shape of a cross. They had also been buried face-up, with their arms stretched above their head and shirts pulled over their faces. Some of the victims showed signs of sexual assault and none had been reported as missing by loved ones. The killer might have gotten away with his crimes, had it not been for several crucial mistakes: leaving a grave open long enough to be discovered, and burying a receipt and bank deposit slip bearing his name in the pocket of victim Melford Sample. The name on the evidence was Juan Corona.

Armed with this evidence, police arrested Corona at his Yuba City home on May 26, 1971. After a search of his home, detectives found a machete that matched the murder weapon and a ledger that contained the names of seven victims. He was charged with twenty-five counts of first-degree murder and he pleaded innocent. His trial was moved to Solano County because of media attention and the proceedings began on September 11, 1972. His defense lawyers attempted to lay the blame for the crimes on Corona's missing brother, Natividad, a known violent offender with homosexual tendencies, but the jury of ten men and two women didn't believe the claims and eventually found him guilty of all charges. On February 7, 1973, he received a sentence of twenty-five consecutive life terms.

While serving his sentence, Corona has been suspected of numerous other murders but has never been officially charged. In 1978, a California Appeals court granted him a new trial based on the incompetence of his legal team. The new trial made no difference and, in 1982, he was again found guilty of the twenty-five murders and sent back to prison to serve out his twenty-five consecutive life terms. Today, Corona is incarcerated at the California State Penitentiary in Corcoran.

1971-1983

THE SCORECARD KILLER

Orange County

Randy Steven Kraft was a quiet and unassuming computer programmer. To the outside world he appeared to be quite normal, but looks can often be very deceiving. What lurked below the surface was a homicidal sexual sadist who would become one of the most prolific serial killers in California history. He is believed to have committed over fifty murders of young men and teenage boys between 1971 and 1983, but those estimates could be much higher. He often raped, tortured, and mutilated his victims. But unlike other serial killers, who often sought out and basked in the notoriety of their crimes, Kraft has never publicly offered an explanation as to why he committed the crimes and has avoided the spotlight since his conviction in 1989.

In the early morning hours of May 14, 1983, California highway patrol officers stopped a suspected drunk driver, who was observed weaving erratically in and out of traffic on the Santa Ana Freeway, near Mission Viejo in South Orange County, California. After being pulled over, the driver, Randy Kraft, immediately exited his vehicle and approached the patrol officers. Growing more apprehensive by the second, officers had Kraft perform a routine sobriety test, which he failed, and was arrested. While Kraft was being placed into the back of the patrol car, another officer approached Kraft's

Serial Killer Randy Kraft from his 1989 trial. *Courtesy of the Orange County Register/Zuma Press.*

vehicle and observed a young male who appeared to be passed out in the front passenger seat. The officer attempted to wake the man but was unable to get a response. Upon closer examination, it was determined that the man was deceased. The dead man was observed to have strangulation marks around his neck, and his hands had been bound and his pants were pulled down. He was later identified as Terry Gambrel, twenty-five, a Marine stationed at nearby Camp Pendleton.

Kraft was born on March 19, 1945, in Long Beach, California. He grew up in a modest home in Midway City. His childhood was considered normal, unlike many other serial killers. He was a bright student and well liked. After graduating from Westminster High School in 1963, he began attending Claremont Men's College in Claremont, California. His first known encounter with the police came three years later when he was arrested for lewd conduct in Huntington Beach, but the charges were dismissed.

After graduating from college in 1968 with a bachelor's degree in economics, Kraft enlisted in the US Air Force, where he earned a top-secret security clearance. But within the year, he was medically discharged after disclosing his homosexual inclinations. After leaving the service, he returned to Southern California and settled in Long Beach. For the next decade, he worked at various jobs as a bartender, truck driver, and computer programmer. From

1980 to 1983, he worked for a Santa Monica-based aerospace company. Just prior to his arrest in 1983, he had been laid off and began a short-lived career as a freelance computer consultant.

In March 1970, Kraft had another run-in with police after meeting thirteen-year-old Joey Fancher in Huntington Beach. The boy told him that he was a runaway and needed a place to stay. Kraft offered to let him stay at his apartment in Belmont Shore. Once in the apartment, Kraft allegedly drugged and sexually assaulted the youth. The next morning, after Kraft left for work, the boy was able to escape and called police. The boy initially told police that Kraft had forced him to take drugs but denied any sexual molestation. However, Fancher later recanted the entire story, confessing that he had voluntarily taken the drugs and, because of this, no charges were ever filed in the case.

During his years in Long Beach, a city with a prominent gay community, Kraft became more open with his homosexuality and began to experience an overwhelming desire to kill. He soon began trolling the gay bars and freeways of Southern California for potential victims. Late at night, armed with a cooler of beer and a glove compartment stocked with drugs, Kraft typically lured young men and teenage boys into his car with the promise of a ride and free alcohol. He would then drug, sexually assault, torture, and strangle them to death. Their bodies were then unceremoniously dumped along the freeways of Southern California.

His murderous crime spree is suspected to have begun as early as October 1971, with the slaying of thirty-year-old Wayne Dukette, a bartender at a well-known Long Beach gay bar. Dukette's body was discovered off the Ortega Highway between Orange and Riverside County. Police later determined that Dukette had likely been Kraft's first homicide victim after deciphering the killer's coded notebook, which detailed all of his crimes.

After Kraft's arrest in 1983, a search of his car uncovered numerous photographs of young men, a few of which appeared to be deceased. Police also found the briefcase that contained the notebook that held the list of mysteriously coded messages. A search of Kraft's home uncovered further evidence that convinced police that they had just apprehended a serial killer. In the photograph collection, investigators were able to easily identify several victims: Robert Loggins, nineteen, a Marine who had been found dead in September 1980; Roger De Vaul, twenty, and Geoffrey Nelson, eighteen, who were found murdered in February 1983; Eric Church, twenty-one, another hitchhiker, who was found dead in Orange County on March 27, 1983; and the body-count kept growing. Police also found DNA evidence at Kraft's home that matched Scott Hughes, eighteen, whose body was found dumped beside the Riverside Freeway in April 1978. Other items found at his home implicated him in the 1982 murders of three Oregon men and one Michigan man. Police learned that Kraft had worked for the aerospace company between June 1980 and January 1983, visiting corporate offices in Oregon and Michigan at the times of these unsolved murders.

As the list of victims increased, police investigators were able to crack the code in Kraft's notebook. They were able to determine that:

- "2 in 1 Hitch" referred to the murders of Nelson and De Vaul
- "Marine Carson" was a reference to Richard Keith, twenty, a young Marine whose strangled body was found in Laguna Hills in June 1978
- "Jail Out" described the case of Ronald Young, twenty-three, found stabbed to death in Irvine, just hours after his release from jail on June 11, 1978
- "Parking Lot" referred to Keith Crotwell, eighteen, who had disappeared on March 26, 1975, and whose severed head was found several days later off the coast of Long Beach

In all, Kraft was charged with sixteen murders but is strongly suspected in fifty-one others.

On September 26, 1988, after five years of delays, Kraft's murder trial finally began in Orange County Superior Court. During the proceedings, which lasted nearly eight months, both the prosecution and defense called over 150 witnesses to testify. On May 12, 1989, Kraft was found guilty of sixteen counts of first-degree murder and was eventually sentenced to death. Today, he remains on death row at San Quentin Prison awaiting appeals. He has continued to deny any involvement in the murders and has refused to comment on the case. In 1993, he filed a multi-million dollar libel suit against the publisher and author of a book about his case, frivolously claiming the volume had unfairly tarnished his character, thereby dashing any future prospects of employment. The lawsuit was dismissed by the California Supreme Court in June 1994.

1972-1973

SLAUGHTER IN SANTA CRUZ

Santa Cruz County

Herbert William Mullin was a star athlete and voted most likely to succeed by his classmates at Santa Cruz High School. At that time, no one could have imagined the horrors that lay ahead. It is because of his homicidal crime spree and those of fellow serial killers Edmund Kemper, John Linley Frazier, and "Trailside Killer" David Carpenter, that Santa Cruz would earn the dubious designation as murder capital of the world and the infamous nickname "Murderville, USA."

Mullin was born April 18, 1947, in the central California farming town of Salinas but was raised in Santa Cruz. He was the son of strict Catholic parents and his early childhood was considered to be quite normal. He was an excellent student and was well-liked by classmates and teachers, but things began to spiral out of control after graduating high school. During the summer of 1965, Mullin's best friend, Dean Richardson, was killed in a motorcycle accident. This tragedy would have a profound and devastating effect on Mullin, who began to withdraw from society. He became obsessed with his dead friend, transforming his bedroom into a shrine with furniture arranged around the dead boy's photograph. He also began to exhibit early signs of schizophrenia, such as hearing voices, and began to question his sexuality.

Becoming fixated with Eastern religions, his family became concerned with his unstable behavior. In 1969, he was persuaded by his parents to check himself into a local mental hospital but soon refused to cooperate with doctors and was released after only six weeks of treatment. In October 1969, he experienced a full-blown paranoid schizophrenic episode, which was worsened by the use of LSD and other drugs. During this period, the voices in his head became more pronounced. They began telling him to do bizarre things, such as self-mutilation and, because of this, he was hospitalized for a short period. After his release in June 1970, Mullin had numerous confrontations with law enforcement and decided to leave Santa Cruz. He bummed around the San Francisco Bay Area for over a year staying in cheap motels but returned to his parents' home in September 1972. By this time, the voices in his head had become more violent and commanded him to kill.

On October 13, 1972, while driving through the Santa Cruz Mountains, he spotted fifty-five-year-old Lawrence White, a transient. Pulling his car to the side of the road, Mullin told the man he was having car trouble and as White looked at the car's engine, he was beat to death with a baseball bat. Eleven days later, on October 24, Mullin ramped up his murderous rampage when he picked up twenty-four-year-old Mary Guilfoyle. The young woman was a student at Cabrillo College and was hitchhiking when Mullin offered her a ride. He drove Guilfoyle to a secluded area near Santa Cruz and stabbed her in the chest and back. He then dissected her remains, scattering the organs along the side of the road. Her skeletal remains wouldn't be discovered for four months.

Mullin now began to hear new voices, which were perceived to be coming from future victims, who were begging him to kill them. On November 2, in an attempt to clear his conscience, Mullin sought out the counsel of sixty-four-year-old Henry Tomei, a priest at St. Mary's of the Immaculate Conception Catholic Church in Los Gatos. After confessing the previous murders, Mullin stabbed Father Tomei to death in the church's confessional booth.

During this period, Mullin stopped using drugs and blamed them for all of his problems. In December, he purchased a handgun and resumed his murder rampage. On January 25, 1973, bent on revenge, he went looking for a former acquaintance whom he blamed for his drug use. Arriving at the last known address of Jim Gianera, he encountered the home's new occupant Kathy Francis, who gave him the former tenant's new address. He then drove to the updated address where he shot Gianera and his wife Joan. To eliminate any witnesses, Mullin drove back to Kathy Francis's home and shot her and her two young sons as they slept.

His homicidal urges still not satiated, on February 6, 1973, Mullin went to Henry Cowell Redwoods State Park for a hike where he encountered four teenage boys: Robert Spector, David Oliker, Brian Card, and Mark Dreibelbis. After striking up a casual conversation with the teens in which he accused them of polluting the forest, Mullins, pulled out his handgun and shot them all to death.

A week after the quadruple homicide on February 13, Mullin, while driving through Santa Cruz, encountered seventy-two-year-old local resident Fred Perez. The elderly man was tending to his front-yard garden when Mullin pulled up and shot him to death. This time, there were witnesses to the murder, who gave police a description of the car and its plate number. Mullin was apprehended a short time later without incident.

While in custody, he confessed to all of the murders and told detectives that he had committed the crimes to prevent a catastrophic earthquake from destroying California. He was charged with ten counts of murder. The first three slayings had taken place in other jurisdictions. His murder trial began on July 30, 1973, in Santa Cruz Superior Court and, after only three weeks of testimony, he was found guilty of the first-degree murders of Jim Gianera and Kathy Francis and second-degree murder of the other eight victims. For these crimes he received a sentence of life in prison. The Santa Cruz County prosecutor later charged him with the murder of Father Tomei, but on the day the trial was to begin (December 11, 1973), Mullin pleaded guilty to second-degree murder and was sentenced to life in prison. Today, he is incarcerated at the Mule Creek State Prison in Ione, California.

1972-1974

SANTA ROSA HITCHHIKER MURDERS

Sonoma County, San Francisco, Redding, and Marysville

In February 1975, California's Department of Justice issued a confidential report stating that fourteen unsolved murders in the past three years had been committed by a single man. Six victims had been found near Santa Rosa in Sonoma County and five were discovered in San Francisco, with one each in Marysville and Redding. The murders were distinguished from a host of other unsolved homicides by similar disposal of the bodies and the killer's fondness for retaining souvenirs of his victims.

The chain of deaths began on February 4, 1972, when two twelve-year-old girls, Maureen Strong and Yvonne Weber, vanished on their way home from a Santa Rosa skating rink. Their remains were found on December 28, on an embankment near a rural country road in eastern Sonoma County. The killer had removed all clothing and a single gold earring from each victim. On March 4, nineteen-year-old co-ed Kim Allen disappeared while hitchhiking in Santa Rosa. Her nude body, strangled with clothesline, was found in a nearby creek bed. There were superficial cuts on her chest and rope burns on her wrists and ankles. Once again, the victim's clothing and one earring were missing. The killer struck again on November 21, when thirteen-year-old Lori Jursa vanished from a Santa Rosa market. Her remains were discovered three weeks later and the cause of death was listed as a broken neck. Like the other victims, one earring was missing and the body was stripped of clothing. The killer then shifted to San Francisco, claiming four victims—Rosa Vasquez, Yvonne Quilintang, Angela Thomas, and Nancy Gidley—between May and July of 1973. Like the other victims, all had been strangled and found nude dumped along roadsides or in deserted parking lots.

The string of unsolved homicides took an occult angle after teenager Caroline Davis was kidnapped on July 15. A runaway from Shasta County, Davis was last seen hitching a ride on Highway 101 near Santa Rosa. Her body was found on July 31, near the spot where Strong and Weber's bodies were dumped seven months earlier. But unlike the other victims, Davis had been poisoned with strychnine and, near her body, police discovered a strange design arranged from twigs, laid out to form two interlocking rectangles. The crude sculpture was described as a witchy symbol and was understood to designate the carrier of spirits. On July 22, 1973, the semi-nude body of Nancy Feusi was found near Redding, California, but because of severe decomposition of the remains, an exact cause of death was not determined.

On November 4, the scene shifted back to San Francisco with the discovery of Laura O'Dell's nude and strangled corpse. The killings continued on December 22, when twenty-two-year-old Theresa Walsh was found raped and strangled to death near the location in Santa Rosa where Kim Allen's body was found in April 1972. The murders continued into 1974, with the discovery of Brenda Merchant's body on February 1, in Marysville. Her semi-nude body was found stabbed to death beside a rural road. Seven months later, on September 29, fourteen-year-old Donna Braun's naked body was found floating in the Salinas River near Monterey. She had been strangled.

And so, presumably the murders then ceased. A fifteenth victim, inadvertently omitted from the government's original report, was twenty-year-old Jeannette Kamahele, a college co-ed who disappeared while hitchhiking near Santa Rosa on April 25, 1972. Her skeletal remains were exhumed on July 6, 1979, in a shallow grave within 100 yards of where Lori Jursa's body was found in November 1972.

The occult theory's chief advocates were detectives at the Sonoma County Sheriff's Department. Impressed by the stick sculpture found near Caroline Davis' body, investigators also found significance in victims being dumped along the east side of various roads. Additionally, they discovered a possible connection in cases from Washington and Oregon between January and July 1974 in which women had been kidnapped during the waning phases of the moon. They went on to theorize that the killer or killers must have been familiar with witchcraft or the occult, because of the symbol found during the Caroline Davis case and the possible occult involvement in the missing females in the states of Oregon and Washington.

Unfortunately, this theory proved to be false when all the Oregon victims were credited to serial killer Ted Bundy, and further investigation determined that time tables and movements cleared Bundy of any involvement in the California crimes. Likewise, the reputed witchcraft symbol from the Davis crime scene was ultimately proved to be a piece of childish art constructed by a small boy on vacation in the likeness of the family's car and trailer.

In the years since the last known victim's body was discovered, police have questioned numerous suspects that include serial killer Harvey Carignan, who was issued a speeding ticket on June 20, 1973, in Solano County, east of Santa Rosa. But no other evidence links him to the crimes, and one week after the traffic violation, he was claiming victims in Minnesota, leading to his arrest in September 1974. Carignan was in custody when Donna Braun was murdered and the other victims showed no traces of his murder weapon of choice: a claw hammer. An intriguing theory published by Robert Graysmith, in 2007, credits the elusive Zodiac killer with these and many other unsolved California homicides, but this theory is a moot point until such time as the killer is actually apprehended. In the meantime, we can only say that one or more sadistic serial killers is still on the loose in the Golden State, and as each year goes by, the trail of this elusive murderer gets colder and colder.

1973

EASTER DAY SHOOTING RAMPAGE

Los Angeles

On Easter Sunday 1973, William Ray Bonner went on a wild shooting spree in south Los Angeles, where he killed seven and wounded ten. At the time of the rampage, Bonner was an unemployed gas station attendant. He was born on March 28, 1948, and had an extensive arrest record dating back to 1966 that included drugs, assault, and auto theft. Acquaintances would later describe him as being a loner and soft-spoken.

The shooting frenzy was precipitated the night before by an argument with a friend and a break-up with his girlfriend. Already agitated by the previous night's events, in the early afternoon of April 22, Bonner got into another argument and shot and killed his mother's friend, Otha Leavitt, fifty-three, at his south Los Angeles home.

Infuriated, Bonner then went outside and shot teenagers Anthony Thomas and Carolyn Cleveland, who had accompanied Leavitt and were waiting in her car. The teens were severely injured but managed to flee the scene and survived the attack. At this point, Bonner got into Leavitt's 1967 Plymouth sedan and, armed with a handgun and shotgun, drove to a local Texaco gas station. Arriving at the station, he entered the service bay and confronted former coworker, Raleigh Henderson, thirty-three, and shot and killed him.

Bonner then approached a female customer, shooting in the air and fled the scene. Next, he drove to a nearby Arco gas station where he attempted to rob the station's attendant and then shot and killed a customer, Vicky Wells, eighteen, and wounded her thirteen-year-old sister Aileen. Bonner had been employed at both service stations and had been fired from both jobs.

After leaving the Arco station, Bonner drove a short distance to the home of Vernon Thompson, with whom he had argued the previous night. Vernon was not home at the time but Bonner shot to death his fifty-seven-year-old father Jevie Thompson, his wife Eddie Mae, and their teenage son Alfred. Bonner then drove to Smitty's Drive-In Liquors, on South Avalon Boulevard, where he shot and killed store owner Smitty Sneed and wounded Duly Bennett. Bonner then headed to Liquorama Liquors on South San Pedro Street, where he took money from the cash register and shot and critically wounded store employee Robert L. Smith and Roosevelt Jenkins. He then drove to the McKinley Avenue home of his former girlfriend twenty-two-year-old Dianne L. Andrea and shot and killed her.

After the shooting rampage, Bonner evaded capture for nearly an hour before being spotted by two Los Angeles police officers near the corner of Manchester Boulevard and Vermont Avenue. Bonner pointed his shotgun at the officers, but the weapon failed to discharge. Throwing the useless weapon to the ground, Bonner sped away in the stolen car. A short time later, he abandoned the vehicle and carjacked Mary Felton, forty-five, as she was waiting at a stoplight. Bonner threatened to kill her and her two daughters if she did not drive away. The incident was witnessed by a security guard, Versell Bennett, fifty-eight, who gave chase to the stolen vehicle and eventually forced it to stop at the corner of Manchester Boulevard and Kansas Avenue. Bonner and Bennett exchanged gunfire. The security guard was initially mistaken for the gunman and was shot by police. Bennett would succumb to his injuries four days later. Bonner jumped from the commandeered car and rolled under it, and opened fire on approaching police. Moments later, he was shot several times and taken into custody.

Bonner was formally charged with seven counts of murder, eight counts of assault with a deadly weapon, and three counts of kidnapping. He initially pleaded innocent by reason of insanity. On November 13, 1973, he pleaded guilty to six counts of first-degree murder, one count of second-degree murder, and assault with a deadly weapon. Bonner was sentenced to life in prison on December 14, in Torrance Superior Court. Today, he remains incarcerated at the California Men's Colony in San Luis Obispo.

1974-1975

THE CURIOUS CASE OF PATTY HEARST

Berkeley, San Francisco, Los Angeles

Patty Hearst was the granddaughter of newspaper mogul William Randolph Hearst, and for more than a year after her abduction, she became a machine-gun wielding bank robber and political activist named Tania. The strange-but-true saga of the newspaper heiress began on February 4, 1974, when the nineteen-year-old was kidnapped from her Berkeley, California, apartment by three armed members of a leftist revolutionary group, who stuffed her half-naked and blindfolded into the trunk of a car. They sped away leaving behind Hearst's brutally beaten boyfriend, Steven Weed. Two days later, a letter arrived at radio station KPFA in Berkeley. It stated that Hearst was a prisoner of the Symbionese Liberation Army, a radical Bay Area group that had been implicated in the assassination of Oakland's superintendent of schools, Dr. Marcus Foster, the previous year.

The letter was followed by a series of taped messages from Hearst and SLA leader Donald DeFreeze, then known as General Field Marshal Cinque. The tapes were filled with the SLA's anti-establishment rhetoric and included a demand that Randolph A. Hearst, Patty's father and chairman of the Hearst publishing empire, buy millions of dollars' worth of food and distribute it among the poor.

The media was already going wild with the story when, on April 3, a rambling communique arrived in which Hearst herself denounced her bourgeois parents and declared that she had willingly chosen to stay and fight for the SLA cause. She began calling herself "Tania" after a comrade who fought alongside Cuban revolutionary Che Guevara.

On the morning of April 15, five SLA members robbed the San Francisco branch of the Hibernia Bank. They all wielded rifles and told patrons to get on the floor. One of the women announced, "This is Tania Hearst!" It was she, a bank guard later testified, who shouted the threat: "Lie down or I'll shoot your (expletive) heads off!" The grainy black-and-white security footage of Tania/Patty cradling a rifle in her arms, anxiously standing guard

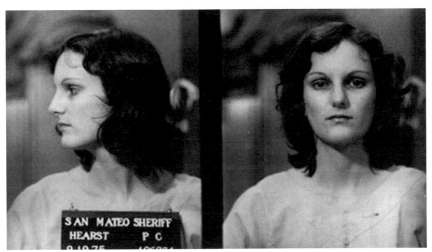

Booking photo of Patty Hearst, San Mateo County Sheriff's Department, September 19, 1975.

while her associates/abductors netted over $10,000 in cash, is arguably the most famous security tape of all time. The heist lasted only five minutes and the members of the gang sped off. Their diversionary gunshots wounded two bystanders. The bank footage revealed the identities of the four other SLA bandits, including that of Field Marshal Cinque. DeFreeze, thirty, was a career criminal who had escaped from California's Soledad Prison in 1973 where he advocated militant politics. After his jail break, he cofounded the SLA. Within days of the Hibernia Bank heist, the FBI issued wanted posters featuring mug shots of all five perpetrators, including Hearst.

The fugitives fled to Los Angeles, where, on May 16, there was another very public, violent incident. Hearst sprayed submachine gunfire across the storefront of Mel's Sporting Goods to assist the escape of SLA members William and Emily Harris, aka Teko and Yolanda, who were being detained for shoplifting. Police worked fast this time, and were determined to find the location of the gang's hideout, and on May 17, surrounded it. A fierce shootout left the building engulfed in flames, and six SLA members, including DeFreeze, were killed. Hearst was not at the hideout but instead watched live TV coverage of the confrontation from a motel room near Disneyland, where she and the Harrises were hiding out. The trio were able to elude law enforcement for several months and they crisscrossed the country throughout the summer of 1974, gathering new followers and scheming more crimes. On April 21, 1975, with Hearst manning the getaway car, a band of masked SLA members robbed the Crocker National Bank in Carmichael, California, near Sacramento, and killed Myrna Opsahl, a forty-two-year-old mother of four who was depositing her church's collection money. Any sympathy the public felt over Hearst's captivity was pretty much erased by this murder, and the manhunt for the SLA intensified. Finally, on September 18, the running came to an end and the remnants of the SLA were apprehended by the FBI at two different apartments in San Francisco. Among those arrested was Patty Hearst.

On February 4, 1976, marking the two-year anniversary of her kidnapping, Patty Hearst, a few weeks shy of twenty-two, went on trial for the armed robbery of the Hibernia Bank. She arrived at the San Francisco courthouse with her family wearing a beige pantsuit—nothing like the urban guerrilla she had listed as her occupation when she was booked. Indeed, Hearst appeared pale and fragile—to some, a sympathetic figure. Over the next nine weeks, as the prosecution portrayed her as a victim turned willful accomplice, her famous attorney, F. Lee Bailey, argued that she had been brainwashed and threatened throughout her ordeal. The jury of seven women and five men deliberated for only twelve hours before returning a guilty verdict. Hearst was sentenced to seven years but served only twenty-one months before her term was commuted by President Jimmy Carter in February of 1979. In January 2001, just hours before turning the White House over to George W. Bush, President Bill Clinton pardoned her.

Today, Hearst lives a quiet life in suburban Connecticut with her husband and remains perhaps the only person on the planet with any real understanding of what truly happened during her nineteen months with the SLA.

1974-1975

THE DOODLER

San Francisco

In the years prior to the AIDS epidemic, the gay community of mid-1970s San Francisco was confronted with another lethal menace. Between January 1974 and September 1975, a knife-wielding stalker was responsible for seventeen attacks, fourteen of which were fatal. The Zodiac killer may have been San Francisco's most infamous serial killer, but another lesser-known madman stalked the streets at the same time and, just like the Zodiac, has never been apprehended for his crimes. The difference is, while the Zodiac's murder spree was heavily publicized, the crimes of this other killer went under-reported by the news media and the story is nearly forgotten today.

When the murder spree began, based on discrepancies in choice of victim, San Francisco police believed they were tracking three different serial killers. Five of the victims were drag queens, mutilated by a killer who apparently hated transvestites. Six others, including high-profile attorney George Gilbert, were selected from the sadomasochistic world of gay bars, clubs with names like Ramrod, Fe'Be's, and Folsom Prison. The last six victims were middle-class businessmen, slain by an assailant who picked them up in Castro Village bars, enticing his prey with cartoon sketches of themselves. Three of the latter victims survived the attacks, and the killer's taste for comic artwork gave the "Doodler" his infamous nickname. The killer would often sketch his victims prior to having sex, then stab them to death. Police theorized that the murderer was ashamed of the homosexual acts he had committed and killed his victims in an attempt to alleviate his conscience.

Over time, as leads were run down and eliminated, police realized they were searching for a single killer in their string of unsolved homicides. In 1976, suspicion focused on a suspect described by authorities as a mental patient with a history of treatment for sex-related issues. Questioned repeatedly, the suspect spoke freely to detectives, but always stopped short of a full confession. Meanwhile, the three surviving victims, which included a well-known entertainer and diplomat, refused to identify their attacker, afraid of ruining their lives by "coming out" in court. On July 8, 1977, frustrated police investigators announced that an unnamed suspect had been linked to fourteen murders and three assaults between 1974 and 1975. Indictment was impossible, they said, without cooperation from survivors of the Doodler's attacks—which never happened. Forty years after the fact, the case remains at a dead end, officially unsolved, with the unnamed suspect, if he still survives, presumably under ongoing surveillance.

1975

ATTEMPTED ASSASSINATIONS OF PRESIDENT GERALD R. FORD

Sacramento and San Francisco

In September 1975, President Gerald R. Ford survived two assassination attempts in California. He had ascended to the presidency on August 9, 1974, after

SHOT PLUS APPROXIMATELY 1 SEC.

Reaction of Secret Service agents, police, and bystanders approximately one second after Sara Jane Moore attempted to assassinate President Gerald R. Ford on September 22, 1975. *Courtesy of the Gerald R. Ford Library.*

the resignation of Richard Nixon. His life could have been ended amid gunshots outside San Francisco's historic St. Francis Hotel on the afternoon of September 22, 1975.

The president was at the hotel to give an address to a World Affairs Council audience and, as he emerged from the hotel's Post Street lobby at around 3:30 p.m., he paused to wave at a large crowd before getting into his limousine. Two shots rang out. The first one narrowly missed Ford and a second was deflected by a bystander who grabbed at the arm of the shooter, forty-five-year-old Sara Jane Moore, a political extremist and FBI informant. A San Francisco policeman subdued Moore before she could fire her .38-caliber handgun again. The president was pushed into his limousine and rushed to San Francisco International Airport. Moore's failed assassination was the second attempt on Ford's life in California in a little over two weeks.

Sara Jane Moore was born on February 15, 1930, in West Virginia. She grew-up in a household of seven children and was quiet and well-liked in school. Following high school graduation, she went through a series of failed marriages and eventually moved to San Francisco where she became involved with several radical left-wing political groups. In the month leading up to her failed assassination attempt on President Ford, Moore worked as a paid FBI informant.

Gerald R. Ford was born on July 14, 1913, in Omaha, Nebraska. He would go on to distinguish himself as a student at the University of Michigan and Yale University Law School. In 1948, he won a seat in Congress from Michigan's 5th Congressional District, a post he would hold for twenty-four years. In 1964, he was appointed by President Lyndon Johnson to the Warren Commission that investigated the assassination of President John F. Kennedy. A conservative Republican, Ford opposed most of LBJ's legislative agendas and

Gerald R. Ford, first official portrait (August 24, 1974). *Courtesy of the Gerald R. Ford Library.*

was critical of his handling of the Vietnam War. He was elected House Minority Leader in 1965. He was a supporter and friend of Richard Nixon and assumed the Vice Presidency in 1973, after the resignation of Spiro Agnew. In the aftermath of the Watergate Affair that forced Nixon to resign the presidency, Ford was sworn in as the thirty-eighth president of the United States on August 9, 1974.

On September 5, 1975, Charles Manson follower twenty-six-year-old Lynette "Squeaky" Fromme attempted to shoot Ford on the state Capitol grounds in Sacramento. Around 10:00 a.m., the president returned to the Senator Hotel after addressing a large gathering of business leaders at the State Fair Host Breakfast at the Sacramento Convention Center. As he was walking from the hotel through Capitol Park to meet with California Gov. Jerry Brown, Fromme, clad in a red robe and armed with a .45-caliber revolver, stepped from behind a tree and, at a range of only two feet, pointed her gun at Ford's back. Secret Service agent Larry Buendorf grabbed the gun

Secret Service agents rush President Ford (center) towards the California State Capitol following the attempt on the president's life on September 5, 1975. *Courtesy of the Gerald R. Ford Library.*

before it went off and wrestled Fromme to the ground. During the scuffle, Fromme was heard to yell, "It didn't go off! It didn't go off." President Ford was quickly whisked away into the safety of the Capitol building. Later that morning, Ford addressed a joint session of the California legislature and made no reference to the incident. Ironically, the topic of his speech was crime in the United States.

Fromme was born on December 22, 1948, in Santa Monica, California. She grew up in a normal household and as a young child performed in various dance troupes. After graduating from high school, she moved to Venice, California, where she befriended Charles Manson. Captivated by his charm and charisma, she joined his Family at the Spahn Ranch north of Los Angeles. It was eighty-year-old George Spahn who gave her the nickname Squeaky due to her high-pitched voice. She managed to avoid arrest during the infamous Tate-LaBianca murder case because she was not present at either crime scene. After Manson's conviction, she and other members of the Family drifted throughout California.

During Fromme's lengthy trial in federal court, she refused to cooperate with defense attorneys and stated that she was relieved not to have shot the gun, but did it to help protect the environment. During the proceedings, which (like the early Manson trials) often took on a circus-like atmosphere, she threw an apple at the lead prosecutor, knocking off his glasses. Fromme was eventually convicted of the attempted assassination of a president and sentenced to life in prison. She was first incarcerated at the Federal Correctional Institution in Dublin, California, but after she attacked another inmate was transferred to the Federal Prison Camp in Alderson, West Virginia. On December 23, 1987, she escaped and attempted to meet Manson but was captured after two days and sent to the Federal Medical Center in Carswell, Texas. She was released on parole on August 14, 2009.

Sara Jane Moore eventually pleaded guilty to the attempted assassination of a president and was sentenced to life in prison. In 1979, she also escaped from the Federal Prison Camp in Alderson, West Virginia, but was captured a few hours later. She was then sent to the Federal Prison Camp in Dublin, California, and on December 31, 2007, was released on parole. Moore has since expressed remorse for the attempted assassination stating she was "blinded by radical political views" at the time.

1976

DEATH OF THE SWITCHBLADE KID

Hollywood

Actor Sal Mineo was murdered on February 12, 1976, in Hollywood, California. He was walking behind his apartment when neighbors heard him scream for help. Witnesses described seeing a white man with long brown hair fleeing the scene.

Sal Mineo, 1973. *Courtesy of Allan Warren.*

Salvatore Mineo Jr. was born on January 10, 1939, in The Bronx, New York. He was a talented actor and teen heartthrob that co-starred opposite James Dean in *Rebel without a Cause* (1955), for which Mineo was nominated for a best

On the night of February 12, 1976, actor Sal Mineo was stabbed to death in this alley behind his West Hollywood apartment.

supporting actor Academy Award, and from which he also gained the nick-name "The Switchblade Kid." He teamed up again with Dean the following year in the critically acclaimed motion picture, *Giant* (1956). His transition to adult film roles was not easy, but he later appeared in films such as *Exodus* (1960), for which he won a Golden Globe for best supporting actor and was nominated for another Academy Award. Other film credits included *The Longest Day* (1962) and *Escape from the Planet of the Apes* (1971). He was also a regular on numerous television series of the late 1960s and early 1970s. On the night of his murder, Mineo was returning home after rehearsing his role in the play *P. S. Your Cat is Dead*.

For several years, police searched for clues to the killer's identity. They suspected that Mineo's volunteer work for prison reform had put him in contact with dangerous acquaintances. They then shifted their focus to his personal life after discovering boxes of photos of nude men in his apartment, but this also failed to turn up any solid leads in the case. A break came in early 1978, when Michigan authorities reported that Lionel Ray Williams, who had been arrested on bad check charges, had been bragging to fellow inmates that he had killed Mineo. Although he later withdrew his statements, his wife back in Los Angeles told police detectives that her husband had come home the night of the murder soaked in blood. However, there was a problem, as Williams was black with an Afro and all of the witnesses had

Grave of Sal Mineo at Gate of Heaven Cemetery in Hawthorne, New York.

described the perpetrator as a white man with long brown hair. Fortunately, police uncovered an old photo of Williams in which his hair had been dyed brown and straightened.

On January 17, 1978, Williams pleaded not guilty to first-degree murder and other charges that included robbery. The latter charges were included when witnesses identified him as the culprit in a string of robberies around the Los Angeles area. Williams's trial began in Los Angeles Superior Court before Judge Ronnie Lee Martin on January 9, 1979. Prosecutors theorized that the defendant had been lying in wait to rob Mineo as he returned home from acting rehearsals on the night of the slaying. Their case relied on several key pieces of evidence that included the statement made by Williams's now-deceased wife Theresa Williams; Allwyn Price Williams, a jail informant; and Los Angeles Medical Examiner Dr. Thomas Noguchi.

During the proceedings, the prosecution presented evidence that supported their theory that Williams stabbed Mineo with a knife similar to the one that Mrs. Williams claimed her husband had on him the night of the murder. Further testimony by Dr. Noguchi revealed that the perforation in the tissue of Mineo's wound and the blade of the replica knife matched perfectly. Allwyn Price Williams testified that the defendant, while incarcerated in Michigan, had bragged to him about killing Mineo. The defense tried to discredit the prosecution's case by presenting three witnesses whose description of the alleged perpetrator didn't match the defendant's appearance. Based on this information, they argued that Williams could not have been the person at the scene of the crime. The prosecution refuted these allegations by showing the jury a picture of Williams in which he had light skin and long straight hair. The jury did not accept the defense's claims and, on March 16, 1979, found the defendant guilty of second-degree murder and ten counts of robbery. He received a sentence of fifty-one years in prison and was eventually released on parole in the early 1990s. Today, his whereabouts are unknown.

Sal Mineo's gravesite can be found at the Gate of Heaven Cemetery in Hawthorne, New York, in section 2, plot 211.

1976

SHOOTING RAMPAGE AT CAL STATE FULLERTON

Orange County

On the morning of July 12, 1976, Edward Charles Allaway, thirty-seven, a custodian at Cal State Fullerton shot and killed seven coworkers and wounded two at the campus library. He had been employed at the university for a year when he became despondent and delusional after the break-up of his marriage. Allaway blamed coworkers for the demise of the relationship and then went on a shooting rampage at the university.

In 1973, Allaway hoped to escape the troubles that were haunting him by moving to Southern California. The move offered the former Marine and Michigan native a chance at a new life. He moved in with his sister Shirley Sabo and her husband and found a job as a janitor at a hardware store in Fullerton. Less than a year later, he began working as a custodian at Knott's Berry Farm in Buena Park. During that time, he met and fell in love with a pretty waitress with strawberry-blonde hair named Bonnie, who was fifteen years his junior. They were married on May 28, 1974, and moved into a modest apartment in Anaheim. In May 1975, he accepted a custodial position at Cal State Fullerton.

Around this same time, he began to suffer from delusions that his wife was being unfaithful. He became enraged by the jealousy, and his explosive temper led to their separation. Bonnie encouraged her husband to seek counseling, but he refused. Allaway moved to the Casa Valencia Motel in Anaheim. His hallucinations and paranoia were becoming more pronounced. As he swept the hallways of Cal State Fullerton's library, he began to hear voices and see shadows. He began to feel persecuted at work and found offensive graffiti, which he believed was intended for him, on the walls and stalls of the men's third-floor restroom. He also thought his coworkers were forcing his estranged wife to participate in pornographic films.

On Thursday night, July 8, Allaway drove to Bonnie's apartment in an attempt to reconcile and offered to take her to dinner, but she declined. That night he couldn't sleep and the voices in his head became more pronounced. Two days later, he went to a local Kmart and purchased a .22 caliber rifle

Cal State Fullerton's Library, where on the morning of July 12, 1976, Edward Charles Allaway shot and killed seven people.

and a box of bullets. In his mind, he thought the gun was needed for protection from his coworkers, whom he believed were his tormentors. He spent the remainder of the weekend locked inside his apartment, ate very little, did not sleep, and kept the loaded rifle by his side. Delusional and distraught, he decided it was time to leave California and move back to Michigan.

On Monday morning, July 12, around 6:00 a.m., Allaway phoned the university to quit his job, but no one answered. He then called Bonnie and told her about his plan to move back to Michigan and asked her to join him, but she declined. This was the defining moment that sent him into a homicidal rage. When he left his apartment several hours later, he felt certain his life was in danger and that he needed to act to save himself from harm. He reached the university around 8:30 a.m. and parked his car along the west side of the Cal State Fullerton library. He then walked into the building carrying the rifle and box of bullets. He made his way to the basement and entered the Instructional Media Center and, without warning, he opened fire.

His first victim, Paul Herzberg, forty-one, an IMC technician was shot and killed at his desk. The second victim, Bruce Jacobsen, thirty-two, also a technician, was shot and killed while attempting to take cover in a nearby conference room. In an adjacent office, Frank Teplansky, fifty-one, a graphic artist, and retired Professor Seth Fessenden, seventy-two, were chatting when the shots rang out. Allaway burst into their office, and with no place to hide, Teplansky and Fessenden were gunned down at point-blank range. Allaway then left the media center and headed to the outdoor hallway on the south side of the library. There he was confronted by fellow custodians, twenty-five-year-old Deborah Paulsen and fifty-one-year-old Donald Karges. Allaway fired several shots at them but missed. Paulsen and Karges attempted to flee, but were quickly pursued and shot to death. Allaway left the basement area and headed to the first-floor lobby of the library. There he encountered associate librarian Donald Keran, fifty-six, library assistant Stephen Becker, thirty-two, and custodial supervisor Maynard Hoffman, sixty-five. Hoffman was shot and wounded as he stood near the elevators, Keran was shot and also wounded while sitting at his desk, and Becker was shot and killed, while attempting to flee through an emergency exit door. Allaway then retraced his steps and fled out the west entrance of the library. Witnesses stated they heard him mutter as he left the building, "I'm going to kill all those SOBs for having sex with my wife." He then got into his car and fled the scene.

The bloody rampage had taken less than ten minutes. In the carnage were left seven people dead or dying, and two seriously wounded. At the time, it was only the second such mass school shooting in United States history... and wouldn't be the last. The first had taken place ten years earlier at the University of Texas, where Charles Whitman shot and killed fourteen people while wounding thirty-two at the university campus in Austin.

After the rampage, Allaway drove a short distance to the Hilton Inn in Anaheim where his wife worked. He found her in a banquet room training a new employee; it was just after 9:00 a.m., he was covered in blood, and Bonnie thought he had been in a fight. He asked to make a phone call. Allaway told Anaheim police dispatchers:

> I went berserk at Cal State Fullerton and I committed some terrible acts; I'd appreciate it if you people would come down and pick me up. I'm unarmed and I'm giving myself up to you.

He then asked for a glass of water and waited. A few minutes later, Anaheim police surrounded the hotel and apprehended Allaway without incident.

Allaway's murder trial began in Orange County Superior Court on August 3, 1977. After several weeks of testimony, a jury of seven women and five men found him guilty of six counts of first-degree murder, one count of second, and two counts of assault with a deadly weapon. At his sanity trial, which began in November, he was found not guilty by reason of insanity. The jury had been hopelessly deadlocked and could not reach a verdict. The defense and prosecution agreed that Superior Court Judge Robert P. Kneeland should decide the sanity issue. After rendering his verdict, Judge Kneeland stated that Allaway should never be released from custody and should always be held at a maximum-security facility. He was then committed to the Atascadero State Hospital. In 1992, mental health professionals determined that he no longer posed a threat to society and it was suggested that he be released from custody. That request and all that have followed have been denied.

1976

CHOWCHILLA SCHOOL BUS KIDNAPPING

Madera County

Prior to the summer of 1976, very few people had ever heard of Chowchilla, a small farming town located in California's central valley. All of that changed when the largest mass kidnapping for ransom in American history occurred there.

Brothers Richard Allen Schoenfeld, twenty-five, and James Leonard Schoenfeld, twenty-three, and their friend Frederick Newhall Woods IV, twenty-four, were from privileged backgrounds and had grown up in the San Francisco Bay Area. All three lived with their parents and made feeble attempts at finding employment. They dreamed of fame and fortune in Hollywood. They hung out and discussed movies featuring crime and car chases, and debated committing the perfect crime. Exactly when these discussions crossed into the realm of reality is not certain. It has been theorized that the trio planned the Chowchilla kidnapping as a mental exercise to see if it could actually be done. The plan was developed over several months: they would hijack a school bus, hide the children somewhere safe, demand a sizable ransom, pick-up the money, and then release the hostages unharmed— all within twenty-four hours. On the late afternoon of July 15, 1976, they implemented their plan.

Part-time school bus driver Ed Ray, fifty-five, was driving down rural Avenue 21 and came upon a broken-down white van in the middle of the road. Once the bus came to a stop, a man, carrying a gun and wearing a nylon stocking stretched over his head, approached. The gunman told Ray to move to the back of the bus and two other masked men appeared from behind the broken-down vehicle and got onto the bus. One of the men drove the school bus, while a second watched Ed Ray and the twenty-six children, who ranged from age six to fourteen. The third man returned to the white van and followed the bus.

After a short distance, the children were transferred to two separate vans whose windows had been blacked out. At 4:15 p.m., the two vans set off on what would be an eleven-hour journey to Livermore, California, to a rock quarry fewer than 100 miles from the site of the abduction. When they arrived, Ed Ray and the children were told to climb down a ladder sticking out of the ground into what appeared to be a cave. The cave turned out to be a buried moving van. The truck was twenty-five feet long and had been equipped with bread, water, mattresses, and a portable toilet.

At 6:00 p.m., worried parents alerted the police that their children had not returned home from school and the bus was found two hours later nine miles west of Chowchilla. The police search was called off temporarily when the area was hit with severe weather. As night fell, Ed Ray and some of the older teenage boys began to dig their way out of the buried truck, but it took nearly sixteen hours. They walked to the guard shack at the entrance to the quarry and police were called. Meanwhile, the kidnappers had been unable to phone in their demands for a $5 million ransom to the Chowchilla police because the phone lines were busy with worried parents and journalists. The kidnappers had not thought their victims would escape and so had made little attempt to disassociate themselves from key evidence, such as the vans or from the buried moving truck.

At 4:00 a.m., on July 17, the children were returned to their parents. Ed Ray was questioned by detectives and under hypnosis was able to recall the license plate number of the first van and all but one number of the second. Both vans were traced to a car dealership in Oakland, California. Police soon discovered that three vehicles had been purchased by Frederick Woods, using the alias Mark Hall. Woods turned out to be the son of the quarry owner. Several of the children remembered that the kidnappers had used the names Fred and James. This led to Richard and James Schoenfeld. Richard surrendered to authorities on July 23, and James was arrested on July 29. That same afternoon, Frederick Woods was arrested in Vancouver, Canada.

Because of pretrial publicity, their trial was moved from Madera County to Alameda County and, on July 25, 1977, all three defendants pleaded guilty to twenty-seven counts of kidnapping for ransom without inflicting injury. On December 15, 1977, after two weeks of testimony, Judge Leo Deegan sentenced all three to life in prison without the possibility of parole. In 1981, these sentences were changed to life with the possibility of parole. On June 20, 2012, after serving thirty-four years behind bars, Richard Schoenfeld was released on parole. Both James Schoenfeld and Frederick Woods have been denied parole numerous times and are currently serving their sentences at the California Men's Colony in San Luis Obispo, California.

On May 17, 2012, at the age of ninety-one, Ed Ray died at a Chowchilla nursing home from cirrhosis of the liver.

1976-1979
THE LOOK-A-LIKE MURDERS
Santa Barbara and Los Angeles County

During the early winter months of 1976 and 1977, fear would strike the picturesque college community surrounding the University of California, Santa Barbara. A serial killer was plucking women off the streets of Isla Vista for his own cruel satisfaction. The slayings of three women, all of whom had striking similarities in appearance were labeled "The Look-a-Like-Murders" by the press.

The community of Isla Vista in the late 1970s was an idyllic and hopeful place. Hitchhiking was common among the students, even though it was known to be dangerous. On November 20, 1976, these dangers were suddenly brought home when the Santa Barbara County Sheriff's office was notified about the disappearance of twenty-one-year-old college coed Jacqueline Rook. She had been last seen at a bus stop on the outskirts of Isla Vista, having told friends she was going shopping. Her disappearance sent shock waves through the student community.

Watching the events with keen interest was a local man named Thor Nis Christiansen. The nineteen-year-old had grown up in the tiny tourist village of Solvang, forty miles north of campus. Born to immigrant Danish parents, Thor grew up working at the family restaurant. His father was an alcoholic and regularly abused his son, while his mother spoiled him out of guilt for working long hours at the family restaurant. As a young child, Thor began to torture and kill small animals, and by his teens was showing characteristics of an addictive personality. He began to drink and take drugs, and although he was a bright student, his grades began to plummet. During high school, he struggled with relationships with girls and became more reclusive. Uninterested in academics, Christiansen dropped out of high school in his junior year, moved out of his parents' house and supported himself through various unskilled jobs.

Two weeks after the disappearance of Jacqueline Rook, a nineteen-year-old waitress named Mary Ann Sarris vanished from plain sight. She disappeared around 4:30 p.m. on December 6, from the busy intersection of Patterson and Hollister Avenues after undergoing some medical tests at Goleta Valley Hospital. Despite an intense and widespread police investigation, law enforcement was baffled by the two disappearances. They had no leads and no suspects. But one man, Thor Christiansen, managed to avoid attention.

Patricia Laney, twenty-one, was an active member of the student community at UC Santa Barbara and was well-liked by her fellow classmates. On January 19, 1977, she vanished while distributing flyers on the previous disappearances. She had astonishingly vanished from the same intersection where Mary Sarris had last been seen six weeks earlier. Sarris' skeletal remains would not be found until May 22, 1978, in Drum Canyon.

Within twenty-four hours of her disappearance, Patricia Laney's nude body was found on an isolated road in Refugio Canyon. She had been shot in the side of the head with a small-caliber handgun. Police found fingerprints on some discarded paper towels in the victim's blood near the scene; however, the Santa Barbara Sheriff's Department was unsuccessful in finding a match for the prints. Apparently, the murderer had never been arrested before. As police continued to search the canyon for clues, they uncovered the partially clothed body of Jacqueline Rook. She had been shot twice in the head.

Thor Christiansen first came to the attention of law enforcement in February 1977, when he and a friend were detained in an isolated area of Goleta. The teens had been drinking beer when a Santa Barbara Sheriff's deputy on routine patrol came upon the scene. He cited the youths for underage drinking and asked to search their car, where he found a .22-caliber pistol. The gun was confiscated and the teens were released without further charges. After this encounter with police, Christiansen moved to Oregon, and the Isla Vista murders abruptly stopped. After several months, he returned to Santa Barbara where he completed his high school degree at a local community college. Christiansen then moved into an apartment in Goleta with his girlfriend, Kerry Soliz, and began making frequent trips to Los Angeles.

Two years after the last-known Isla Vista murder, a prostitute working the streets of Hollywood would provide the solution to the mystery of the unsolved killings. On the evening of April 18, 1979, Linda Preston, twenty-four, of Baldwin Park was approached by Christiansen on Hollywood Boulevard and solicited for sex. She got into his car and the pair drove into the nearby Hollywood Hills where Christiansen pulled out a gun and shot her in the left ear. Preston grabbed the steering wheel of the car and the vehicle spun out of control and crashed. She was able to escape the car and ran to a nearby house for help. Although seriously injured, she survived the attack. Christiansen fled the scene.

Three months later, on July 13, Preston was back in Hollywood and hanging out at the Bottom Line Bar, when she spotted the man who had attacked her. She notified police and Christiansen was arrested a short time later. He was arraigned for the assault in Beverly Hills Municipal Court on July 13. Because he had a Goleta address and there were similarities to the unsolved Isla Vista slayings, Los Angeles police detectives contacted the Santa Barbara County Sheriff's Department. On July 27, Christiansen was booked for the murders of the three Goleta women. Los Angeles police soon learned that he had also been killing in Los Angeles. On May 26, the body of known prostitute Laura Sue Benjamin, twenty-two, was found dead in a drainage channel near Big Tujunga Dam, north of Los Angeles. She had been shot and sexually assaulted. On August 21, Christiansen was charged in connection with her murder.

Christiansen's trial for the murder of Laura Benjamin and assault on Linda Preston began on March 13, 1980, before Los Angeles Superior Court Judge Charles Woodmansee. After a two-month trial, in which Christiansen flip-flopped his pleas, he was eventually found guilty of one count of first-degree murder and another of assault with intent to commit murder. On May 15, he was formally sentenced to twenty-seven years to life in prison. He was then transferred to Santa Barbara to stand trial for the slayings of Jacqueline Rook, Mary Ann Sarris, and Patricia Laney. On June 8, he pleaded guilty to those charges and calmly told the trial judge that after shooting each victim in the head, he had sex with their corpses. For these crimes he was sentenced to life in prison. Eight months later, on March 31, 1981, he was stabbed to death in the main exercise yard at Folsom Prison. His attacker was never identified.

1977-1979

THE HILLSIDE STRANGLERS

Los Angeles County

Between October 1977 and early 1979, a dozen young women were murdered in and around Los Angeles and Washington State. The killer was dubbed "The Hillside Strangler" by the press, because the victims were often strangled and dumped along hillsides. Police also thought the slayings were committed by one person, which ultimately proved to be wrong when cousins Kenneth Bianchi and Angelo Buono confessed and were convicted of the homicides.

Kenneth Alessio Bianchi was born on May 22, 1951, in Rochester, New York, to an unwed prostitute. He was later adopted by Nicolas and Frances Bianchi and raised in Rochester. From an early age he showed signs of trouble, and although he was an intelligent student, he failed to apply himself in school. In the mid-1970s, he moved to Southern California and began spending time with his older cousin. He had a lifelong interest in law enforcement, but never found employment and settled on low-paying security guard positions.

Angelo Anthony Buono Jr. was born on October 5, 1934, in Rochester, New York, the son of immigrant parents. After his parents' divorce, he moved with his mother and sister to Glendale, California. At an early age he began to exhibit a deep hatred towards all women that was seeded in his complicated relationship with his mother. Buono was married and divorced several times and fathered numerous children. He was extremely arrogant, and teenage girls were often very attracted to him. By the time his cousin Kenneth Bianchi arrived in Los Angeles in 1975, he had already amassed a long history of criminal activity that included theft, assault, and rape. Buono became a mentor and role model for the mild-mannered and impressionable Bianchi.

When the cousins found themselves short of cash, they hatched a scheme to start a prostitution ring. Bianchi used his charisma to recruit girls and Buono used his connections to get customers. In October 1978, they purchased a list of potential clients from a local prostitute named Deborah Noble. When they found out that the list was phony, they decided to take revenge on Noble. Unable to locate her, they took their rage out on another prostitute instead: nineteen-year-old Yolanda Washington. Her naked and badly battered body was found on October 18, 1977, near Forest Lawn Cemetery in Glendale. She had ligature marks around her neck, wrists, and ankles. The duo's perverse thirst for sadistic sexual thrills and homicidal blood lust had begun.

Buono and Bianchi soon began cruising around Los Angeles looking for victims. They used fake badges to persuade girls that they were undercover police officers and ordered them into their car, which resembled an unmarked squad car. Once they had subdued their victim, they would drive to their home where they would sexually torture and eventually murder their victims, most often through strangulation. The bodies were then disposed of along various hillsides throughout the Los Angeles area.

Thirteen days after the body of Yolanda Washington had been found, Judith Ann Miller, fifteen, was found dead in La Crescenta. The killers struck for a third time on November 6, when Lissa Teresa Kastin, twenty-one, a dancer and waitress, was found dead near Chevy Chase Country Club in Glendale. Like the other victims, she had been raped and strangled. Four days later, on November 10, Jill Barcomb, eighteen, a known prostitute, was found nude and strangled near Mullholland Drive in Sherman Oaks. A week later,

Body of Hillside Strangler victim Kimberly Diane Martin is removed by coroner's office personnel. *Courtesy of the Los Angeles Public Library, Herald-Examiner Collection.*

on November 17, Kathleen Robinson, seventeen, was found strangled to death in the mid-Wilshire District. On November 20, the bodies of Sonja Johnson, fourteen, and Dolores Cepeda, twelve, were found by two boys in a remote ravine west of Elysian Park. The girls had vanished on November 13, after boarding a bus in Eagle Rock.

Later that same day, twenty-year-old Kristina Weckler was found naked and strangled to death in Highland Park. On November 23, the decomposing body of Jane King, twenty-eight, a model, was discovered off the 5 Freeway in Glendale. Six days later, the body of Lauren Wagner, eighteen, was found off Cliff Drive in Glendale, and like the other victims, she had been tortured and strangled. On December 13, two newspaper delivery men discovered the body of Kimberly Diane Martin, seventeen, on a steep slope in a residential area in Silver Lake. She was a known prostitute and had lived in Los Angeles for only a year. The last confirmed Los Angeles area victim of the Hillside Stranglers was Cindy Lee Hudspeth, twenty, a bank clerk. Her nude and ligature-marked body was found in the trunk of her car, down an embankment off the Angeles Crest Highway near La Canada on February 16, 1978. What interested police investigators was that she lived directly across the street from victim number eight, Kristina Weckler, in Silver Lake.

Then, as quickly as the homicidal rampage had begun, the slayings abruptly stopped. Police investigators had few leads and were stymied in apprehending the killers. Eleven months would pass before a break in the case occurred.

Angelo Buono (left) leaving Los Angeles Superior Court after his arraignment on ten counts of murder, October 31, 1979. *Courtesy of the Los Angeles Public Library, Herald-Examiner Collection.*

On the evening of January 11, 1979, college students Karen Mandic, twenty-two, and her friend Diane Wilder, twenty-seven, were lured into a house that was being watched by Kenneth Bianchi in Wallingham, Washington. Bianchi had relocated to Washington in May 1978 to be near his girlfriend Kelli Boyd and their newborn son. At 11:00 p.m., Karen's friend, Steve Hardwick, was concerned that she had not contacted him and he called police. Just after 4:30 p.m., on January 12, the strangled bodies of the two women were found in Karen's car. Bianchi had left many clues at the crime scene and police apprehended him the next day. On March 21, 1979, as Bianchi was being prepared for trial, he was hypnotized by court appointed psychiatrists and became another personality named "Steve," who was a foul-mouthed braggart and boasted of the Los Angeles and Bellingham, Washington, murders. He also claimed that he had a partner in crime, his cousin Angelo Buono.

In October 1979, Bianchi pleaded guilty to the Bellingham slayings and was extradited back to Los Angeles to stand trial for five of the "Hillside Strangler" murders. Meanwhile, Angelo Buono was arrested and charged with ten of the slayings. Bianchi at first pleaded innocent by reason of insanity, claiming his alter ego Steve had committed the crimes but later agreed to plead guilty and testify against Buono in exchange for leniency.

Kenneth Bianchi, the Hillside Strangler, testifies in a courtroom against his cousin and accomplice Angelo Buono on July 6, 1981. *Courtesy of Bettman/Corbis.*

Angelo Buono's murder trial began in Los Angeles Superior Court on November 16, 1981, before Judge Ronald M. George. The proceedings would be one of the longest in California history. Bianchi hoped to avoid being the ultimate cause of his cousin's conviction but that failed. On January 9, 1984, Buono was found guilty of nine murders and sentenced to life in prison. Bianchi was also sentenced to life, but because he had not been forthcoming and truthful in his testimony, he was ordered to serve his sentence in Washington State rather than California as had been previously agreed upon. On September 21, 2002, Angelo Buono died of a heart attack at Calipatria State Prison in Imperial County, California. Bianchi is currently serving his life sentence at the Washington State Penitentiary in Walla Walla, Washington.

1977-1979

THE ORANGE COAST KILLER

Orange County

The latter 1970s produced a sudden rash of random homicidal violence in America, alerting criminologists to a disturbing rise in the incidence of serial murder. Some regions of the United States suffered more than others, but none compared to Southern California, where the Freeway Killer, the Hillside Strangler, the Skid Row Slasher, and a host of others practiced their ghastly trade. One such fiend, the "Orange Coast Killer," outmaneuvered his rivals by slithering out of newspaper headlines into legend as the one who got away. Between August 1977 and October 1979, the Orange Coast Killer claimed seven known victims. Most were young women who were raped and beaten to death in their first-floor apartments in and around Orange County.

In retrospect, law enforcement officials agree that the murder rampage most likely began on August 2, 1977, with the murder of twenty-nine-year-old Jane Bennington. The victim was a part-time student and waitress who was found raped and bludgeoned to death at her Corona Del Mar apartment. Bennington's killer left no clues behind, and in the fifteen-month gap before he struck again, other homicides took precedence that demanded the attention of Orange County police investigators.

The killer made his second-known appearance on November 22, 1978, when Patricia Neufeld, thirty-four, was found bludgeoned to death at her Garden Grove home. The serial murderer struck again on March 8, 1979, when Joan Virginia Anderson, twenty-eight, a housewife and mother of two small children, was found beaten to death at her home in Fountain Valley. Anderson's pajama-clad body was discovered in her bedroom by neighbors after the victim's five-year-old son was found wandering the streets. The victim's husband was traveling on business at the time of the attack.

On May 14, 1979, twenty-two-year-old Savannah Leigh Anderson, a credit checking service secretary was sexually assaulted and bludgeoned to death at her Irvine apartment. Her body was found by her boyfriend, who had gone to the dead woman's apartment to pick her up for a date. After he got no answer at the front door and saw that Anderson's car was parked nearby, he became suspicious and called police. Anderson's nude body was found in the bedroom of her apartment. Although this murder was initially attributed to the Orange Coast Killer case, it was solved seven years later. A part-time security guard at Anderson's apartment complex, Robert L. Sellers, was arrested and convicted of the slaying in November 1986.

Ten days after Anderson's murder, on May 24, 1979, Kim Whitecotton, twenty, survived an attack in her Santa Ana Heights home and provided a graphic account of the attack to police, which panicked her neighbors. After this incident, there was an upsurge in gun sales and purchase of guard dogs in the neighborhoods that seemed to be the killer's chosen hunting grounds. Local newspaper articles alerted women to be cautious and lock all windows and doors, while police distributed sketches of the suspect who was described as a white male in his early thirties, with dark hair, a mustache, and pock-marked face. Even with such scrutiny, the killer remained invisible to everyone except his victims, seemingly free to come and go at will. The killer struck for the last known time on July 19, 1979, when he assaulted twenty-four-year-old Jan Pettingill at her Costa Mesa home, but she survived the attack.

A special police task force was formed to track the killer and they waded through a maze of useless tips from terrified members of the public, all of which turned out to be of no use. As the autumn of 1979 faded into a warm California winter, it became apparent that the killer had vanished or relocated. This time his disappearance was no trick, no holiday, and as far as Orange County Sheriff's homicide detectives know, the Orange Coast Killer still remains at large. In recent years, Gerald Parker the infamous "Bedroom Basher," has been considered a prime suspect in some of these crimes but has never been charged.

1977-1978

A THIRST FOR BLOOD—THE VAMPIRE OF SACRAMENTO

Sacramento

During the early winter of 1977–1978, Richard Trenton Chase went on a one-month murder rampage in Sacramento. Nicknamed the "Vampire of Sacramento," Chase mutilated, drank the blood and cannibalized several of his six victims.

Richard Trenton Chase was born on May 23, 1950, in Santa Clara, California, and grew up in what was later determined to be an ordinarily dysfunctional home. There was some abuse but nothing out of the norm for the time. At an early age he began exhibiting sociopathic characteristics that included torturing and killing small animals. In high school, he began experimenting with marijuana and LSD. As he grew into adulthood, his behavior became more pronounced and bizarre. He thought he was being poisoned by aliens and Nazis, and that his internal organs were being stolen. To alleviate the pain he was feeling, he needed to kill animals and drink their blood.

In 1975, because of this harmful behavior, Chase was involuntarily institutionalized at the Beverly Manor Psychiatric Hospital in Riverside, California. At the institution, fellow patients nicknamed him "Dracula," for his penchant for killing birds and drinking their blood. He continued to suffer from severe paranoid delusions and was diagnosed a paranoid schizophrenic and prescribed anti-psychotic medication. A year after his hospitalization, Chase was no longer considered a threat to himself, or others, and released to the care of his mother. Shortly after coming home to Sacramento, his mother helped him move into an apartment and he stopped taking his medication. His paranoid delusions soon returned with renewed vengeance. He continued to believe that Nazis, aliens, and the FBI were out to get him and the only way to protect himself was with fresh blood. During this same period, he purchased several guns and began to practice shooting.

On August 3, 1977, while on routine patrol near Pyramid Lake, Nevada, several Bureau of Indian Affairs officers noticed a pick up truck stuck in some sand on the side of the road. Looking inside the abandoned vehicle, officers found blood stains, several rifles, and a bucket containing what appeared to be a human liver. They scanned the area with their binoculars and perched on a rock a half-mile away was Richard Chase. He was naked and covered in blood. Certain that he had committed a murder, officers took him into custody. Chase claimed that the blood on his body was his own and that it had seeped out of him. The liver and blood were tested and it was determined to have come from a cow. Chase was then released without charges being filed. Things were quickly spiraling out of control and after years of hunting animals, Chase was about to graduate to more serious game.

His rage and paranoia became homicidal on the afternoon of December 29, 1977, when he shot and killed fifty-one-year-old Ambrose Griffin in a random drive-by shooting. The victim was unloading groceries from the trunk of his car at his East Sacramento home when Chase pulled up and shot him. At the time, police had no obvious suspects or reasons why anyone would have wanted to kill Griffin. Law enforcement didn't know it, but a murder spree was about to begin that would shake Sacramento to the core. Chase would strike again, but this time it wouldn't be a simple drive-by shooting.

On the evening of January 23, 1978, Chase broke into the North Sacramento home of twenty-four-year-old Teresa Wallin and shot her in the head as she was taking out the trash. Wallin, who was three months pregnant at the time, was dragged back into the house, where her body was mutilated and partially cannibalized. Chase used an empty yogurt container to drink some of her blood.

Police knew they had a psychotic killer on the loose and needed to act fast. A large task force was formed. As news of the murder spread, so too did the fear among the public. What law enforcement didn't know was that Chase was about to strike yet again with even more ferocity.

Four days later, on January 27, Chase broke into the home of thirty-six-year-old Evelyn Miroth, who was babysitting her twenty-two-month-old nephew. The house was located only one mile from the previous murder scene. There Chase shot Miroth in the head and mutilated her body. There were signs that she had been raped and partially cannibalized. Miroth's six-year-old son Jason, and Daniel Meredith, fifty-two, a family friend were both shot to death. David Ferriera, Miroth's infant nephew, was kidnapped from the scene. His decapitated corpse was found two months later at the Arcade Wesleyan Church.

Unlike most serial killers, Chase was murdering indiscriminately and wasn't following a pattern. The random nature of the slayings meant that there were very few clues, and terror within the community was reaching a fever pitch. As police canvassed the area, several witnesses came forward and described seeing a white male with an orange parka in the area on the night of the murders. Despite this description, law enforcement struggled to identify the killer.

Then detectives got the break they needed; a woman came forward stating that she had gone to high school with a man who fit the description of the killer. His name was Richard Chase. She had just run into him at a local strip mall. Armed with a name and an address, detectives went to Chase's Watt Avenue apartment. The officers knocked on his door but got no response, although they could hear that someone was obviously home. The officers pulled back out of sight and waited for instructions from superiors. The silence outside led Chase to believe that the police had left the scene. He came out of the front door and was immediately apprehended and arrested after a brief scuffle. When investigators entered Chase's apartment, they encountered a scene right out of a Hollywood horror film. The apartment was filthy with every square inch of the home covered in fresh and dried blood. They also found the murder weapons and personal effects from some of the victims. A calendar hanging on the wall of the apartment chillingly detailed the dates of the previous slayings, and forty-four other unspecified murder dates yet to come. During a period of intense interrogation, Chase only admitted to killing dogs, but never confessed to killing people. He was charged with six counts of first-degree murder.

Because of intense media coverage of the case, Chase's murder trial was moved to Santa Clara County and began on January 2, 1979. His defense attorneys asked for a verdict of second-degree murder to spare him the death penalty, since he was clearly insane at the time of the murders. The prosecution argued that the defendant was a sexual sadist, who knew exactly what he was doing at the time of the killings. Chase took the stand in his own defense and admitted to drinking the blood of his victims and to the decapitation of the infant. He described himself as a good person, who had a weak heart and mind.

On May 8, after five months of testimony, and after only five hours of deliberation, the jury sided with prosecutors and found Chase guilty of six counts of first-degree murder. One month later, after a brief sanity hearing, Chase was formally sentenced to death in the gas chamber and transported to San Quentin Prison. On the morning of December 26, 1980, one day shy of the third anniversary of the murder of Evelyn Miroth and three others, Chase was found dead in his cell from an overdose of drugs. He had been prescribed a daily dose of antidepressants and had been hoarding the pills prior to his suicide.

1977-1979

THE DATING GAME KILLER

Orange County and Los Angeles

On June 20, 1979, twelve-year-old Robin Christine Samsoe and several friends went to Huntington Beach for a day of fun in the sun. At some point during the afternoon, the girls were approached by a man, later identified as Rodney James Alcala. He wanted to take pictures, but was scared off by an adult friend of the girls. In the late afternoon, Robin had to leave for dance practice. She had forgotten her dance outfit at home and, fearing that it would take too much time to walk, asked to borrow a friend's bicycle. As she pedaled off for home, this would be the last time Robin was seen alive.

For several weeks police conducted an intensive search for the young girl, and on July 2, 1979, her remains were discovered by a state forestry employee in the foothills near Sierra Madre. At the Chantry Flat campgrounds, north of Los Angeles County, police officials identified the skeletal remains as that of the missing young girl.

On July 24, 1979, based on a composite drawing, tips from several informants, and other physical evidence, Rodney Alcala was arrested and charged with Samsoe's murder. He was a 1968 graduate of UCLA's theater arts department and a part-time photographer who lived with his parents at the time of his arrest. He was born Rodrigo Jacques Alcala Buquor on August 23, 1943, in San Antonio, Texas, but was raised in Los Angeles. In 1964, he was medically discharged from the US Army for undisclosed psychiatric reasons.

In 1968, Alcala committed his first documented crime when a passing motorist witnessed him lure eight-year-old Tali Shapiro into his Hollywood apartment and called police. The girl was found in the apartment raped and beaten, but Alcala was nowhere to be found. He had fled to the East Coast and enrolled in the film school at New York University using an alias. Alcala was eventually arrested and extradited back to California in 1971. Because the victim refused to testify, prosecutors allowed Alcala to plead guilty to a lesser charge. In 1974, he was paroled after serving less than three years in prison.

Two months after his release, Alcala was rearrested for violating parole and providing marijuana to a thirteen-year-old girl who claimed she had been kidnapped. Once again, he was sent to prison but paroled after serving only two years. In 1977, after his release, he was hired as a typesetter at the *Los Angeles Times* in the midst of their coverage of the Hillside Strangler murders. During this same time period, Alcala persuaded dozens of young women that he was a professional fashion photographer and photographed them.

On September 13, 1978, despite his criminal record, Alcala appeared as a contestant on *The Dating Game* television show. He won the contest and a date with Cheryl Bradshaw, who subsequently refused to go out with him,

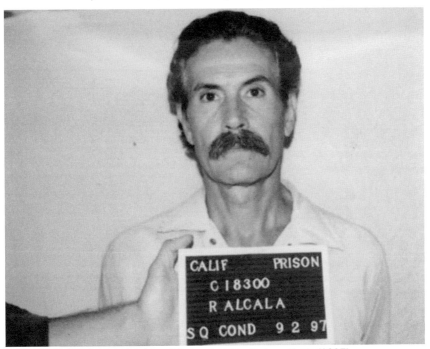

California State Prison photo of convicted serial killer Rodney Alcala (1997).

because she found him to be too creepy. This rejection may have been the inciting factor that led Alcala to murder Robin Samsoe and at least two others soon after the show's taping.

After a lengthy trial in Orange County Superior Court, in which Alcala did not testify in his own defense, he was found guilty of the first-degree murder of Robin Samsoe on June 20, 1980, and sentenced to death by Judge Philip E. Schwab. In a shocking turn of events on August 23, 1984, Alcala's murder conviction was overturned by the California State Supreme Court. The court ruled that the jury had been improperly told of Alcala's prior sex-related crimes and ordered a new trial. In the second trial, new physical evidence surfaced that showed Alcala had been present at Sunset Beach and had taken pictures at the location the day Robin Samsoe disappeared. On May 28, 1986, his second trial ended with another first-degree murder conviction, and he was again sentenced to death.

Then on April 2, 2001, the unthinkable happened again when the California State Appeals Court overturned Alcala's second conviction and ordered another trial. This time, the defense had been precluded from developing and presenting evidence material to significant issues in the case.

In other developments, Los Angeles police detectives linked Alcala through DNA evidence to the sexual assault murders of four additional women:

1. Jill Barcomb, eighteen, whose beaten and strangled body was discovered off Mulholland Drive in 1977, originally thought to have been a victim of the Hillside Strangler
2. Georgia Wixted, twenty-seven, a registered nurse, found bludgeoned to death at her Malibu apartment in December 1977
3. Charlotte Lamb, thirty-two, a legal secretary, raped and strangled at her El Segundo apartment in June 1978
4. Jill Parenteau, twenty-one, a computer programmer, found dead at her Burbank apartment in June 1979

In June of 2008, it was agreed that Alcala would be tried again for Robin Samsoe's murder and would also stand trial for the other four homicides.

At the third trial, which began in Orange County Superior Court in February 2010, Alcala acted as his own attorney. He offered no defense in the four additional murder charges and was eventually convicted of five counts of first-degree murder. On March 9, 2010, he was again sentenced to death. While on death row at San Quentin Prison awaiting appeals of his conviction and sentence, Alcala has penned a book in which he pins the Samsoe murder on someone else and has filed several frivolous lawsuits against the California State Penal System for an alleged slip-and-fall, and for failing to provide him with proper nutrition. Alcala is also considered a prime suspect in five other murders:

1. TWA Flight attendant Cornelia Crilley, 1971, New York
2. Ciro's Night Club Heiress Ellen Jane Hoover, 1977, New York
3. Pamela Jean Lambson, 1977, Marin County, California
4. Antoinette Wittaker, 1977, Seattle, Washington
5. Joyce Gaunt, 1978, Seattle, Washington

Alcala continues to maintain his innocence in all of these cases.

1978

THE HILLTOP RAPIST

Shasta County

With a revered white eagle feather laid across his chest to signify his Native American birthright, and strapped to a gurney, convicted serial killer and rapist Darrell Keith Rich made one final statement to the world: "Peace," then quietly drew his last breath and was put to death by lethal injection at San Quentin Prison on March 15, 2000. Known as the "Hilltop Rapist," Rich was convicted of the rape and murder of four women in Shasta County during the summer of 1978. He was also convicted of five other sexual assaults.

He was born on February 14, 1955, adopted at a young age and raised in the tiny Northern California town of Cottonwood. He grew up in a Mormon household, but knew very little about his biological father's Native American heritage and only became aware of his one-quarter Cherokee ancestry after many years on death row. In school, he was a poor student and had very few friends. After his parent's divorce, he began to drink heavily and became progressively more violent. He was first arrested at age seventeen for assault with a deadly weapon, and sent to the California Youth Authority. There he was diagnosed with numerous psychological issues. After his release in late 1975, he attempted to turn his life around by marrying his longtime girlfriend and having a child. Things began to deteriorate in April 1976, when he was injured in a car crash. After the accident, he became severely depressed and began to verbally and physically abuse his wife. Over the next two years, the couple would split-up and reunite numerous times. They split-up for the final time in the early summer of 1978, after she began to fear for her life.

The marital discourse and demise of the marriage might have been the spark that sent Rich over the edge and into a two-month frenzy of murder and rape. He committed his first-known adult crime on June 13, 1978, when he assaulted a twenty-five-year-old woman as she was walking down the street in Redding, California. After she refused his sexual advances, he became enraged and savagely beat the young woman, pushing her down an embankment. The victim survived the attack and was rescued twelve hours later. For the next two months, his attacks on women worsened under the scorching sun of Shasta County. Several of the assaults took place around Redding's Hilltop Drive, and the local news media began calling the unknown assailant the Hilltop Rapist.

Rich would kill for the first time on July 4, 1978, only hours after sexually assaulting a teenager on Hilltop Drive. Annette Fay Edwards, nineteen, was kidnapped by Rich as she walked home from a local fireworks show in Redding. Her body was discovered three days later on the side of a nearby county road. She had been raped and beaten to death with a rock.

His homicidal urges and rage out of control, Rich struck again in early August when he abducted Patricia Ann Moore, seventeen, as she hitchhiked through Cottonwood. Her nude and battered body was found two weeks later at the West Central Landfill in Igo, California. An autopsy revealed that she had been beaten, raped, and strangled to death. A few days later, still not satiated, Rich met Linda Diane Slovik, twenty-six, at a bar in Chico. After leaving the establishment together, he drove Slovik to the West Central landfill, where he raped her in plain sight of Patricia Moore's body. After finishing with her, he shot her twice in the head and left the body where it landed.

In mid-August, eleven-year-old Annette Lynn Selix was abducted by Rich in the early evening as the young girl walked home from a grocery store in Cottonwood. He took her back to his home where he repeatedly raped and beat her. He then drove with the girl thirty miles on Interstate 5 to a bridge near Lake Shasta, where he threw her to the rocks 100 feet below. Selix's body was found the next day, and an autopsy later determined that the girl had been alive at the time she was tossed from the overpass. During this same period, Rich committed at least four other sexual assaults.

Things began to unravel on the morning of August 23, 1978, when Rich asked a friend if he wanted to ride motorcycles. The friend declined and Rich rode off. About twenty to thirty minutes later, he returned and, for some reason, told the same friend that he had found two dead bodies at the local dump. They then called police. Later that afternoon, Shasta County Sheriff's detectives interviewed Rich and asked him if he'd be willing to take a polygraph examination about the bodies he had found at the landfill. He agreed to the test and was taken to the room where the polygraph examination was administered. One of the questions asked of him was whether he had murdered the women he claimed to have found. He vehemently denied any involvement in the crime, but the polygraph determined he was being deceptive. Detectives informed him that he had failed the test. He acknowledged that the exam had been administered fairly, but could not explain why he had failed it. He abruptly got up and informed investigators he had something to tell them, but couldn't right then. He stated he'd call them in three days. Because they had no physical evidence linking him to the murders, police were forced to allow him to leave.

Later that evening, Rich, overcome with guilt, confessed to his girlfriend Gale Croxell and a friend that he had taken and failed a polygraph examination about the murdered women he had found at the dump. He went on to tell them he had been paid $7,000 by a local motorcycle gang to kill one of the women. When pressed about the other girl, he admitted that he had killed her because she was in the wrong place at the wrong time. Croxell's friend then contacted police and gave a written statement that included where one of the murder weapons could be found. Around 9:00 p.m., Rich approached several acquaintances at a local liquor store and told them that he had failed a lie-detector test. He also told them that he had until the next day to come up with an alibi or he was going to be arrested for murder. After he left the scene, the acquaintances telephoned police. When detectives received this additional information, they knew it was time to take action. At 11:00 p.m., sheriff's deputies arrested Rich at the Oarlock Bar in Redding. He was taken back to the Shasta County Sheriff's department, where, after several hours of intense questioning, Rich confessed to the murders of Moore and Slovik. In the coming weeks, he also admitted to killing Annette Edwards and Annette Selix.

Because of intense media publicity, Rich's murder trial was moved to Yolo County, which began in December 1980. Although he confessed to the crimes, his defense attorneys contended that he was legally insane when they were committed and was unable to comprehend the gravity of the offenses. The jury was not convinced, and Rich was convicted of three counts of first-degree murder and one of second degree for the murder of Patricia Moore. On January 23, 1981, he was formally sentenced to death.

In late December 1980, after he had already been convicted and was awaiting sentencing, he married twenty-five-year-old Loretta Summers at the Yolo County Jail. During his twenty years on death row, Rich embraced his Native American ancestry and adopted the name "Young Elk." He was remorseful for the crimes he had committed and spent the last day of his life visiting with relatives and a Native American spiritual advisor. Shortly after midnight on March 15, 2000, he was led into the death chamber at San Quentin Prison. He was strapped into the lethal injection gurney and administered a fatal cocktail of drugs. Darrell Keith Rich, the Hillside Rapist, was the ninth person executed in California since the death penalty was reinstated in 1977.

1978

ROBERT ALTON HARRIS

San Diego

Robert Alton Harris's life held two truths: the twin homicides he committed were merciless, and he was fated to meet his end in an execution chamber.

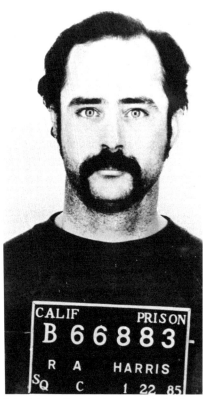

Robert Alton Harris' prison mug shot, taken on January 22, 1985.

His pitiful life began in mayhem on January 15, 1953, in an Army hospital at Fort Bragg, North Carolina. His father, Kenneth Harris, a decorated World War II veteran and career soldier, had assaulted his wife, who was drunk, and sent her into premature labor. Harris's inauspicious beginning was trumped in early childhood by a severe speech impediment and learning disabilities. He was also abused emotionally and physically by both parents.

After Kenneth Harris's discharge from the Army in 1962, the family moved to Visalia, California. In December 1964, Kenneth was convicted of sexually assaulting his daughter (Robert's sister) and was sent to state prison. During this same period, Robert began to exhibit sociopathic characteristics, such as the torture and slaughter of small animals. He also began experimenting with drugs and had numerous encounters with law enforcement.

In May 1967, frustrated with Robert's continued misbehavior and criminal activity, his mother (by then divorced), abandoned the fourteen-year-old in Sacramento to fend for himself. Robert made his way to Oklahoma, where he briefly lived with his older brother and sister. He was kicked out of school there and ran away to Florida where he was arrested for stealing a car. Harris spent the next four years in juvenile detention centers, where he attempted to commit suicide and was diagnosed with a schizophrenic personality. In 1972, at the age of nineteen, he was released from juvenile detention and returned to California where he found employment as a welder, married, and fathered a child. Three years later, he found himself unemployed with a severe drinking problem.

One drunken evening in 1975, while living in a trailer in Imperial County, California, Harris got into a fight with his brother's roommate, James Wheeler, and beat him to death. Harris was convicted of voluntary manslaughter and served two and a half years in state prison.

On July 5, 1978, five months after his release from prison, Robert and his brother Daniel, eighteen, kidnapped John Mayeski and Michael Baker, both sixteen, from a parking lot of a fast-food restaurant in Mira Mesa, a suburb of San Diego. The teens had been sitting in their car eating hamburgers when they were approached by the Harris brothers. At gunpoint, Robert commandeered the boys' car and drove them to Miramar Lake. Daniel Harris followed close behind in another vehicle. Robert told the boys that he had no intention of hurting them and only needed their car for a bank robbery. Once at the secluded area, he ordered the boys out of the car and shot them execution style. The Harris brothers then drove back to their apartment and finished the boys' hamburgers. Once done with their meal, at 12:30 p.m., they drove to the San Diego Trust Savings & Loan Bank, near where the earlier abduction had occurred, and robbed it. A witness to the robbery followed the Harrises back to their apartment and phoned police. A half-hour later, San Diego SWAT officers surrounded the apartment and apprehended them without incident.

In a twist of fate, one of the responding officers was Stephen Baker, the father of one of the murdered victims. He was unaware at the time that his son had been slain by the man he had just arrested. Later that evening, Daniel Harris, under intense interrogation, confessed to the murders of Baker and Mayeski, and instructed detectives where they could find the bodies.

Robert Harris's murder trial began on January 8, 1979, in San Diego Superior Court. Daniel Harris was the prosecution's star witness in the proceedings. He had agreed to testify against his brother in exchange for a reduced sentence. Robert Harris took the witness stand in his own defense and attempted to pin the murders on his brother. He testified that he had robbed the bank and had only confessed to the murders to protect his younger brother and denied being at the scene of the slayings. On January 24, a little over two weeks after the trial had begun, a jury of seven men and four women found Harris guilty of two counts of first-degree murder and two counts of kidnapping. On March 6, 1979, Judge Eli Levensen sentenced him to death in the gas chamber. Daniel Harris, for his testimony, was charged with one count of kidnapping and sentenced to six years in prison. He was released on parole in 1983.

On April 21, 1992, thirteen years after his conviction, Robert Alton Harris was executed in the gas chamber of San Quentin Prison. His last words were, "You can be a king or a street sweeper, but everyone dances with the grim reaper." He was the first man executed in California after the death penalty was reinstated in 1977.

1978-1980

TWISTED TWOSOME— THE SACRAMENTO SEX SLAVE MURDERS

Sacramento County

On the morning of September 11, 1978, Gerald Gallego woke his twenty-one-year-old girlfriend, Charlene Williams, and told her that today was the day to make his sexual fantasies a reality.

L ater that same day, Sacramento police received a call about two missing teenage girls: Kippi Vaughn and Rhonda Scheffler. The teens had gone shopping at the Country Club Plaza Mall and had failed to come home. Their car was found abandoned at the mall and there was no trace of the girls. Two days after they were reported missing, a migrant farm worker found their bodies in a meadow twenty miles southeast of Sacramento. An autopsy revealed that both girls had been raped, bludgeoned, and shot to death. The brutality of the crime did not go unnoticed by the public, but the case soon went cold with no clues or suspects.

Meanwhile, Gerald Gallego's appetite for rape and murder had just begun. He was the quintessential sexual sadist and sociopath, who found great pleasure in inflicting pain on others. Although Charlene Williams was at first shocked by the savagery of the murders, she too became caught up in the whole process. She later stated that she continued to help Gerald in making his homicidal fantasies a reality because she feared she might be his next victim.

A few weeks after the murder of Scheffler and Vaughn, on September 30, Gallego and Williams decided to get married. Eager to spread the good news, they decided to visit his fourteen-year-old daughter at his mother's house in Chico, California. He had been molesting his daughter since she was six, and when the couple showed up at his mother's home, she immediately called police as she had just recently become aware of the molestations. Gallego and his new bride left before police arrived, and an arrest warrant was issued for Gallego for multiple felony counts for the assault of his daughter. When Chico police attempted to serve the warrant at Gallego's last-known address, he was nowhere to be found. Gallego and Williams had already fled to Reno, Nevada, and remarried under the assumed names of Mr. and Mrs. Stephen Feil.

Gerald Armond Gallego was born on July 17, 1946, in Sacramento, California, and grew up in an abusive and neglectful household. As an adult, he was no stranger to crime, having been arrested twenty-three times for crimes ranging from robbery to sexual assault to escaping prison. His father, Gerald Sr., was the first man executed in Mississippi's gas chamber in 1955 for the murder of two police officers.

Gallego met Charlene Williams on September 10, 1977, at the Black Stallion Card Room in Sacramento. She was a few weeks shy of her twenty-first birthday. Born on October 10, 1956, she was the only child of Charles and Mercedes Williams. Charlene grew up in an upper middle-class atmosphere. She was well-educated and made her way through life by pleasing others, but she also had a wild streak and wanted more out of life. In high school, she began experimenting with drugs and dreamed of escaping the boredom and constraints of suburbia. In Gerald Gallego, she found the bad boy she had always desired. A few weeks after meeting, Gerald and Charlene moved in together. Their relationship began to sour when he became abusive and controlling. This was compounded by Gerald's impotency issues, and Charlene tried to solve these problems by feeding his fantasies about keeping young girls as sex slaves. She was happy and all too eager to turn these sexual illusions into reality to take pressure off herself.

After leaving his mother's home, the Gallegos fled to Reno, Nevada, and laid low and out of sight for nine months. This changed on June 24, 1979, when Charlene approached fourteen-year-old Brenda Lynn Judd and thirteen-year-old Sandra Cooley at the Washoe County Fair. She asked the girls if they wanted to make some money distributing flyers. The girls accepted and followed her to her van, where Gallego was waiting with a gun. He ordered the girls into the van and tied them up. Charlene drove down Route 395, twenty-five miles northwest of Reno. When they arrived at a secluded area, Gerald ordered the girls out of the van and walked with them into the brush. He raped and then killed both of them with hammer blows to the head and buried their bodies in a shallow grave.

Three months after the murder of Judd and Cooley, the Gallegos left Reno and returned to Sacramento using their new assumed names. They tried to live as normal a life as possible, but Gerald was addicted to killing. Ten months later, on the morning of April 24, 1980, Gerald again woke Charlene and told her it was time to go shopping for victims. They spent a good part of the morning trolling various malls but couldn't find anyone suitable. Eventually, they made their way to the Sunrise Mall in Citrus Heights, a suburb of Sacramento, where they spotted Karen Chipman-Twiggs and Stacy Ann Redican, both seventeen, as they were leaving a bookstore. As before, Charlene approached the two girls, this time with an offer of smoking some free marijuana. They both agreed and followed her back to the van, where Gerald was again waiting with a gun. The girls were tied up, and Charlene drove to a secluded area of Limerick Canyon, near Lovelock, Nevada. Once at the location, Gerald led each girl into the deep underbrush where he raped and beat them to death. He then buried them together in a shallow grave. Because the girls had a history of running away, they were at first just listed as missing persons. Four months later, on July 27, hikers discovered the girls' skeletal remains.

In June, Gerald and newly pregnant Charlene drove to Oregon for a vacation. Along the way, they spotted another expectant mother, Linda Aguilar, thirty-four, hitchhiking on the side of the road near Gold Beach, Oregon. Once she was inside the van, Gerald took her to the back and tried to rape her but couldn't perform. Charlene drove to a secluded section of beach, and Gerald killed Aguilar by smashing her head with a large rock. Two weeks later, on June 22, tourists found Aguilar's body in a shallow grave. An autopsy later determined that she was still alive when she was buried in the sand. By the time the details of her agonizing death were revealed, Gerald and Charlene were already back in Sacramento looking for their next sex slave. While committing seven murders in less than two years, Gerald and Charlene Gallego remained invisible to local law enforcement agencies.

On July 16, after spending the day fishing, Gerald and Charlene went to the Sail Inn in West Sacramento. There they met thirty-four-year-old Virginia Mochel, the mother of two and a favorite of the regulars at the bar. Charlene engaged her in casual conversation and invited her back to their apartment for drugs and sex. Once back at the Gallegos' apartment, Mochel was repeatedly raped by Gerald and eventually strangled to death. They then disposed of the body. Unfortunately for the Gallegos, Mochel's disappearance didn't go unnoticed by friends and acquaintances. Sacramento police were informed of the disappearance and went to the Sail Inn to interview every person who might have information. Several witnesses remembered seeing Mochel talking to an extremely loud couple named Stephen and Charlene Feil. Police detectives were able to track down Charlene and ask her to come in for questioning. She admitted that she and her husband had stopped at the bar for a few drinks after a long day of fishing, but knew nothing about Mochel's disappearance.

Then on July 27, the bodies of Karen Twiggs and Stacy Redican, who had gone missing three months earlier, were found in Limerick Canyon, Nevada. Both victims were found bound with their hands behind their backs and had been bludgeoned to death. Nevada investigators were unaware of the connection between their victims and the others in surrounding areas. Back in Sacramento, police got a break in the Virginia Mochel case when her body was found near the Sacramento River on October 2, ten weeks after she disappeared. She had been bound with fishing line and investigators remembered that the only people in the bar the night of the disappearance with fishing equipment had been Charlene and Stephen Feil. As police combed their files to track down the Feils, they were unaware that Gerald and Charlene had split up. Charlene had sold the couples' van and moved back into her parents' home while Gerald began living in a series of low-rent apartments and motels. Even though they had split up, Gerald and Charlene were still in limited contact.

When he got the urge to kill again, Gerald knew who to call; Charlene was too close to the action to just walk away from it all. Gerald was now losing complete control and was willing to go after any victim without regard to the consequences. On the evening of November 1, Gerald and still-pregnant Charlene set out in search of another sex slave. As they drove around Sacramento, almost ready to give up for the night, Gerald spotted a young couple sitting in their car at the Arden Fair Mall. Craig Miller, twenty-two, and his fiancée, Mary Beth Sowers, twenty-one, students at Sacramento State University, had just left a fraternity party and were talking when Gallego approached the couple, pulled a handgun, and ordered them both into his car. Not wanting to anger him, Miller and Sowers complied with his demands. After driving to a secluded area near Bass Lake in El Dorado County, Gerald ordered Miller out of the car and shot him twice in the back of the head execution style. He then got back into the car and ordered Charlene to drive to their apartment, where he raped Sowers for several hours. After he was fully satiated, he and Charlene drove their victim to a secluded area in Placer County, near Loomis, where Sowers was shot and killed. By the next morning, the couple has been reported missing. Miller's body was found the following day, but there was no sign of Sowers. They had been abducted in plain view of witnesses who wrote down the license plate number of the vehicle. This information led directly to Charlene, and when police showed up at her parents' home, she told investigators that the car had been stolen. Police believed her story and as soon as they left, she phoned Gerald. Knowing that law enforcement was closing in, they decided to ditch their car and hopped a bus for Salt Lake City.

For several weeks, they remained fugitives from justice, moving from place to place, finally ending up in Omaha, Nebraska, where Charlene phoned her parents and asked for money. They agreed to help, but unknown to Charlene, they were already cooperating with the FBI. On November 17, the murderous duo appeared at a Western Union office in Omaha to claim their cash and were immediately apprehended by FBI agents without incident. Five days after their arrests, on November 22, the body of Mary Beth Sowers was found in a pasture outside Sacramento. She had been shot three times in the head.

Even though they were now in jail, Gerald still continued to manipulate Charlene. They corresponded by letters, where he wrote how he was going to protect her and loved her. While in custody, Charlene gave birth to a son on January 17, 1981, and her parents were given custody of the baby. As time passed, Gerald began to lose his hold over Charlene and, facing a possible death sentence, she decided it was best to save herself and agreed to cooperate with investigators in exchange for a lenient sentence. She revealed that there were eight other victims.

Authorities in ten jurisdictions across three states now had the difficult decision of how to proceed with prosecutions. It was finally agreed that Gallego would be first prosecuted in California and then Nevada for the murders of Miller, Sowers, Twiggs, and Redican. For her cooperation, Charlene would be spared the death penalty and given a sixteen-year sentence without the possibility of parole.

After a year of interviews and investigations, Gerald Gallego's trial finally began in the spring of 1983 in California. He ill-advisedly decided to serve as his own attorney and, on April 11, the jury convicted him of the first-degree murders of Miller and Sowers. Two months later, he was formally sentenced to death in the gas chamber. He was then extradited to Nevada to stand trial for the murders of Stacy Redican and Karen Twiggs. These proceedings began on May 23, 1984, in Pershing County, Nevada, before Judge Lewelyn Young. This time, Gallego allowed a public defender to handle the case. The defense's strategy was to discredit Charlene's testimony, which ultimately failed. On June 7, after deliberating for less than four hours, the jury convicted him of another two counts of first-degree murder and two counts of kidnapping. One month later, he received another death sentence. Gallego now had the dubious distinction of being sentenced to death in two states at the same time.

After testifying at the second trial, Charlene returned to California to serve out her sentence. In August 1997, at the age of forty, she was released on parole. In November 1999, twenty years after vanishing from the Washoe County Fair, the skeletal remains of Brenda Judd and Sandra Colley were finally discovered. On July 18, 2002, after successfully putting off his execution for more than two decades, Gerald Gallego, age fifty-six, died from rectal cancer at a Nevada state prison medical facility.

1978-1979

SOULS FOR SATAN

Los Angeles

Four years after the Skid Row Slasher terrorized the city of Los Angeles, yet another sadistic serial killer began hunting vagrants in the homeless encampments and historic core area of the city. Local news media quickly nicknamed him the "Skid Row Stabber," to avoid confusion with the earlier case. The "Stabber" proved to be just as prolific as his predecessor, claiming eleven victims and wounding two others between October 1978 and January 1979. All of the victims were attacked with knives and several of the murders appeared to be satanic in nature.

The list of victims include:
1. Jessie Martinez, fifty, (October 23, 1978)
2. Jose Cortez, thirty-two, (October 28, 1978)
3. Bruce Emmett Drake, forty-six, (October 30, 1978)
4. J.P. Henderson, sixty-five, (November 4, 1978)
5. David Martin Jones, thirty-nine, (November 9, 1978), his body was found on a walkway near the Central Public Library. An eyewitness to Jones' murder told police that he saw a black man flee the scene of the slaying mumbling, "I'm Luther; I'm the peacemaker."

The slaughter continued with the murders of four more victims:
1. Francisco Perez Rodriquez, fifty-seven, (November 11, 1978)
2. Frank Lloyd Reed, thirty-six, (November 12, 1978)
3. Augustine E. Luna, forty-nine, (November 12, 1978)
4. Jimmy White Buffalo, thirty-four, (November 17, 1978)

Two days later, the killer attacked Jose Ramirez, twenty-seven, and Ricardo Seja, twenty-six, near the corner of Main and 3rd Streets. Both victims managed to survive the attack and, scrawled on the wall of a nearby Greyhound Bus Station restroom, police found a message from the killer that read: "My name is Luther, I kill winos to put them out of their misery." The Stabber's next victim, Frank Garcia, forty-five, was murdered on Thanksgiving night, November 23, 1978. His body was found on a bench in City Hall Plaza opposite Parker Center Police headquarters. A palm print from the probable killer was found on the bench.

After the murder of Garcia, the killings abruptly stopped for two months, but picked up again on January 21, 1978, when Luis Alvarez was found stabbed to death in an alley near Harlem Place. Police began to speculate as to why the killings had ceased for two months and assumed the perpetrator had been incarcerated during the murder hiatus. A thorough search of jail records uncovered information on twenty-eight-year-old Bobby Joe Maxwell, a transient, who had an extensive criminal record that included burglary and armed robbery. He had moved to Los Angeles in 1977 after being released from prison in Tennessee. Maxwell had been arrested on December 14, 1978, near Skid Row, while standing with a knife over a sleeping derelict. He pleaded guilty to a misdemeanor charge of carrying a concealed weapon and was sentenced to sixty days in jail. Maxwell was released from custody on January 18, 1979, three days before the murder of Luis Alvarez.

Detectives knew they had a prime suspect in the Skid Row Stabber case, but lacked evidence to make an immediate arrest, and for the next two months secretly watched Maxwell. Then, on the afternoon of April 4, 1979, confident that they had enough evidence, detectives secured a probable cause arrest warrant and Maxwell was taken into custody without incident. A subsequent search of his various residences uncovered several possible murder weapons and other physical evidence. After an eyewitness to the murder of David Jones identified Maxwell in a lineup, and his palm print was found to match the one found at the scene of the murder of Frank Garcia, he was charged with ten counts of murder and other crimes.

Because of legal issues, Maxwell's murder trial was delayed for over four years and finally began on November 16, 1983. Over the next seven months, a jury of seven women and five men heard testimony in Los Angeles Superior Court. The prosecution contended that Maxwell had committed the crimes for several reasons: to obtain souls for Satan, to put transients out of their misery, and to rob them. While in custody, he confessed to a cellmate that he had killed the vagrants "to obtain souls for Satan." Several former cellmates from Tennessee testified that they'd observed Maxwell worshipping Satan while in custody. They also stated that they'd observed him use the name "Luther" as a variation of Lucifer. On July 12, the jury reached a split-decision verdict after deliberating for twenty-five days. They found Maxwell guilty of the first-degree murder and robbery of Frank Garcia and David Jones; they acquitted him of three murders and deadlocked on the remaining five. On September 6, Superior Court Judge David J. Aisenson sentenced Maxwell to life in prison without the possibility of parole. The prosecution requested that the five remaining deadlocked charges be dismissed.

In 2010, after more than twenty-five years in prison, Maxwell's murder convictions were overturned by the 9th Circuit Court of Appeals. They found that a key prosecution witness, notorious jailhouse informant Sidney Storch, had committed perjury during the trial and that prosecutors had failed to disclose that he had gotten benefits from authorities in exchange for his testimony. In February 2013, Los Angeles County prosecutors secured a grand jury indictment of Maxwell for the murders of Jose Cortez, Bruce Drake, and Frank Reed. At the time of the publishing of this book, no retrial date has been set and Maxwell is currently incarcerated at the California State Prison facility in Lancaster.

1978

DAN WHITE AND THE TWINKIE DEFENSE

San Francisco

When former San Francisco City Supervisor Dan White assassinated America's first openly gay elected official, Harvey Milk, and Mayor George Moscone on November 27, 1978, the case caused a sensation that would go down in the annals of US jurisprudence as one of the most bizarre in history. The tragedy would also propel Harvey Milk to legendary status within the gay and lesbian community.

Daniel James White was born on September 2, 1946, in San Francisco. He was often described as being the all-American boy. In high school, he was an excellent student and star athlete. White would serve in the Vietnam War as a paratrooper and, upon his return home, would work as a police officer and then as a fireman in San Francisco. In 1977, he was elected to the San Francisco Board of Supervisors. White was a conservative Democrat who was troubled by the growing tolerance of elected officials towards homosexuality and crime within the city. He represented a district of predominantly white working-class people and became part of a loosely formed coalition that opposed Mayor George Moscone and his liberal politics. White had frequent disagreements on policy with fellow supervisor Harvey Milk.

In the 1970s, many people still believed homosexuality was an illness and there were those who still thought it could be corrected by intense psychiatric care. At the time, there were no unified national gay organizations. George Moscone had been elected mayor of San Francisco in 1976 and was an early supporter of gay rights, managing to abolish a city law against sodomy. He was also the first mayor to appoint large numbers of minority groups, including gays and lesbians, to influential positions within the City of San Francisco.

Harvey Milk was the first openly gay man to be elected to an official position of any significance in the United States. He was born on May 22, 1930, in Woodmere, New York. A veteran of the Korean War, upon his discharge from the service, he returned to Manhattan where he became a Wall Street investment banker. He soon tired of the monotony of it all and, in 1972, moved to the Castro District, in the center of San Francisco's gay community. There he became a vocal advocate for gay rights and was nicknamed "The Mayor of Castro Street." His relentless pursuit for attention led many to label Milk as a publicity seeker, but he knew that the root cause of the gay dilemma was invisibility and lack of exposure. He ran for election as a city supervisor three times before finally succeeding in January 1978.

When Dan White was elected supervisor from San Francisco's 8th district in 1977, he was forced to resign his job as a fireman due to a provision in the city charter that barred anybody from holding two city jobs. As a result, he started a small restaurant at Fishermen's Wharf, but it failed due to the pressures of being a supervisor. Finding it impossible to support his family on the limited salary of a city supervisor and the increasing backseat he felt he was being forced into by Moscone, Milk, and other progressive board members, White abruptly resigned his seat on November 10, 1978. Numerous colleagues and constituents influenced his decision to try and retract his resignation, and White approached Mayor Moscone and asked to be re-appointed to the board. Although Moscone considered White's plea, he had already been strongly influenced by Milk and others to appoint another liberal, Federal Housing official Don Horanzy, to the post.

On the morning of November 27, 1978, a frustrated and delusional White went to San Francisco City Hall with a loaded .38-caliber handgun. In order to avoid the metal detectors, he entered through a basement window that had been neglectfully left open for air circulation. He proceeded to the mayor's office where he began to openly argue with Moscone. It was suggested

San Francisco City Hall from east end of Civic Center Plaza. It was here, on November 27, 1978, that Dan White shot and killed Mayor George Moscone and Supervisor Harvey Milk.

that they go to a more private room to continue the conversation. Once there, White pleaded to be re-instated to the board of supervisors, but Moscone refused. Feeling he had no other choice, White pulled out his concealed handgun and shot Moscone four times at point blank range—twice in the chest and twice in the head—killing him instantly. White then calmly walked down the corridor and shot Harvey Milk five times—twice in the chest, once in the back and twice again in the head. After that, he fled City Hall and, a short-time later, surrendered at a local police station where he was formerly employed.

White's murder trial began on May 1, 1979, and it was revealed during testimony that he had also planned to kill California State Assembly Speaker Willie Brown and fellow supervisor and attorney Carol Ruth Silver, but couldn't find them the day of the shooting. During videotaped police interrogation sessions that were replayed for the jury, White came across as a pathetic man who was barely able to explain why he had shot Milk and Moscone. His defense attorney claimed he had acted in the heat of passion and not out of malice. They claimed that diminished capacity caused by extreme stress in White's home life and depression caused him to commit murder. While describing White's emotional state at the time of the crimes, psychiatrist Martin Blinder testified that in the days leading up to the shootings, the defendant had become severely depressed. He had abandoned his usual healthy diet and overindulged in a diet of junk food that included soda and

Twinkies. Newspapers across the country picked-up on this, sensationalized their headlines and created the term "Twinkie defense" as an insulting label implying that a criminal defense was fake or ridiculous. On May 21, after only thirty-six hours of deliberation, the jury found White guilty of voluntary manslaughter instead of first-degree murder, despite his obvious premeditation. White was sentenced to a maximum of seven years and eight months in prison on July 3, 1979, and never expressed any public remorse for the crimes.

In the aftermath of what was perceived by many to be a very light sentence, protestors took to the streets of downtown San Francisco and became violent. Thousands of policemen responded to the riots and hundreds of protestors were injured and arrested. Dan White served only five years of his sentence and was released on parole on January 6, 1984. After his release, he moved to Los Angeles for a year using an assumed name and then moved back to the Bay Area. When San Francisco Mayor Dianne Feinstein became aware of this, she issued a public statement asking him not to return. In defiance, White still moved back to San Francisco and attempted to reconcile with his wife and children, but the marriage never recovered. On October 21, 1985, a despondent and depressed White committed suicide inside the garage of his home. He had run a garden hose from the exhaust pipe of his car to the inside of the vehicle. His body was found early the next day by his brother.

1978-1979

THE BEDROOM BASHER

Orange County

Known as the "Bedroom Basher" for breaking into women's apartments and beating them to death, Gerald Parker thought he had gotten away with murder, until DNA evidence linked him to the murder of five women and an unborn child in Orange County, between 1978 and 1979.

During his seven-and-one-half years of service in the Marine Corps, Parker was based at the El Toro Marine Corps Air Station, as well as other military bases throughout the country. In 1980, he was convicted in the rape of a thirteen-year-old Tustin, California, girl.

That same year, in what appeared to be an unrelated case, twenty-two-year-old Tustin Marine Corporal Kevin Lee Green was convicted of assault and second-degree murder for the September 30, 1979, attack on his nine-and-one-half-month pregnant wife, which led to the death of their unborn child. Dianna Green, twenty-one, was unconscious for a month after her attack and suffered a significant loss of memory because of her injuries. When she finally regained consciousness and spoke with police investigators, she misidentified her husband as the assailant. She stated that during an argument, he had struck her on the head with a large key ring, causing severe trauma. Kevin Green was arrested and charged with second-degree murder and assault. He vehemently denied any involvement in his wife's attack and stated that he was not home at their Tustin apartment at the time of the crime.

Prior to his trial, which began in September 1980, Green's defense attorneys administered a polygraph test to their client, which he passed. The jury of seven men and five women eventually sided with the prosecution's claims and convicted Green of all the charges. On November 7, Superior Court Judge Luis A. Cardenas sentenced him to fifteen years to life in prison. While incarcerated, Kevin Green attempted to have DNA tests performed on the semen police investigators had collected at the scene of his wife's attack. Unfortunately, he could not afford the cost of these tests. Luckily, this crucial DNA evidence was never destroyed.

In 1996, using newly developed forensic technology, police began using DNA samples of convicted criminals to solve numerous crimes. Some of this evidence linked Gerald Parker to a string of unsolved murders in Orange County. On June 14, 1996, detectives met with Parker at Avenal State Prison, where he was incarcerated for a parole violation. There he confessed to five murders, and the assault on Dianna Green. With this new evidence, Kevin Green was released from prison after serving over seventeen years behind bars for a crime he did not commit.

Parker's murderous rampage had begun on December 2, 1978, when he raped and bludgeoned to death seventeen-year-old department store clerk Sandra Kay Fry at her Anaheim apartment. Four months later, on April 1, 1979, the body of twenty-one-year-old shipping clerk Kimberly Gaye Rawlins, was found beaten to death at her Costa Mesa apartment. Parker struck again on September 14, when Marolyn Carleton, a thirty-one-year-old widow, was raped and murdered at her Avocado Street apartment in Costa Mesa, and her body was discovered by her nine-year-old son. The killer then moved on to Tustin, where he assaulted Dianna Green on September 30. A week later, on October 7, twenty-four-year-old Debra Jean Kennedy, a cassette tape assembler at Memorex, was slain at her Tustin home. The victim's body was found in the house she shared with her sister. Parker struck for the last known time on October 21, when seventeen-year-old Debra Lynn Senior, an Orange Coast College student, was raped and murdered at her Costa Mesa apartment.

Parker's murder trial began in Orange County Superior Court before Judge Francisco Briseno on September 17, 1998. After a four-week trial, the jury took only two hours to convict him of six counts of first-degree murder with special circumstances. He was sentenced to death on January 22, 1999, and is currently incarcerated on death row at San Quentin Prison pending appeal of his conviction and sentence. Parker has also been considered a prime suspect in another string of unsolved murders that are associated with the Orange Coast Killer case.

1979
I DON'T LIKE MONDAYS
San Diego

Brenda Ann Spencer was born on April 3, 1962, in San Diego, California. After her parents separated, she lived with her father, Wally Spencer, in near poverty in the San Carlos section of the city. She was an awkward teen, unusually thin with stringy, red hair. She was a loner and uninterested in school. In December 1978, a psychiatrist recommended she be admitted to a mental hospital for severe depression, but her father refused to give permission. Friends later said she often expressed hostility toward authority figures and expressed a desire to do something big to get on television. For Christmas 1978, her father gave her a .22-caliber rifle. Spencer would later state, "I asked for a radio and he bought me a gun." When asked why he might have done that, she answered, "I felt like he wanted me to kill myself."

A month later, on Monday January 29, 1979, at 8:30 a.m., sixteen-year-old Spencer achieved the notoriety she desired when she began shooting at the Cleveland Elementary School, which was located directly across the street from her home. She began firing her rifle at students and teachers as they were lining up for morning classes. Spencer shot and killed principal Burton Wragg, fifty-three, as he tried to shield students. Custodian Mike Suchar, fifty-six, was also shot and killed as he attempted to aid the stricken principal. During the shooting rampage, eight children and a San Diego police officer, twenty-eight-year-old Robert Robb, were also injured. Twenty minutes after it had begun, San Diego police surrounded Spencer's home

Brenda Spencer leaves the Orange County courthouse, on October 1, 1979. Spencer plead guilty to two counts of first-degree murder in the schoolyard sniper attack in San Diego that killed two men. *Courtesy of Bettmann/Corbis.*

and laid siege for more than six hours. During the standoff, a *San Diego Tribune* reporter phoned Spencer and asked why she had done it. Her matter-of-fact reply was, "I don't like Mondays. This livens up the day." She concluded the conversation by saying, "I have to go now. I shot a pig [a policeman] I think, and I want to shoot some more." No further shots were fired and Spencer surrendered in the early afternoon. She calmly exited the front door of her house and carefully laid her rifle on the driveway. SWAT officers then rushed in and placed her under arrest.

Because of media coverage, Spencer's trial was moved to Orange County, and on October 1, 1979, she pleaded guilty to two counts of first-degree murder. Under the plea agreement, she received a twenty-five-years-to-life sentence and would be eligible for parole after serving sixteen years. Spencer first became eligible for parole in 1993, but was denied early release and has been unsuccessful at four additional parole hearings. She is currently incarcerated at the California Institute for Women in Chino, California.

Spencer's comments during the shooting rampage were immortalized and cited as the inspiration behind the song "I Don't Like Mondays," written by Bob Geldof for his band the Boomtown Rats, which was released in the summer of 1979 and was a number one hit in the UK and #73 on the US Billboard chart. Geldof later clarified why he wrote the song:

> I was doing a radio interview in Atlanta…and there was a telex machine beside me. I read it as it came out. Not liking Mondays as a reason for doing somebody in is a bit strange. I was thinking about it on the way back to the hotel and I just said, "Silicon chip inside her head had switched to overload." I wrote that down. And the journalists interviewing her said, "Tell me why?" It was such a senseless act. It was the perfect senseless act and this was the perfect senseless reason for doing it. So perhaps I wrote the perfect senseless song to illustrate it. It wasn't an attempt to exploit tragedy.

1979-1980
THE FREEWAY KILLERS
Southern California

Between 1972 and 1980, nearly four dozen young men were murdered and raped in and around Southern California. The victims had often been strangled, sadistically tortured, and dumped along freeways throughout the region. Law enforcement believed that

more than one perpetrator was at large. The authorities
agreed that several dozen of the slayings were almost
certainly connected. Sixteen of these murders would
be solved in 1983, and attributed to Scorecard Killer
Randy Kraft. The Los Angeles media quickly dubbed
this murderer "The Freeway Killer."

William George Bonin was born on January 8, 1947 in Connecticut,
and grew up in a very chaotic and abusive home. He spent significant
time as a young child in the care of his grandfather, a convicted child
molester, and spent several years in foster care before being reunited with his
mother. At an early age, he began molesting other kids. After graduating from
high school, he joined the US Air Force and served with distinction during
the Vietnam War. He was honorably discharged from the service in 1968 and
moved to California. Between 1968 and 1974, he was arrested and convicted
in several sexual-assault cases. Bonin was paroled in October 1978 and moved
to Downey, finding employment as a truck driver. Shortly after the move,
he became friends with Vernon Butts and Gregory Miley. The triumvirate
of evil that would eventually become known as The Freeway Killers had
united.

Between late May and November 1979, Bonin and Butts abducted and
murdered seven victims that included:
1. Thomas Lundgren, fourteen
2. Mark Shelton, seventeen
3. Markus Grabs, seventeen
4. Donald Hyden, fifteen
5. David Murillo, seventeen
6. Robert Wirostek, eighteen
7. An unidentified male whose body was found in Kern County

On November 30, operating alone, Bonin kidnapped and murdered
seventeen-year-old Frank Fox. The teen's body was discovered several days
later in San Diego County. Bonin struck again on December 10, when he
murdered John Kilpatrick, fifteen. His remains were later found in an isolated
area near Rialto. On January 1, 1980, Bonin still acting alone, kidnapped and
murdered sixteen-year-old Michael McDonald of Rialto. His mutilated body
was found two days later in San Bernardino County.

On February 3, 1980, Bonin teamed-up with Gregory Miley and abducted
and murdered fourteen-year-old Charles Miranda as the teen was walking
along Santa Monica Boulevard. The boy's battered body was later discovered
in an alley in Hollywood. Several hours after murdering Miranda, Bonin and
Miley drove to Huntington Beach where they kidnapped and killed twelve-
year-old James McCabe as he hitchhiked to Disneyland. His body was found
three days later in the city of Walnut.

Bonin struck out on his own again between March 14 and 21, killing three teenagers, Ronald Gatlin, Glenn Barker, and Russell Rugh. On March 24, Bonin and another accomplice, William Pugh, seventeen, abducted and murdered fifteen-year-old Harry Todd Turner in Los Angeles. Pugh had been picked up by Bonin in early March, but for some reason, was not killed. The pair quickly bonded and became good friends.

On April 10, Bonin again struck out on his own, murdering teenagers Steven Wood and Lawrence Sharp. Nineteen days later, Bonin and Vernon Butts teamed up to kill Darin Kendrick, nineteen, whose body was found dumped along the Artesia freeway in Carson. On May 19, Bonin acting alone, abducted fourteen-year-old Sean King from a bus stop in Downey. The boy's badly mutilated body was later found dumped in rural San Bernardino County.

On May 29, things began to unravel when William Pugh confided to his therapist that his friend William Bonin was the Freeway Killer. The therapist immediately contacted law enforcement with this information. The Freeway Killers struck for the last known time on June 2, 1980, when Bonin, along with yet another accomplice, James Munro, abducted Steven Wells, eighteen, from a bus stop in Los Angeles. Wells's body was found the next day dumped behind a gas station in Huntington Beach. Police began their covert surveillance of Bonin the following day.

Nine days later, on June 11, Bonin was observed assaulting a young man in his van and was arrested. While in custody, he confessed to nearly two dozen abduction murders and named Vernon Butts as his main accomplice—all the while never expressing any remorse for any of his alleged crimes. Bonin was eventually charged with twelve counts of first-degree murder and various other crimes. Vernon Butts was arrested on July 25, and charged as an accomplice in five murders. He would later be charged with an additional four. James Munro was arrested in Michigan on July 31, for the murder of Stephen Wells and extradited back to California. On August 22, Gregory Miley was arrested in Texas for the murder of Charles Miranda and James McCabe. In December, Butts, Munro, and Miley all agreed to plead guilty and testify against Bonin to avoid the death penalty. On January 11, 1981, Vernon Butts committed suicide by hanging himself at the Los Angeles County jail.

William Bonin's murder trial began on November 4, 1981, in Los Angeles Superior Court. On January 5, 1982, after two months of sensational testimony in which Greg Miley and James Munro appeared as star witnesses for the prosecution, Bonin was found guilty of ten counts of first-degree murder and other crimes. He was acquitted in the deaths of Thomas Lundgren and Sean King. He was formally sentenced to death on March 12, 1982, by Superior Court Judge William Keene. Miley and Munro were later sentenced

Los Angeles County Sheriff's Department booking photo of William Bonin (left) and Vernon Butts (right). *Courtesy of Bettmann/Corbis.*

to twenty-five years to life and fifteen years to life, respectively, for their roles in the murders, and both are currently incarcerated at Mule Creek State Prison. William Pugh was eventually convicted of voluntary manslaughter in the murder of Harry Turner and sentenced to six years in prison. His whereabouts today are unknown. On February 23, 1996, William Bonin was put to death at San Quentin Prison. His execution was the first use of lethal injection in the state of California.

1979-1981

THE TRAILSIDE MURDERS

Marin and Santa Cruz County

Serial Killer David Joseph Carpenter, "The Trailside Killer," was convicted of murdering seven people between 1980 and 1981 in Santa Cruz and Marin County. Although the actual number of victims is not known, the number is estimated to be as high as eleven.

Carpenter was born on May 6, 1930, in San Francisco, California. In childhood, he was subjected to severe emotional and physical abuse at the hands of his parents and, because of this trauma, developed a severe speech impediment. He also suffered psychological damage that resulted in the development of anti-social characteristics. In his late teens, he was incarcerated for molesting two female relatives. After his release from prison, he appeared to turn his life around. He married in 1955 and fathered three children. This all came to a crashing end in 1960, when he was arrested for another assault. He received a fourteen-year sentence, but was released on parole in 1967, after serving only half of the original punishment. Three years later, he was arrested again and charged with rape and parole violations for which he received another lengthy prison sentence.

Carpenter was released from custody in 1979 and began living with his elderly parents in Glen Park. During the three years he was not in custody, between 1967–1970, he was considered a prime suspect in the Zodiac murders. Although he was eventually cleared in those slayings, it wasn't long before he made a name for himself in the annals of American crime history.

His first suspected murder victim was Anne Menjivar, a longtime friend. She disappeared while hiking in Mount Tamalpais State Park in Marin County, north of San Francisco. Her body was found on June 4, 1979, but her slaying would never be officially linked to Carpenter, although police considered him the prime suspect. On August 1979, forty-four-year-old Edda Kane disappeared while hiking in the same park. Her body was found on August 20. She had been shot to death execution style. Carpenter would also be considered a suspect in this case but was never charged. Seven months later, in the same park, Barbara Schwartz, twenty-three, was found shot and stabbed to death. Again, Carpenter is considered the prime suspect in this murder but was never formally charged with the slaying.

Carpenter's first confirmed murder took place on October 15, 1980, when twenty-six-year-old Anne Alderson was found raped and shot to death after vanishing from a hike at Mount Tamalpais State Park. His next victim, Mary Frances Bennett, twenty-three, was found stabbed to death on October 21, 1979, while hiking at the Lands End Park in San Francisco. This murder was established through DNA evidence in 2010. As of the date of this book, Carpenter has not been charged with the slaying. His next confirmed victim, Shauna May, twenty-five, disappeared on November 27, 1980, while hiking in Point Reyes National Seashore State Park in Marin County. Her body was discovered in a shallow grave two days later. She had been shot to death. Nearby, police discovered the remains of yet another victim: Diane O'Connell, twenty-two, had vanished a month earlier from the park. She too had been shot to death and raped. That same day, two more victims were discovered in the same park. Cynthia Moreland, eighteen, and Richard Stowers, nineteen, had apparently been murdered on the same weekend as Anne Alderson. The discovery of four murder victims on the same day in the same park sparked a media frenzy and sent shock waves through the Marin County area.

Carpenter did not wait long to strike again. Moving his hunting ground south on March 29, 1981, he encountered two University of California, Davis students, Ellen Hansen and Stephen Haertle, while they were hiking at the Henry Cowell Redwoods State Park near Santa Cruz. Both victims were shot and Hansen was raped. Although severely injured, Haertle survived the attack and was able to give police a detailed description of the attacker. Other witnesses also provided information about a small red car leaving the scene of the crime.

Police got a break in the case on May 1, 1981, when twenty-year-old Heather Scaggs was reported missing by her boyfriend. She had gone to buy a car from David Carpenter, a co-worker at the California Trade School in Hayward. Police went to Carpenter's home in Glen Park to question him about the disappearance and immediately noticed a resemblance to composite sketches of the Trailside Killer. Parked in the driveway of the home was a red sports car. Police showed Stephen Haertle a photo of Carpenter, who he immediately recognized as the killer. Carpenter was taken into custody on May 15, and ten days later, the remains of Heather Scaggs were found by hikers in Big Basin Redwood State Park, north of San Francisco. Autopsy reports found that the same gun had been used in the deaths of Scaggs and Hansen, but despite a thorough search of the suspect's home, no weapons were found. A short time later, testimony from a suspect facing trial for robbery revealed that Carpenter had sold the thief a .38 caliber handgun. The weapon was recovered and its barrel markings matched the bullets fired at Hansen, Scaggs, and Haertle.

Carpenter's first murder trial was moved from Santa Cruz County to Los Angeles because of widespread news coverage and began on May 23, 1984, before Superior Court Judge Dion G. Morrow. On July 6, he was convicted of the rape and murder of Ellen Hansen and Heather Scaggs, as well as the attempted murder of Stephen Haertle. On November 16, 1984, Carpenter was sentenced to death in the gas chamber. His second trial for the murders of Richard Stowers, Cynthia Moreland, Anne Alderson, Diane O'Connell, and Shauna May, was moved from Marin County to San Diego County. The proceedings began on January 5, 1988, before Superior Court Judge Herbert Hoffman. On May 10, he was found guilty of five counts of first-degree murder and he received another sentence of death. Today, Carpenter remains on death row at San Quentin Prison pending appeals of his convictions.

1979

THE TOOL BOX KILLERS

Los Angeles County

In 1978, Lawrence Bittaker was serving time at the California Men's Colony in San Luis Obispo for assault when he met Roy Norris, a convicted rapist. They became best friends and conceived a scheme to rape and murder teenage girls. They also planned to document the savagery on film. Paroled on November 15, 1978, Bittaker began to make preparations for the crime spree. Norris was released on June 15, 1979, and joined Bittaker in Los Angeles, excited to begin carrying out their evil plans. They would be dubbed the "Tool Box Killers" because the majority of the murder weapons they used were stored inside a tool box.

Lawrence Sigmund Bittaker was born on September 27, 1940, in Pittsburgh, Pennsylvania, and was adopted by Mr. and Mrs. George Bittaker. The family moved often and finally settled in California. Bittaker's teenage years were filled with numerous run-ins with law enforcement. He dropped out of high school in 1957 and, within the year, was arrested for several crimes. Over the next two decades, he was arrested and imprisoned frequently for various felonies. In 1966, he was examined by several psychiatrists who declared him to be borderline psychotic, highly manipulative, and unable to acknowledge responsibility for his actions. In 1974, he was arrested and convicted for attempted murder and sent to the California Men's Colony in San Luis Obispo.

Roy Lewis Norris was born on February 2, 1948, in Greeley, Colorado, and would spend the majority of his childhood in and out of foster care homes. In 1965, after dropping out of high school, he joined the US Navy. He was arrested for his first-known sexual assault in 1969. Military psychologists diagnosed him as schizophrenic, and he was given an administrative discharge from the service. Over the next decade, he committed more sexual assaults and was incarcerated for several years at the Atascadero State Hospital. In 1975, just three months after his release, Norris raped a Redondo Beach woman, but was not arrested for a year. For this crime, he was convicted and sent to the California Men's Colony in San Luis Obispo, where he and Lawrence Bittaker became close friends.

The duo's homicidal rampage began on June 24, 1979, when they abducted Lucinda Lynn Schaeffer, sixteen, as she walked home from a church outing in Redondo Beach. They drove to a remote location in the San Gabriel Mountains where they strangled Schaeffer and left her body in a hidden ravine. Two weeks later, on July 8, they struck again, kidnapping Andrea Joy Hall, eighteen, as she hitchhiked along the Pacific Coast Highway in Redondo Beach. Norris and Bittaker drove to the same area as the previous murder where they proceeded to rape and strangle their victim before dumping the body.

On September 3, Jacqueline Leah Lamp, thirteen, and Jackie Doris Gilliam, fifteen, were abducted as they sat at a bus stop in Hermosa Beach. The victims were driven to the San Gabriel Mountains where they were held captive for two days. During this time, both girls were tortured and forced to pose for photographs. They were eventually bludgeoned to death. The final victim of the Tool Box Killers was Shirley Lynette Ledford, sixteen, who was abducted, raped, and tortured to death on October 31 after hitching a ride from her job as a waitress in Sunland. Unlike their previous victims, Ledford's body was dumped in plain view on a lawn in Sunland. The killers had wanted to see how the newspapers would sensationalize the crime.

On November 30, police got the break they needed when Bittaker and Norris were arrested for assault, drug possession, and various parole violations. While in custody, Norris began to crack under pressure, and at his preliminary hearing in Hermosa Beach, he offered an impromptu apology for what he claimed was "his insanity," and began confessing his role in the murder spree. According to his statements, young girls were approached on the streets, offered rides, free drugs, and possible modeling jobs. Most turned down the offers, but others were forcibly kidnapped. The victims were driven to remote locations in the San Gabriel Mountains where they were raped and murdered. Tape recordings of Jacqueline Lamp's murder and hundreds of photographs of young women were recovered from Norris and Bittaker's van.

On February 9, 1980, Norris led detectives to the San Gabriel Mountains where the skeletal remains of Jacqueline Lamp and Jackie Gilliam were recovered in shallow graves. The bodies of Lucinda Schaeffer and Andrea Hall were never found. The Los Angeles County Sheriff's Department then announced that Bittaker and Norris might be linked to the disappearance of as many as forty victims. On March 18, Norris pleaded guilty to five counts of first-degree murder and turned state's evidence against Bittaker. In return for his cooperation, he received a sentence of forty-five years to life, with parole possible after thirty years.

Lawrence Bittaker's murder trial began on January 19, 1981, in Torrance Superior Court. During the proceedings, he testified in his own defense stating that he knew nothing about the murders and only became aware of the crimes after he was arrested. On February 17, 1981, he was found guilty of five counts of first-degree murder. He was sentenced to death on March 24, 1980, by Superior Court Judge Thomas W. Fredricks. The judge also imposed an alternate sentence of 199 years and four months, to take effect in the event that the defendant's death sentence was ever commuted to life imprisonment. Today, Bittaker sits on death row at San Quentin Prison awaiting appeals and has never expressed any remorse for the crimes, while Roy Norris is presently incarcerated at the Richard J. Donovan Correctional Facility in San Diego.

1979-1986

THE ORIGINAL NIGHT STALKER MURDERS

Orange, Ventura, and Santa Barbara County

From 1979 to 1986, a serial killer stalked the bedroom communities of Southern California. The Original Night Stalker (not to be confused with serial killer Richard Ramirez) has been linked through DNA evidence to ten murders. The killer has also been linked to the "East Bay Rapists" series of crimes (1976-1979), in which nearly fifty burglaries and rapes were committed in the San Francisco Bay and Sacramento areas. This killer is considered to be one of the worst unapprehended serial criminals in American history.

The first known incident occurred on October 1, 1979, when an intruder broke into a Goleta home and tied-up its occupants. The attacker alarmed the couple by chanting "I'm going to kill them" to himself. When the female victim began to scream for help, the attacker fled the scene. Physical evidence from this incident was later linked to the murders of Robert Offerman and Debra Manning.

In the early morning hours of December 30, 1979, Dr. Robert Offerman, forty-four, and his girlfriend, Debra Manning, thirty-five, of Goleta, were shot and killed in their condominium. That same night, the killer allegedly broke into a neighbor's house and stole a bicycle that was later found abandoned on a street near the murder scene. The killer struck again on March 16, 1980, when he bludgeoned to death prominent Santa Paula attorney Lyman Smith, forty-three, and his wife Charlene Smith, thirty-three, in their Ventura home. A log

Gravesite of Keith and Patrice Harrington at Pacific View Memorial Park in Newport Beach, California.

from the fireplace was used to beat both victims. The couple's bodies were discovered by their twelve-year-old son. At the time of the murder, Lyman Smith had been under consideration for appointment to a judicial post by Gov. Jerry Brown.

Five months later, on August 21, 1980, Keith and Patrice Harrington were found bludgeoned to death in their home in the upscale, gated community of Niguel Shores in Laguna Niguel. Keith, twenty-four, was a fourth-year medical student at the University of California, Irvine, and Patrice, twenty-seven, was a pediatric nurse; they had been married for only four months before their murders. The killer struck again on February 6, 1981, when Manuela Elenore Witthuhn, twenty-eight, was raped and beaten to death at her Irvine home. The victim's husband was out of town when the murder occurred. The killing spree then switched to Central California when another couple, Cheri Domingo, thirty-five, and Gregory Sanchez, twenty-seven, were found shot and beaten to death on July 27, 1981, at their home in Goleta, California. These murders took place just a few blocks away from where Robert Offerman and Debra Manning had been slain.

The final murder linked to the Original Night Stalker case occurred on May 4, 1986, when Janelle Lisa Cruz, eighteen, was found raped and clubbed to death in her parent's home in Irvine, California. The teenager had been left home alone while her parents vacationed in Mexico. A suspect, Gregory Jesus Gonzalez, the young woman's boyfriend, was briefly detained by police, but was later released for lack of evidence. Apparently, the boy had visited Cruz earlier in the evening and soon after he left, she had been attacked.

After Janelle Cruz's murder, the killing spree abruptly ended, and no further evidence links the killer to other crimes. Over the years, police have interviewed numerous suspects, but no one has ever been arrested in connection with the crimes. It has been speculated that either the killer is in prison, has died, or just stopped killing. News coverage and a television program entitled *True Hollywood Stories Investigates: The Original Night Stalker,* which aired in May 2009 on the "E" Entertainment channel, brought renewed interest to the unsolved string of murders. Then on May 20, 2009, a Ventura area couple was found brutally stabbed to death by an unknown intruder. The slayings of Brock and Davina Husted at their upscale seaside home in a gated community of Ventura, California, bears eerie similarities to the Original Night Stalker crimes. Police say there was no motive for the killings and it appears to be a random crime.

Was this the work of the Original Night Stalker? Was the renewed publicity associated with the earlier killings enough to bring the murderer out of retirement? No one knows for sure, but if the Husted murders are related to the Original Night Stalker case, the killer's methods have not changed much over the years. He has primarily stalked middle-class couples who live in single-story homes, which were often for sale. He entered the victim's homes through unlocked doors and windows in the middle of the night, killed or subdued the male victim, then raped and bludgeoned to death the female.

This string of slayings was one of the motivating factors in the passage of California Prop 69 in 2004. This legislation authorized the collection of DNA from some accused and all convicted felons in California. While this database has solved numerous cold cases across the country, it has not yet helped apprehend the Original Night Stalker.

Conclusion

It is indeed strange that with all the knowledge we have gained in the past hundred years we preserve and practice the methods of an ancient and barbarous world in our dealing with crime. So long as this is observed and exercised there can be no change except to heap more cruelties and more wretchedness upon those who are the victims of our foolish system.

—Clarence Darrow
American Lawyer (1857-1938) from *The Story of My Life*.

The crime stories examined within the preceding pages were some of the most horrifying ever committed in California. In choosing which crimes to include, an eye was kept on the well-known and obvious, as well as more obscure stories that may surprise. The main intent of this book was not to glorify crime or criminals, but it was intended to be an unbiased description of facts and events. It is hoped that the reader has gotten a better understanding of the psychology and senselessness of it all.

Millions have come to California's golden shores in search of fame and fortune, but scores have found misery and pain. Some of the crimes mentioned in this book were more sensational than others, some more baffling, some more audacious, while others were sickening and appalling. The notorious crimes detailed within the previous pages were all of these things and more; but the end of this book is not the conclusion of the story. In the remaining two decades of the twentieth century, California would play host to an overabundance of sensational and notorious crimes that include:

- Douglas Clark and Carol Bundy, "The Sunset Slayers," were convicted of seven serial killings in Los Angeles between June and August 1980.
- The murder of Playboy Playmate of the Year Dorothy Stratton: she was killed by her estranged boyfriend Paul Snider at her Los Angeles home on August 4, 1980. Snider committed suicide after the slaying.
- Between 1982 and 1988, Dorthea Puente, dubbed the "Death House Lady," was responsible for the murder of nine elderly and mentally ill people who lived at her board and care home in Sacramento, California. She killed them for their social security checks and buried their bodies in her backyard. She was convicted of three murders and sentenced to life in prison without the possibility of parole. In 2011, she died in prison from natural causes.
- Vicki Lynn Morgan was a model and wannabe socialite. She was a former mistress of financier Alfred Bloomingdale, a member of the famed department store chain family. She was beaten to death by her jealous boyfriend Marvin Pancoast at her Los Angeles apartment on July 7, 1983. He was convicted of the crime and sentenced to twenty-five years to life and died in prison in 1991 from AIDS.
- Between 1983 and 1985, serial killers Charles Ng and Leonard Lake raped and murdered twenty-five people at a rented cabin in rural Calaveras County, California. Lake committed suicide while in custody, and Ng was convicted and sentenced to death for the crimes.
- Richard Ramirez, the infamous "Night Stalker," who terrorized Southern California between June 1984 and August 1985, was convicted of thirteen murders and numerous other crimes and sentenced to death. He died at San Quentin Prison in 2013.
- San Ysidro massacre: on July 18, 1984, James Huberty entered a San Diego-area McDonald's restaurant and shot and killed twenty-one people and

injured nineteen others before being killed by a SWAT team member.

- Between 1985 and 2007, the "Grim Sleeper" serial killer was responsible for at least ten unsolved murders in Los Angeles. In 2010, Lonnie David Franklin was arrested in connection with the crimes and is still awaiting trial.

- Serial killer Morris Solomon Jr., dubbed "The Sacramento Slayer," was responsible for at least seven murders in Sacramento between June 1986 and April 1987. He was sentenced to death and is still awaiting execution.

- Television and film star Rebecca Schaeffer was shot to death by a crazed stalker in the doorway of her Hollywood apartment on July 18, 1989. Schaeffer was best known for her role on the hit CBS sitcom *My Sister Sam*. Her murderer, Robert John Bardo, had stalked Schaeffer for three years prior to the attack and was convicted and sentenced to life in prison for the slaying.

- On August 20, 1989, brothers Lyle and Eric Menendez shot their wealthy parents to death at their Beverly Hills mansion. Their subsequent trial created a firestorm of sensation in the national media. In 1996, they were both convicted of first-degree murder and sentenced to life in prison.

- Cleophus Prince Jr., "The Clairemont Killer," was responsible for the rape and murder of six women in San Diego County between January and September 1990. He was convicted and sentenced to death and is still awaiting execution.

- John Famalaro, "The Cold Storage Killer," abducted twenty-three-year-old Denise Huber from an Orange County, freeway after her car became disabled. Her battered body was discovered three years later in a locked freezer at Famalaro's Prescott, Arizona, home. He was convicted in 1997 and sentenced to death.

- On June 10, 1991, eleven-year-old Jaycee Lee Dugard was abducted while she walked home from school in South Lake Tahoe. She remained missing for eighteen years. Her abductors, Phillip and Nancy Garrido, were arrested and pleaded guilty to rape and kidnapping charges. Phillip received a sentence of 400 plus years, while Nancy was sentenced to thirty-six years to life behind bars.

- Heidi Fleiss, "The Hollywood Madam," ran a high-end prostitution service in Los Angeles from 1990 to 1993. She was convicted of pandering and tax evasion and sentenced to seven years in prison.

- On October 1, 1993, twelve-year-old Polly Klaas was abducted from her Petaluma, California, home. Two months later, Richard Allen Davis confessed to the murder of Klaas and led police to a shallow grave off Highway 101 near Cloverdale, where the young girl's body was discovered. Davis was convicted of first-degree murder and sentenced to death.

- Between 1993 and 1995, a killer dubbed "The Pomona Strangler," was responsible for the murder of four Pomona, area prostitutes. No one has been arrested in connection with the crimes and the case remains open and unsolved.

- On June 12, 1994, Nicole Brown Simpson, the ex-wife of NFL football legend O. J. Simpson, and her friend Ronald Goldman were brutally murdered at her Brentwood townhouse. O. J. Simpson was eventually charged with the murders, and his slow-speed chase through the freeways of Los Angeles and sensational trial have been credited by many as the beginning of reality television. Simpson was eventually acquitted of the double homicide, but later held liable for their deaths in a civil case.

- On the morning of February 28, 1997, Larry Phillips Jr. and Emil Matasareanu robbed the North Hollywood Bank of America. Attempting to flee the scene, they were confronted by Los Angeles police and killed in a wild shootout.

- Rapper Notorious B.I.G., Christopher Wallace, was gunned down in a drive-by shooting by an unknown assailant on March 9, 1997, in Los Angeles. His death has been attributed to the East Coast/West Coast hip-hop feud that claimed the lives of other rap stars such as Tupac Shakur in 1996.

- Cary Stayner, "The Yosemite Killer," a handyman at the Cedar Lodge Motel outside of Yosemite National Park, was responsible for the abduction and murder of Carole Sund, Juli Sund, Silvina Pelosso, and Joie Armstrong between February and July 1999. Stayner was arrested on July 24, 1999, and eventually was convicted of the murders and sentenced to death.

Bibliography

Adams, Charles F. *Murder by the Bay: Historic Homicide in and About the City of San Francisco*. Word Dancer Press, 2005.

Babyak, Jolene. *Breaking the Rock: The Great Escape from Alcatraz*. Oakland CA: Ariel Vamp, 2001.

Barnes, Gene. *I, Witness. Accessed February 14, 2014.* http://iwitnesslife. wordpress.com/2012/09/09/mass-murderer-steve-nash-1957/.

Boulton, David. *The Making of Tania Hearst*. London: New English Library, *1974.*

Cairns, Kathleen A. *Proof of Guilt: Barbara Graham and the Politics of Executing Women in America*. Lincoln, NE: University of Nebraska Press, 2013.

Campbell, Bruce J. *Escape from Alcatraz*. Danvers MA: Ten Speed Press, 2005.

Cheney, Margaret. *Why—The Serial Killer in America*. Backinprint.com, 2000.

Clarke, Thurston. *The Last Campaign: Robert F. Kennedy and 82 Days That Inspired America*. New York NY: Macmillan, 2008.

Cliser, Gary. "The Many Faces of Carole Tregoff Pappa." Accessed February 27, 2014. http://caroletregoff.blogspot.com/.

Craib, Ralph. "An Appetite for Murder." *SF Gate*, 7 May 1995. Accessed February 10, 2014. www.sfgate.com/news/article/An-Appetite-for-Murder-As-the-nation-feasts-on- 3034433.php#page-1.

Crane, Cheryl. *Detour: A Hollywood Story*. New York NY: Arbor House/William Morrow, 1988.

Crane, Cheryl. *Lana: The Memories, the Myths, the Movies*. Philadelphia PA: Running Press, 2008.

Cray, Ed. *Burden of Proof: The Case of Juan Corona*. New York NY: Macmillan, 1973.

Cuthbert, David. "Cheryl Crane: Past Can't Hurt Me Now." *Spokane Chronicle*. January 12, 1988. p. F4.

"Crime: Young Man with a Gun." *Time*, 22 January 1951. Accessed February 4, 2014. http://content.time.com/time/subscriber/article/0,33009,888880,00.html.

Dickensheet, Dean W. *Great Crimes of San Francisco*. Comstock, 1984.

Donnelley, Paul. *501 Most Notorious Crimes*. London: Bounty Books, 2009.

Eggar, Steven A. *The Killers Among Us: Examination of Serial Murder and Its Investigations*. Prentice Hall, 2002.

Ellenberger, Allan R. *Ramon Novarro: A Biography of the Silent Film Idol, 1899–1968*. Jefferson, NC: McFarland, 2009.

Evans, Colin. "Raymond Bernard Finch and Carole Tregoff Trials: 1960 & 1961." Great American Trials. 2002. Encyclopedia.com. Accessed February 27, 2014. www.encyclopedia.com/doc/1G2-3498200213.html.

Flowers, R. Barri. *The Sex Slave Murders*, New York NY: St. Martins Press, 1996.

Gaute, J.H.H. and Robin Odell. *The Murderers' Who's Who*. London: W. H. Allen, 1989.

Gillespie, Kay L. *Dancehall Ladies: The Crimes and Executions of America's Condemned Women*. University Press of America, 1997.

Gilmore, John. *L.A. Despair: A Landscape of Crimes & Bad Times*. Los Angeles, CA: Amok Books, 2005.

Graebner, William. *Patty's Got a Gun: Patricia Hearst in 1970s America*. Chicago IL: University of Chicago Press, 2008.

Graysmith, Robert. *The Sleeping Lady: The Trailside Murders Above the Golden Gate*. Onyx Press, 1991.

Graysmith, Robert. *Zodiac*. New York, NY: Berkley Books, 2007.

Haugen, Brenda. *The Zodiac Killer: Terror and Mystery*. North Mankato, MN: Capstone Press, 2010.

Hearst, Patricia Campbell, with Alvin Moscow. *Patty Hearst: Her Own Story*. New York NY: Avon, 1988.

"Investigations: Death Wish." *Time*, 6 November 1964. Accessed March 26, 2014. http://content.time.com/time/subscriber/article/0,33009,876374,00.html.

Jeffers, H. Paul. *Sal Mineo: His Life, Murder, and Mystery*, Philadelphia, PA: Running Press, 2002.

Justia US Law. "People v. Walker 112 Cal. App. 2d 462." Accessed February 4, 2014. http://law.justia.com/cases/california/calapp2d/112/462.html.

Kidder, Tracy. *The Road to Yuba City: A Journey into the Juan Corona Murders.* New York NY: Doubleday, 1974.

Leader-Post. "Life in Prison for Mass Killing." 17 December 1973. Accessed May 27, 2014. http://news.google.com/newspapers?id=ofdUAAAAIBAJ&sjid=3TwNAAAAIBAJ&pg=4891,3484647.

Lester, David. *Serial Killers*. Philadelphia PA: The Charles Press, 1995.

Lewis, Brad. *Hollywood's Celebrity Gangster. The Incredible Life and Times of Mickey Cohen*. New York NY: Enigma Books, 2007.

Lodi News-Sentinel. "Father Confesses Murder of His Three Children." 25 May 1964.

Long Beach Press-Telegram, Various dates and years.

Los Angeles Times. Various Dates and Years.

Maloney, J. J. "Randy Kraft: The Southern California Strangler." www.crimemagazine.com. Accessed March 20, 2014. http://crimemagazine.com/randy-kraft-southern-california-strangler.

Marzilli, Alan. *Famous Crimes of the 20th Century*. Philadelphia PA: Chelsea House, 2003.

McDougal, Dennis. *Angel of Darkness: The True Story of Randy Kraft and the Most Heinous Murder Spree*. New York NY: Grand Central, 1991.

McFadden, Robert D. "Tale of 3 Inmates Who Vanished from Alcatraz Maintains Intrigue 50 Years Later." *New York Times*, 9 June 2012. Accessed February 28, 2014.

McLellan, Vin; and Paul Avery. *The Voices of Guns: The Definitive and Dramatic Story of the Twenty-two-month Career of the Symbionese Liberation Army, One of the Most Bizarre Chapters in the History of the American Left*. New York: Putnam, 1977.

Michaud, Michael Gregg. *Sal Mineo: A Biography*. Harmony, 2010.

Moldea, Dan E. *The Killing of Robert F. Kennedy: An Investigation of Motive, Means, and Opportunity*. New York: Norton, 1995. www.nytimes.com/2012/06/10/us/anniversary-of-a-mystery-at-alcatraz.html?_r=0.

Nash, Jay Robert. *Bloodletters and Badmen: A Narrative Encyclopedia of American Criminals from the Pilgrims to the Present*. M. Evans & Company, 1995.

"National Affairs: 300 Years is Not Enough." *Time*, 2 April 1951. Accessed February 4, 2014. http://content.time.com/time/subscriber/article/0,33009,814483,00.html.

Newton, Michael. *Hunting Humans: An Encyclopedia of Modern Serial Killers*. Breakout Publications, 1990.

Newton, Michael. *The Encyclopedia of Unsolved Crimes*. New York NY: Checkmark Books, 2004.

"People v. Finch." *Leagal.com*. Accessed February 27, 2014. www.leagle.com/decision/1963965213CalApp2d752_1854.xml/PEOPLE%20v.%20FINCH.

Oakland Tribune, Various years and dates.

Orange County Register, Various years and dates.

O'Shea, Kathleen A. *Women and the Death Penalty in the United States, 1900–1998*. Greenwood, 1999.

Ramsland, Katherine. "Killer Prophet." *Crimelibrary.com*. Accessed March 19, 2014. www.crimelibrary.com/notorious_murders/mass/john_frazier/4.html.

Rawson, T. *I Want to Live: The Analysis of a Murder*. New York: New American Library, 1958.

Ressler, Robert K. *Whoever Fights Monsters: My Twenty Years Tracking Serial Killers for The FBI*. New York, NY: St. Martin's Press, 2003.

Schechter, Harold. *The Serial Killer Files: The Who, What, How, and Why of the World's Most Terrifying Murderers*. Random House, 2003.

Schmidt, William E. "First Woman is Executed in US Since 1962." *New York Times*, 3 November 1984. *SCOCAL. "People v. Abbott , 47 Cal.2d 362."* Accessed February 10, 2014. http://scocal.stanford.edu/opinion/people-v-abbott-24137.

Scott, Shirley Lynn. "Unnatural Disasters." *TruTV Crime Library*. crimelibrary.com. Accessed April 14, 2014. http://www.crimelibrary.com/serial_killers/weird/mullin/index_1.html.

"Sequels: Billy's Last Words." *Time*, 22 December 1952. Accessed February 4, 2014. http://content.time.com/time/subscriber/article/0,33009,889546,00.html.

Silva, Deborah. "Santa Rosa Hitchhiker Murders." Santarosahitchikermurders.com. Accessed April 15, 2014. www.santarosahitchhikermurders.com/.

Smith, Nicole. "History of a Cal State Fullerton Killer." DailyTitan.com, 15 May 2006. Accessed April 24, 2014. www.dailytitan.com/2006/05/history-of-a-cal-state-fullerton-killer/.

Smith, Nicole. "Blood Spills in Library Hallways." *DailyTitan.com*, 16 May 2006. Accessed April 24, 2014. www.dailytitan.com/2006/05/bloodspillsinlibraryhallways/.

Squires, Jennifer. "Police: Mass Murderer John Linley Frazier Hanged Himself in Prison." *Santa Cruz Sentinel*. Accessed March 19, 2014. www.santacruzsentinel.com/ci_13156087.

Stephens, Hugh. "I'll Show You Where I Buried the Pieces of Their Bodies." *Inside Detective*. August 1973. Accessed March 4, 2014. www.truecrime.net/kemper/article.htm.

Sullivan, Robert, ed. *The Most Notorious Crimes in American History*. New York: Life Books, 2010.

Talbitzer, Bill. *Too Much Blood*. New York NY: Vantage Press, 1978.

Turner, Lana. *Lana: The Lady, The Truth, The Legend, The Truth*. Dutton Publishing, 1982.

Van Derbeken, Jaxon. "DNA Ties Trailside Killer to '79 S.F. Slaying." SFGate.com, 24 February 2010. Accessed May 28, 2014. www.sfgate.com/crime/article/DNA-ties-Trailside-Killer-to-79-S-F-slaying-3198511.php.

Von Beroldingen, Marj. "Edmund Kemper Interview." *Front Page Detective, March 1974,* Accessed March 4, 2014. www.truecrime.net/kemper/interview.htm.

Vronsky, Peter. *Serial Killers: The Method and Madness of Monsters*. New York NY: Berkley Books, 2004.

Wagner, Diane. *Corpus Dilecti*. New York NY: St. Martin's Press, 1986.

Walker, Bill. *The Case of Barbara Graham*. New York NY: Ballantine Books, 1961.

Weed, Steven; with Scott Swanton. *My Search for Patty Hearst*. New York NY: Crown, 1976.

Weiss, Mike. *Double Play: The Hidden Passions Behind the Double Assassination of George Moscone and Harvey Milk*. San Francisco CA: Vince Emery Productions, 2010.

Wilkes, Roger, Ed. *The Giant Book of Unsolved Crimes*. London: Magpie Books, 2005.

Williams, Bryan. "Hacked Girls to Death Whenever He Got the Urge." *True Detective Magazine*. October 1971.

Witcover, Jules. *85 Days: The Last Campaign of Robert Kennedy*. New York NY: Putnam, 1969.

Index

OTHER SCHIFFER BOOKS
BY THE AUTHOR

**MURDER
AND MAYHEM**
52 Crimes that
Shocked Early
California
1849-1949
978-0-7643-3968-4

**FINAL RESTING
PLACES**
Orange County's
Dead and Famous
978-0-7643-3421-4

FADE TO BLACK
Graveside
Memories of
Hollywood Greats
1927 - 1950
978-0-7643-3709-3

**GREAT BRITAIN'S ROYAL
TOMBS**
A Guide to the Lives
and Burial Places of
British Monarchs
978-0-7643-4129-8

**LITERARY LEGENDS
OF THE BRITISH ISLES**
The Lives & Burial Places
of 50 Great Writers
978-0-7643-4438-1

OTHER SCHIFFER BOOKS
ON RELATED SUBJECTS

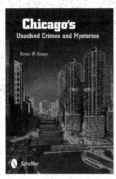

CHICAGO'S UNSOLVED CRIMES & MYSTERIES
Bryan W. Alaspa
978-0-7643-4311-7

CHICAGO CRIME STORIES
Rich Gone Wrong
Bryan W. Alaspa
978-0-7643-3114-5

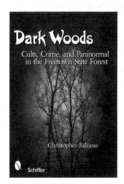

DARK WOODS
Cults, Crime, and the Paranormal in the Freetown State Forest
Christopher Balzano
978-0-7643-2799-5

CHESAPEAKE CRIMES II
Donna Andrews
& Maria Y. Lim, Editors
978-0-87033-582-2

About the Author

Award-winning author and columnist **Michael Thomas Barry** is a graduate of California State University, Fullerton, with degrees in criminal justice and history. Michael is a columnist for CrimeMagazine.com where he pens "This Week in Crime History." He is the author of six nonfiction books that include *Murder & Mayhem: 52 Crimes that Shocked Early California, 1849-1949* (2012); *Literary Legends of the British Isles: The Lives & Burial Places of 50 Great Writers* (2013); and *America's Literary Legends: The Lives & Burial Places of 50 Great Writers* (2015). Among his many literary awards are the 2011 and 2014 Readers' Favorite International Book Awards (silver and gold medals); 2012 and 2013 International Book Awards (winner); 2013 and 2014 Next Generation Indie Book Awards (finalist); and 2013 National Beverly Hills Book Awards (winner). He resides with his wife, Christyn, and their two golden retrievers, Jake and Madison (in spirit), in Orange, California.

Visit his website www.michaelthomasbarry.com for more information.